More Praise for Jon Kerstetter's

CROSSINGS

Finalist for the 2018 Colby Award

"Grave and pensive, but always engaging . . . [*Crossings*] offers intimate portraits of lives shaped by war. . . . A new generation of storytellers will emerge from this latest iteration of the terror wars. . . . [*Crossings* is a] powerful reminder of why we should listen."

—*Wall Street Journal*

"*Crossings* is an intimate and compelling look at how a Native American served his country as a combat medic and overcame the generational odds against success in his personal, professional, and spiritual life. [An] inspiring, transformational story."

—*San Antonio Express-News*

"Kerstetter's remarkable story of courage and resilience provides a detailed look at the life and work of a combat physician. . . . Though this is his first book, Kerstetter is a compelling writer, and not just of war stories. Kerstetter emotionally describes his recovery, the end of his medical career, and the process of relearning that led to this memoir. . . . Recommended for readers who enjoy war memoirs and for anyone looking for a moving life story."

—*Library Journal*

"The author's emergence as a military doctor makes for interesting reading . . . but what is of greatest value in this narrative is Kerstetter's ongoing, twofold recovery from a stroke on one hand and PTSD on the other. . . . The author's medical perspective on his own condition and critical therapeutic moments adds depth to an already solid story. An inspiring memoir."

—*Kirkus Reviews*

"Kerstetter has written a fascinating and nuanced edge-of-your-seat tale about the humanity of medicine amidst the inhumanity of war. Your heart will be pounding on every page. I couldn't put this wonderful book down."

—Matt McCarthy, author of *The Real Doctor Will See You Shortly*

CROSSINGS

A Doctor-Soldier's Story

JON KERSTETTER

B \ D \ W \ Y

BROADWAY BOOKS

NEW YORK

I have changed the names of some people and dates or locations to provide anonymity and security, especially as it relates to Iraq and my tours of duty there.

Published in the United States by Broadway Books, an imprint of the Crown Publishing Group, a division of Penguin Random House LLC, New York. broadwaybooks.com

Broadway Books and its logo, B \ D \ W \ Y, are trademarks of Penguin Random House LLC.

Originally published in hardcover in the United States by Crown, an imprint of the Crown Publishing Group, a division of Penguin Random House LLC, New York, in 2017.

The following chapters were previously published as essays: "Ballistic Maneuvers" first appeared in *Emrys Journal* (2013). "Prologue" first appeared as the 2014 nonfiction prize winner "Learning to Breathe" in *The Normal School* (Fall 2014). "The List" first appeared as finalist for the 2014 Diana Woods Memorial Award, in *Lunch Ticket* (Summer/Fall 2014). "Thinking Level 5.3" first appeared as "Thinking" in *The Examined Life Journal* (January 2014). "Triage" first appeared in *River Teeth* (Spring 2012).

Library of Congress Cataloging-in-Publication data is available upon request.

ISBN 978-1-101-90439-8
Ebook ISBN 978-1-101-90438-1

Printed in the United States of America

Book design by Lauren Dong
Cover design by Keith Hayes
Cover photograph: Raphye Alexius/Blend Images/Getty Images

10 9 8 7 6 5 4 3 2 1

First Paperback Edition

For Collin and my children:
Justin, Darren, Jordan, and Katelyn

Contents

Stroke School   227
Reading   246
Winter Dream   253
St. Luke's   262
Elephant Man   278
Therapy: VA Style   285
The List   299
Thinking Level 5.3   305
Wride (Write)   311

PART FOUR: OVERCOME
Beyond the Crossings   327

Author's Note   339
Acknowledgments   341

Prologue

Iraq, 2003

A SOLDIER LIES IN the sand, blood pooling beneath his head, mouth gulping at the air. His eyes fixed, head tilted off to one side, legs and arms motionless. He's a young soldier in his early twenties, late teens, a young man who should be a freshman in college or finding a summer job while deciding what to do after high school. In less than five minutes he'll probably die right there in the dirt, right at your feet. You will carry his bloodstains on your boots and on the sleeves of your uniform.

You possess the medical skills to save his life and your training as a warfighter helps you think and act decisively. You respond confidently, even brazenly, yet you understand that saving a patient with a head injury involves lots of luck. Maybe this is one of those lucky days and your patient survives. You feel good. But you also feel that this soldier with a shrapnel hole in his skull and a bit of brain oozing and lots of blood dripping might eventually wish you had let him die in the sand, thousands of miles from home with the other soldiers looking on. Your gut tells you this one particular patient has a chance of survival. It also tells you if he ever makes it home, he will live in pain for the rest of his life.

SOLDIERS REQUIRE ONE kind of breathing, doctors quite another. And soldier-doctors, well, they require a fusion of types: the ability to use one lung for soldiering and one lung for doctoring, a unique chimeric breathing shaped from the twisted strands of wildly dissimilar DNA.

It's natural and unnatural, that genetic code, to know as much about killing as healing, to listen for the sounds of bullets in one moment, then listen for the sounds of the wounded in the next; to love each strand with rabid dedication and to hate them both; to cross back and forth between the two. Pull a trigger—Pack a wound. First one, then the other, the prime necessity of war, that instant crossing from doctor to soldier and soldier to doctor without focusing on the difference between the two, because in the end all that matters is just one thing: breathing like a soldier in one breath, then breathing like a doctor in the next. War—Medicine. Inhale—Exhale.

SOLDIER-DOCTOR BREATHING requires large, bold breaths. Breathe in war like you breathe in air. Memorize the shapes of all the aircraft. Learn psyops and night ops and commo and intel. Become a student of ballistics and small-unit tactics. Study the beauty and balance of the human body: skin, heart, lungs, and brain. Learn the chemistry of blood and the physics of circulation. Observe the mechanics of a perfect gait. Smear camouflage paint on your face and your ears and on the backs of your hands. Let your muscles learn the speed of close-quarters combat. Work them until the movements become natural, like reflexes. Train your mind for war, your legs for battle, your hands for surgery. Teach your fingers to feel the smallest lump of pathology and the steady rhythm of a beating heart, then teach them to feel the knurled steel of triggers and the full metal jacket of bullets.

Hearing is a form of breathing. Listen. The sounds tell you when to fight and when to weep—even when to die. The sounds are your friends. As long as you hear them, it means you're alive. Listen to the clamor of surgical instruments or to the prayers of chaplains or to the quiet whispers of Army nurses talking to their patients, even though their patients cannot hear because hearing has left their bodies. Spend your days listening for the monotone warnings of cardiac monitors. And when you hear that flatline sound and it doesn't stop, hit the silent-mode button, then fill in the official medical forms with checkboxes for DOW and KIA (died of wounds, killed in action). Try to minimize the DOW count. Sleep when you can, but wake to the sounds of incoming helicopters. Wake to the cries of the wounded and to the silent screams of soldiers whose limbs and guts had been burned or torn or separated from their bodies. Respond to the high-pitched wind of an RPG, the explosive rattle of small-arms fire, and the bone-breaking blast of an IED. Alert your mind to the rustle of boots and the too-quiet stillness just before a battle.

Fear makes its own kind of sound. Listen for the patterns, the ones that whisper about going home without legs or arms and the ones that mourn the painful deaths of soldiers. Learn to live with those deafening sounds, especially the ones telling you your medical skills may never be enough—that because of you a soldier may die. Shake your fear and keep moving forward.

A SOLDIER WITH a salvageable injury lies at your feet. Iraqi insurgents are attacking your position and you need to clear the area fast. You stop to return fire. Even though you are trained to heal, you are also trained to kill, and that fact makes you a bit hesitant. You lay your hesitation aside for a moment and put your warrior hat on—because, after all, you are in a war. Your gut tightens as you fire a round or two. You grab the soldier by the collar of her uniform and jerk her torso up and off the sand, then sprint as fast as you can for twenty yards.

As you run, the soldier's legs drag and slow you down. Other soldiers help you throw her on a field litter so you can get the hell out of the kill zone. Her right leg dangles off to the side. A medic grabs it and plops it back onto the litter. She screams so violently you can see the vessels in her neck distend and pulse. The leg is barely attached. It's covered with dirt and sand. The bones look like broken spears as they poke through her skin and the burned fabric of her uniform. Your patient is losing blood faster than you know is sustainable for life, and you know if you don't get a tourniquet on her thigh right now—right in the middle of this attack—she'll just bleed out and die. So you slap one on and tighten it up.

You're in this fight. The tourniquet slips. Bones slice against her open wound. The soldier starts bleeding again. Draw your long-blade knife from its sheath, grip the handle as tightly as you can, then reach down and cut the soldier's leg off, right from where it is barely attached and dangling—just cut the goddamned thing off and leave it in the sand, and when she keeps crying and screaming, yell at her, "Shut the hell up!" Imagine that she does. When you finally manage to get the tourniquet tightened again, you're relieved that you made that decision—the one about using your knife, because you had no more time to dink around. You needed to move and the dragging leg was slowing everybody down, and the soldier was better off alive—even without her leg.

LEARN HOW YOUR enemy breathes. Study how they do war—how they treat their wounded and gather their dead. Observe where they live and where their poets gather for coffee; know why they write letters to their wives, what they say, what they leave out. Understand their prayers and their dreams and their fears and their families. Learn how they cuss in their native language, how they read their scriptures and their newspapers and their children's schoolwork. Absorb the color of their land and the smell of their trees. Discover where their rivers bend and their deserts turn to hills.

Read the Geneva Conventions. For the record, sign the Red Cross card that identifies you as medical personnel. Rip it and toss it. Learn the law of war well enough to know when to bend it. Study the manual governing enemy detainees and prisoners of war. Know the rules that define how you must treat them, even when they spit on your skin and call you a murderer. Apply escalation of force, but know when to open fire and ask questions later. Learn how to hate your enemy without crossing the line between soldiering and savagery. Control your breathing. Use your doctor mind and your soldier mind. Focus. Let them become one. Release your body and mind into the hands of war.

It's possible you could end up in the middle of a firefight. Don't flinch. Soldiers will depend on you to make all the right decisions. You may feel that all the "right" decisions are a blur, even though you've spent years in training just so your mind can never get blurred—so you can think without hesitation in the chaos and screaming of combat. You trained well, but now you think all those war games and evac scenarios didn't prepare you. You're right. How could they? This is real. The fear and the blood and the shit are real. Death is real. War is real. And all you can do is adapt and breathe and try to hold on. So you grasp your weapon and your ammo, your knives and your body armor. You carry them next to your medic bag, next to the bandages and tourniquets and morphine. When you grab your gear, it feels like you're grabbing fear or emptiness. Despite what you feel, you move out anyway. As you do, you sense that the mysterious alchemy of war has transformed your nature.

You're up for a mission. You jump in a Humvee or a medevac helicopter. Time warps. You hold the bodies of soldiers you will never know except for that brief moment when they look into your eyes. After less than an hour, you hold their dog tags and their final letters home. You recall a chaplain's eulogy for a soldier: God made us from dust and returns us to dust. It's true. War proves it.

When you think you've held enough of war and your hands lack the strength to hold on to anything more, not even the air, then hold on with your mind and with your soul and with your prayers, if you can find them. And if your mind and your prayers are gone, then hold on with the nails of your fingers or with the soles of your boots, and breathe. Inhale—exhale; soldier—doctor; war—medicine.

ANOTHER PATIENT BLEEDING at your feet says he managed to return fire and that he might have killed one of those bastards. Then he grabs your arm and asks you if he's going to make it. You tell him yes. "Damn right you're going to make it." And then you tell him to take some real deep breaths and that a medevac chopper is just two minutes out and to hold on just a bit longer. You inject him with morphine and maybe you crack a little smile, to which he responds by asking you to tell his mom that he loves her and to tell his dad that he was a good soldier. You say, "Knock it off. Tell 'em yourself." And you know he knows you have to say things like that because you need to keep everybody hoping for the best. You also know he wants to be real and honest, and you want to be real and honest too, but it doesn't come easy.

Later in the day, you see a soldier who had just arrived in theater and on his third day in combat his brain was shot clean out of its skull. His gray matter embedded itself in the crevices of his Humvee. You did absolutely nothing to save him; instead, you ordered your medics to put him in a body bag.

You had another patient last week whose legs literally exploded from his body. He lived less than four minutes—just long enough to say half the Lord's Prayer. A nearby soldier who had taken the four-day combat lifesaver course stood rigid, numb from panic, frozen in time like a terracotta warrior. He couldn't remember how to use tourniquets and just started yelling "Oh my God—oh my God!" until you screamed, "Hey! Get your shit together!" And he did. Then he made the sign of the cross and helped you with another wounded soldier.

For the sake of argument, suppose you live through these and similar scenarios—some from last week, some from prior deployments. In a moment of reflection, you conclude that as long as war continues there will always be Army doctors who will have patients at their feet. You remember all the soldiers who died, and all the efforts of the medic teams and the medevac pilots and the nurses and the surgeons. You realize that despite killing more of the enemy, they are still killing you—and you get a disturbing feeling that war might go on forever.

All your experience from multiple deployments has paid off and your medic teams are damn good: the best. You manage to get soldiers into surgery faster than in any other war—before they have a chance to die in the field. All the medical resources and medical staff work as they should and very few patients actually die in the combat surgical hospitals. But suppose some soldiers do die during surgery or in post-op care or even months later, stateside. They die of infections or lung complications or breathing complications and you feel if you had done just one more thing, spent one more minute of time, made one more vital decision, things would have turned out differently. Slowly, you begin to realize you never had enough time to do everything for your patients. Your thoughts leave you with a fading image of the doctor you thought you were and you come to an understanding that you know more about the practice of war than the practice of medicine.

FROM THE FIRST day of war to the last day of war, you have these soldiers at your feet. You stand over them and look down. The sand darkens as it outlines their bodies. You hesitate just for a moment, then you move your hands swiftly and decisively—like a doctor. And you breathe. You breathe like a soldier.

Part One

LEARN

Near the Edge of a Boundary

Oneida Indian Reservation, Wisconsin

O N A MIDSUMMER day in 1954, my brother Jimmy coaxed me into riding on the lawnmower. I was four years old. Jimmy was a skinny nine-year-old who wore high-top tennis shoes and striped bib overalls everywhere he went. Mom had sent us outdoors after lunch, Jimmy to mow the backyard, me to pick up sticks and stay out of the way. As he mowed, I played alongside him in the fresh-cut grass tossing handfuls of clippings into the air. The sun had warmed most of the lawn, but it was still cool near the house. After making several passes along the border of the yard, Jimmy stopped and wiped his brow, then called me over. I still recall two of his words: "ride" and "fun."

Jimmy helped me set my feet on the mower by placing them on the steel frame where the wooden prongs of the push handle were bolted behind the wheels. I remember how careful we were to avoid the curved blades. I spread my legs like a wishbone and rested my haunches right where the handle forked. I struggled to balance myself, but I learned quickly after a few trial runs. Off we rode.

My brother was right: it was fun. He pushed slowly at first and then quickly picked up speed. He told me to hang on tight, then he would suddenly veer to the left or right so I would go flying off to the side. I tumbled to the grass laughing with joy. Down on the grass, up on the mower I went. Laughing, running, falling, our large backyard sloping and green. The midday sun warmed our skin.

Up on the mower, I watched the blades spin and cut, clippings flying out the back onto my legs. The faster Jimmy pushed, the higher the clippings flew. The smell of cut grass filled the yard. The scissoring sound of the blades rose and fell with the speed of the mower.

The uneven ground made the mower dip and heave and it was hard to keep my feet from sliding off. At one point I may have let out a brief whimper of fear instead of a laugh. That part is unclear, but this part I do remember well: in an instant, like the defined moment in the snap of a twig, the mower stopped. I remember the wild movement of my body falling forward, the rush of fear and the mower blades jammed by a large brown stick. My feet flew and my arms flailed. I felt and heard the dull thud that bodies make when they hit the ground. There was a fleeting moment of silence—and then a flood of pain. My left wrist lay open, pulsing and red. And I lay screaming and crying in a heap. Jimmy ran. I bled on my overalls, on the grass, and on my bare feet. The blood scared me. Instinctively, I felt something was wrong and dangerous. It was the first time I felt so afraid of something I didn't understand.

The trip to the hospital was a blur except for one detail. Suddenly my mother was kneeling beside me inside the house, pressing a large white cloth around my wrist. In the many times she retold the story, she always mentioned that the white cloth I remembered so well was a Kotex pad wrapped around my wrist. She held it in place and "pressed for dear life." One of our neighbors drove us to the hospital in Green Bay. There, a surgeon repaired my lacerated artery, stitched me up, and put a soft-shell cast on my arm.

Many years later, when I was old enough to mow the lawn on my own, Mom would remind me of the Oneida lawnmower incident whenever I brought the mower from the shed for the summer's first mowing. She always mentioned how "deathly afraid" she was that I would lose my hand and how fortunate I was that I did not. She told me how she had prayed to God for the bleeding to stop and how grateful she was for the neighbor's and the doctor's help. As she relived the story she often made a face—half smile, half frown. I interpreted it as part gratitude and part rebuke. When she got that look, she tightened her lips and said some Oneida words that roughly translated meant "Dammit the hell anyway" or another phrase that meant "Oh, the devil." Then in English she said, "Thank the good Lord." Often she took my hand and rubbed the scar on my wrist. Then, after a pause, she would shake her head and laugh just a bit. It was the kind of laughter that buffered memories of near disasters and made them seem less frightening, while also reminding me that I was still vulnerable.

THOSE EARLY ONEIDA years also brought good things, like eating Sealtest ice cream bars while sitting on a milk box near the storefront window of Mom's "drugstore," a small, poorly stocked rural store that sold over-the-counter medications, veterinary supplies, and a limited variety of sundries and groceries. The store belonged to my father, Lawrence Baines Kerstetter, who had left it to my mother, Margaret Archiquette Kerstetter, after their divorce. She was pregnant with me during the last year of their marriage, and soon after I was born, Mom was left with the store, child-support payments, and three children: Jimmy, five years old; Joanne, nine; and me, months old. She was always reticent to discuss exactly why the marriage failed, except to say it was complicated by the day-to-day pressures of living on an Indian reservation with little prospect of anything except month-by-month survival. "Those were hard days," she occasionally reminded me when I was older. And when she did so, her voice cracked and the furrowed lines in her forehead deepened.

Mom did what was necessary to get by. We lived upstairs from the store. She mended our clothes, planted a vegetable garden that my brother and sister tended, and dried corn and fruit at harvest. At times we had enough of whatever we needed. Often we did not. During the harder times, Mom borrowed from neighbors; they borrowed from us. Mom spent nothing on things regarded as unnecessary, fancy clothes or entertainment or travel, yet she was able to save enough money to buy occasional ice cream treats and shoes once a year for each of her kids. She made toy dogs from the oxtail soup bones left over from dinner. She dried them on the windowsill and used India ink to paint faces on them. I used to line those bone dogs up and pretend they were a family.

Eventually, perhaps naturally, Mom decided that she needed to leave Oneida for a steady job and the possibility of a better life. That is what she told me when, as a senior high school student, I asked her why she left Oneida and if she ever regretted her decision. "Leaving home was the only way," she said with resolve. Some choices were hard and painful but they had to be made, because not choosing could "make you or break you."

Despite whatever hesitation she may have felt, in the early summer of 1955, Mom left the Oneida Indian reservation for a job at a Bureau of Indian Affairs boarding school in Brigham City, Utah. With borrowed money for tickets, she took a bus from Green Bay to Chicago's Union Station, where she loaded two steamer trunks, three large suitcases, and her children onto a Union Pacific passenger train westbound for Utah.

Our first home in Brigham City was located at the corner of Seventh South and Main, about a quarter mile from the guarded entrance of the federal Indian school property. Mom rented the rear portion of a filling station. Instead of a front yard, we had blacktop, gas pumps, and a bell that dinged when cars pulled in for service. The house had a large basement with a coal bin and a small root cellar where Mom stored vegetables and canned goods. Some evenings we ate dinner on the screened-in back porch. It had holes in the screen and slanted a bit toward the backyard. During summer evenings after the gas station closed, I played "kick-the-can" with my brother and sister and the neighborhood kids. We used the gas pumps as home plate, and when we stole home we jumped on the black rubber hose that made the service bell ring.

The neighbor kept chickens in his backyard and traded one chicken for two pints of jam or a quart of Mom's bread-and-butter pickles. He used a large tree stump as a chopping block. Hatchet in one hand, flapping bird in the other, he pressed its neck on the stump. Whack! He tossed the headless bird to the grass, where it ran crazed until it finally keeled over and twitched its final twitch. Jimmy and I laughed and chased that wild, possessed carcass, flapping and falling and running in circles. When it stopped, I grabbed it by the legs and marched it to the back of the yard where we all plucked it. I hated that part because the chicken stank of blood and its feathers would stick to my overalls and shirt. Jimmy said I was born to be a chicken plucker.

My first birthday in Utah was November 15, 1955. About a week later I became sick with a sore throat and a cough. Mom rubbed Mentholatum on my neck and had me gargle with salt water. The minty smell of the thick ointment seemed to make it easier to breathe, but within a few days I developed a high fever and painful lumps in my neck. Mom thought I had the mumps. She made Joanne stay home from school to watch me for a few days. Mostly I slept, but Joanne woke me frequently to feed me sips of broth and put cool washcloths on my forehead. When Mom got home from work, she bathed me in cool water and gave me Aspergum to break my fever. I could hear myself wheezing, especially when I took big breaths. I don't recall exactly how many days I was sick, but I remember Mom coming home from work at lunchtime to check on me. I could tell she was worried because her face became stiff and she spoke abruptly to Joanne using Oneida words.

That evening a doctor came to our house carrying a black leather bag. I was lying on the bed in the bedroom next to the kitchen. I had thought perhaps a country doctor might be thin and small, with gray hair and dark glasses, but this man was a tall, black-haired giant with thick hands and a deep voice. He spoke gently yet with authority. I felt apprehensive and shy, but also comforted. He introduced himself as Dr. Smith.

"Johnny," he said, "can you sit up straight on the edge of the bed for me?"

Dr. Smith felt my neck and checked my ears. He asked me to open wide and pressed an oversize Popsicle stick on my tongue. "Say 'Ahhh,'" he said, as he looked down my throat with a bright light he had strapped around his head. He listened to my chest with a cold stethoscope, thumped my back, and asked me to breathe deeply.

"Take a deep breath," he said. "Breathe deep . . . Again."

While he was taking my temperature he whispered to my mother, "Diphtheria," and told her I needed a shot of penicillin. My eyes tracked his face and hands as he spoke. As Mom listened, she frowned and bit the corner of her lip. I had never heard such complicated words or the tone the doctor used to describe my illness. I gathered both meant something serious. He had that concerned look that gave cause for worry, yet he also projected a sense of confidence that made me feel like things would work out okay.

I watched intently as Dr. Smith opened his black bag and pulled out a tiny bottle of white medicine that looked to me like thick creamy milk. He cradled the bottle with his left hand, holding it upside down at eye level, then plunged a needle through its tiny rubber-stopped neck. The needle seemed to me at least six or eight inches long. He filled a glass syringe by placing his right thumb through a metal ring and slowly drawing it back. He flicked his finger against the sides of the syringe and then gave a small squirt that made a vanishing white arc over my bed.

I cried and stiffened as my mom laid me over her lap and pulled my underpants down. Dr. Smith tried to assure me. "Hold still, now, we're almost done." I felt the cold wet swab of alcohol on my skin and then the sharp stab of a needle deep in my right buttock. And as quickly as it had begun, the shot was finished. I didn't know that milk would sting and burn more than anything I had ever felt before.

Dr. Smith made several more house calls during the following week. He smiled warmly and said very few words. He always carried his black bag with its creases and scuffs. It smelled like a cross between my mom's leather work gloves and medicinal alcohol. Its snap-open top held the bag wide open, the fat leather grip resting against its thick black seams. He put the bag on the side of my bed one day. I peeked in. Bandages—lots of bandages. Dark purple iodine bottles from which he doused gauze pads clamped on a medical instrument to paint my throat. Several bottles of milky penicillin, glass syringes, and all sorts of gadgets. I recognized the stethoscope that he always pulled out first then strung around his neck like an extra necktie. A small brown bottle with a lid full of holes was the alcohol dispenser that he so vigorously pumped, saturating three or four cotton balls to clean my skin before giving me a shot. Once I learned what penicillin felt like, the word "shot" was enough to start a few tears running and a total-body stiffening. The smell of the alcohol dispenser would trigger the same response.

The entire experience with Dr. Smith captivated me. His professional demeanor and his authoritative yet soothing voice, his black bag with its blend of medicinal smells, the precision instruments and the medicine with its sting. Whatever the reason, whatever the magic, what I experienced as a child in the care of a country doctor was something I felt a connection to, however rudimentary or childlike in understanding. Doctoring drew me in. It seeded my mind with an interest for all things medical and scientific.

WE LIVED IN the gas station house for five years until the late fall of 1960, when Mom found a better house for us on East 5th South, just a few blocks from Fife Sand and Gravel Pit and across the street from the cemetery. The house was a two-hundred-eighty-square-foot shoe box with cracked asbestos siding and a flat, tar-papered roof that leaked like a sieve when it rained. Mom converted the dugout basement into bedrooms for Jimmy and Joanne. The only indoor plumbing ran to the enamel kitchen sink in Mom's bedroom. Sometimes, especially in winter, I used to piss in a green Mason jar because I didn't want to use the outhouse at night.

In the early summer of 1962, Mom decided to move back to Oneida. Jimmy was a junior in high school. Joanne had left home to attend a licensed practical nurses training program at Holy Cross Hospital in Salt Lake City, Utah. I had just finished the fifth grade. Mom boarded up the house and booked a train to Chicago and a bus to Green Bay. As she would later explain, it was more a move to overcome her isolation as a single parent and reconnect with friends back home. She also wanted one more chance at making a living at Oneida. Mostly, the move held the promise of a place where we could all belong. I didn't know much about belonging, but it did seem like we were always struggling to fit in as an Indian family in a larger, non-Indian community.

When we arrived, we stayed at the farmhouse of Mom's closest friend, Priscilla Manders. I had never seen my mother happier. Priscilla and Mom stayed up late and talked for endless hours speaking in the Oneida language. The strange-sounding words had a musical rhythm that English did not. I noticed the tonal rise at the ends of some words, and how that inflection could alter the meanings of things. Mom and Priscilla told stories around the kitchen table, sometimes laughing, sometimes crying. They traded memories about Indian relatives who had died. They retold stories about reservation life during the Great Depression, how families gathered wild berries and survived by eating corn husk soup and dried squash. Men left Oneida to find work in the big cities like Chicago or Detroit. Their families banded together and waited. Some of the men never came home.

"Those were hard times and sad times," I heard them say before lapsing into silence.

Priscilla drove us around to see old Indian relatives. I met elderly men and women who greeted me in the Oneida language, then pulled me close and hugged me. One elder, who was a traditional healer, spoke in soft Oneida phrases and smoked a pipe. When I told him I wanted to be a doctor, he put his wrinkled brown hands on my head and prayed. After he prayed, he reached in his pocket and pulled out a small medicine bag and took a pinch of tobacco in his fingers. He rubbed it on my hands and I could smell the earthy aroma. Later, my mom told me he knew I wanted to become a doctor even before I had said anything and that he was blessing my hands to do good things. For days after, when I rubbed my hands together, I thought of them as doctor hands.

My mother wanted to rent a place of her own but couldn't afford the available houses. She always stressed the importance of being independent, insisting on doing things without having to use friends or handouts. She had been a young adult during the Depression, and her family had been hurt by their dependency on Indian Affairs officials whose promises had no more substance than dried husks of corn. She wanted reasonable help but shunned dependency on friends and the not-to-be trusted government officials.

"You can't depend on anybody," she would say as she shook her head. "Learn to do things on your own."

One Friday, Priscilla drove Mom through the entire reservation. Mom knocked on doors and asked around. She found a small acreage for sale that had been the site of a cheese factory run by a local non-Indian couple. The abandoned factory stood in shambles. When my mother returned for lunch, she made a barrage of phone calls. No, the owner of the cheese factory would not loan her the money to buy the land. No, she could not get a loan from a bank. Her friends advised her to avoid that acreage because the house needed too much work, but Mom told them it had land for farming and plenty of wood for heating. By the next day Mom had made arrangements with the owner. She gave him a one-hundred-dollar deposit to hold the land for ninety days, after which she would have to buy it or rent it. She talked the landowner into letting her move into the upstairs home during the ninety-day hold. No, he would not turn the electricity on. No, he would not fix the plumbing. Yes, she would have to build her own outhouse. The following day we moved in. For me, it was a great idea. Nobody I knew had their own live-in cheese factory.

The first floor was the business end of the old factory, complete with remnants of stainless steel gutters that ran along the floor and a large flat bin where curds had been stirred. Near the ceilings, attached to the walls by metal hangers, hung disintegrating tubes and hoses that ran to processing vats. A worn and chipped cement ramp stood where trucks once delivered raw milk.

The living quarters were on the second story. A wooden stairway led to a landing midway up. Beyond that, several steps were missing and we climbed carefully to avoid falling. At the top of the stairs was a large room with splintered floorboards. A wood-burning stove doubled as a heater when needed. There was no plumbing: no water, no toilet, no sink. Two large bedrooms lay adjacent to the great room. The windowpanes were empty; their shattered, dirty glass lay in heaps on the floor. My brother and I cleaned the rooms and hauled the glass out in a bucket. Mom had borrowed some military-style cots with sheets and blankets. We slept as if we were camping. On a few cool nights we arranged the cots in a semicircle around the stove. Every few days we would return to Priscilla Manders's house to shower and clean up.

About a month into our ninety-day squatter venture, Mom planned a July Fourth picnic as a thank-you to all who had helped us. People started arriving at noon and stayed until late in the evening. We cooked hamburgers and hot dogs on an open-pit fire. Friends brought fat yellow onions and red and white radishes, boiled potatoes and stalks of celery. There were plates of deviled eggs, jars of sweet and dill pickles, and several muskmelons. Mom made her potato salad with fresh handmade mayonnaise and a sprinkle of cayenne pepper that I could smell over the onions and radishes. Throughout the day we ate and laughed, sitting in a circle on folding lawn chairs and blankets. Stories floated back and forth. Oneida words mingled with English words. The tales seemed to enlarge themselves with each new storyteller. Some of the older people gave accounts of young Oneida Indians who joined the Marines or the Army and went off to war and died in battle somewhere in the front lines on D-Day or in the Korean War. They told about military funerals and twenty-one-gun salutes and mothers who received American flags and letters from war officials. The elders named those Oneida warriors one by one, along with the names of the foreign places where they had died.

One of the named was Oliver Bernard Beechtree, who on October 24, 1952, had sent a telegram to the Oneida drug store from Japan telling my mother that he was outbound for Korea and would send her his address as soon as he could. Oliver had been Mom's closest friend. If he had returned from the war as planned, they might have married and started a new life together. During the naming, when Mom heard Oliver's name, she closed her eyes as if to hold back the tears that began to flow down the soft lines of her face. She brushed a few tears away at first, but then just let them fall. When the elders finished, everybody sat still and said nothing. Several minutes later one of the elders spoke an Oneida prayer and then started to sing a chant. Then after a while the stories began to flow once more and the people wiped their tears and laughed again.

The trip back home to Oneida had been somewhat confusing for me. An adventure for sure, but I also sensed that we lived from day to day never really knowing when and where we would settle, never completely understanding who we were or where we were going. We had arrived at a tribal place of belonging, but I didn't know, and it seemed Mom didn't know, what that belonging meant or how we fit in. When I heard those old Oneida people talk and laugh, I could see that they all belonged together and it made me want the richness that they shared: laughter and food and stories and smoke. I saw and felt the special respect and honor they held for their warriors and for themselves. And it felt good—that rich bond of culture and history and family that connected us all.

MOM NEVER MADE her ninety-day cheese factory deadline, but the owner let her rent it for as long as she needed. We stayed an additional two months as she looked for a suitable job and a house that never materialized. In the wake of our failed resettling, Mom packed us up and we left the Oneida Indian reservation once again, returning to Brigham City, in September 1962. Mom went back to work at the Intermountain Indian School as a food-service worker. I joined the sixth-grade class at Mountain View Elementary.

That year, I read Homer, *The Iliad* and *The Odyssey*. I saw my first science documentary about the physiology of blood, *Hemo the Magnificent*, which featured short video clips of the human heart in motion and red blood cells flowing in single file through microscopic capillaries. The narrator, Dr. Research, used graphics and cartoons to illustrate the structure and function of the blood, heart, and circulatory system. The film lasted about an hour. I sat on the edge of my chair, leaning forward and listening to every word. As the credits rolled at the end of the film, I felt compelled to become a scientist just like Dr. Research. And what I felt wasn't just an idea about an interesting job or a fleeting fancy about the future; it felt more like an anointing with the holy oil of science, maybe like the traditional blessing I had received while at Oneida. After seeing the documentary I wanted to run off to college immediately and study physiology and circulation and healing. Science held the promise of something great and wonderful.

On Saturdays I would walk the short mile to the public library, where the librarian, who always smiled warmly when I told her I was going to be a doctor, put books aside for me about the history of science. My favorite one told the story of William Harvey and his research on the human heart and circulatory system. I read it three or four times, all but memorizing the artist's renderings of Harvey's drawings. I also read about Leeuwenhoek and his invention of the microscope, about Galileo and the telescope, and about Fleming's 1928 discovery of penicillin. I learned how physicians used folk medicine, herbs, bleeding, and surgery to cure their patients. Some explored how the human body worked, and that was my greatest fascination. I needed to know how the science of medicine worked, how it healed the body.

I would pull *Gray's Anatomy* off the library shelf and seclude myself in a quiet corner to absorb as many of the pages as I could in a Saturday morning or afternoon. I don't know that I read the book as much as just looked at the fascinating drawings—the interstices and the shapes, the intricate weave of anatomy and the ordered structure of the human body. I traced the blood vessels and organs with my fingertips and marveled at the beautiful four-color overlays. I saturated my mind with the mystique of the body. Anatomy and physiology mattered to me because they defined the rules of injury and healing; they controlled how skin made scars and bones grew back together. The more I read, the more I had to read and the more I wanted to comprehend it all.

For my twelfth birthday, Mom bought me a model of the human body called the Visible Man. It had a clear plastic shell that mimicked human skin. All the internal organs were there: brain, heart, lungs, liver, intestines, and a semblance of reproductive organs. I painted each one with its corresponding color in the included study guide, taking extra time to add the tiny intricate vessels with a toothpick dipped in red or blue model paint. The chest and abdominal cavity opened by gently flexing the tabs of the overlying plastic chest and abdominal wall. The lungs folded on a bivalve hinge, exposing the bronchial tree. I fancied myself an anatomist. I did simulated dissections almost every day and performed mock surgery on the Visible Man. I took him apart and put him back together. Apart—together; carefully—precisely. And each time I dissected the model, I learned more about the human body, became more of a scientist, more of a doctor.

That Christmas I asked for a microscope. Mom cautioned me that she couldn't afford it and that maybe next year she would have more money. "Don't be disappointed," she said with a frown. On Christmas morning, I spotted a large box under the tree. She made me open it last. When I unwrapped it, I knew immediately what it was. I was ecstatic; Mom had put the microscope on layaway at a department store in Ogden and paid for it over the prior six months.

I mounted my own specimens of cells—studied them for hours. I gathered leaves and butterfly wings and samples of vegetable pigments. I would prick my fingertip with one of my mother's sewing needles, dab the blood on a slide, add a cover slip, and observe. Often the heat from the stage lamp caused the red cells to dry and lose their color before I got enough time to study them in detail. I learned to work fast and change my techniques to protect the kinds of samples I was studying. My time was never dull or wasted. At school, my science teacher took an interest in what I was doing at home and gave me premounted slides of different kinds of tissues from plants and animals. I wrote reports about my findings. He said I was a natural scientist and should plan on going to college.

THE SUMMER BEFORE I started the seventh grade, Mom decided to build a twelve-foot addition on the back of the house. She also added an enclosed stairway for the dugout basement, a slanted roof, and plumbing for our own indoor toilet. She had saved enough money for most of the project and arranged with a friend of a friend to do the construction. She paid him in monthly installments, plus interest, over a year. I helped with odd jobs and painting without pay. A supervisor from Fife's Gravel Pit agreed to give Mom a load of leftover cement for a poured foundation. He said they would have just washed it out at a dumpsite anyway, and since it was paid for, she might as well have it. She thanked him with a jar of homemade pickles.

Beyond all the uncertainties of growing up in those early houses, each one fixed in the inertia of disrepair, I had a feeling a house could define me, at least partially. The physical nature of a house was one thing; the emotional nature of living in that house was a quite different thing. Where you lived mattered. The houses we lived in were small, old, decrepit, and peculiar. They held a history of the impoverished people who lived in them, and to anybody listening, especially to me, those houses shouted that we lived in poverty, both on and off the reservation. As I grew older, I became aware of the dark physics of that poverty. Starting in the sixth grade, and especially as I entered junior high and high school, I felt increasingly embarrassed and even ashamed that we lived as we did. I rarely brought school friends home to play or study; instead I went to their houses, to their yards and their living rooms. I ate their moms' snacks, listened to their stories, and wanted to insert myself into *their* family narratives. At the end of each day, though, I returned to our Fifth South home, because it was what my mother could provide, and because it was where I belonged.

Against that backdrop of constant struggle, I was confronted with watching my mother's stubborn doggedness at providing a home for her children. I knew her life was not easy. I could see it in her worn shoes and in her threadbare dresses, in the way she paid her bills at the end of the month, often paying one bill instead of another, always making sure her checking account had just enough money to cover the checks she had written. In the years spanning 1954 to 1969, the wages from her food-service job ranged from seventy-five cents to less than two dollars per hour. I saw her pay stubs that she kept in shoeboxes. Her work included scrubbing floors and loading and unloading racks of dirty dishes into an industrial dishwasher. She wore long rubber gloves to protect her hands from the heat and detergents. On weekends she often worked as a cleaning lady in private homes.

When she was having a particularly hard time keeping up with finances, she told me she just wanted to give up and die; then she would go to her room and lie on her bed. Occasionally I heard her cry. I never knew what to do, so I took the dog for a long walk and gathered wild asparagus or elderberries. When I returned, I found her at her sewing machine making aprons or kitchen towels out of flour sacks, or in the kitchen canning fruit and vegetables for winter. As she looked up to see what I brought home, she told me how beautiful it looked and how I had a knack for discovering things, and then she would make an elderberry pie or steam the asparagus for dinner.

As a young man, I never fully understood the hardship my mother endured as a single parent. After I left home, I often reflected on the kind of life she lived. She endured the squelch of poverty and the harsh burden of isolation. Her Indian school job perpetuated its own kind of dependency and subsistence living. Much like an Indian reservation, it constantly abraded the bodies and minds of people who had no choice but to remain and endure. And when that struggle wore Mom to the edge of despair, she would sometimes lash out at anything that pushed her just one more inch. Once, Jimmy hounded her for a pair of new Levi's jeans for the start of school. "Everybody in school has new jeans," he kept insisting. Mom told him she simply didn't have the money. Jimmy talked back and said something about her stinking Indian school job. Mom spun around and pinned him to the wall with her thumb.

"Don't you ever talk back to me if you know what's good for you!" she shouted in Oneida and English. "You're not everybody. I'm not everybody. I don't have the money. If you want new jeans, then get your own money and buy them yourself."

I listened from the edge of the sofa. Jimmy was shaking. It felt like all the oxygen in the house had been replaced by a poisonous gas that would kill us if we breathed too deeply. I could see Jimmy swallow hard. He was taller and stronger than Mom, yet she had reduced him to someone small and weak.

Mom gave us both the lecture about "money not growing on trees" and the one that reminded us that we were "good for nothing," and another one about how "we never helped around the house." She yelled that we didn't know what it was like to work until we were "bone-tired" and then have to crawl home from work and cook and clean and hold a family together. She finally let Jimmy go and told us go clean our rooms, and then she turned toward the front door. "I'm going to the store. Maybe I'll just keep on walking," she said, her words high pitched and tremulous.

Jimmy and I were both sweating and trembling. There was an overbearing stillness in the house and I could hear my heartbeat. I struggled with Mom's words, "good for nothing," and I knew they weren't true, that she had lost herself in anger, but I also knew that it wasn't the first time they had been said and that they carried at least some fragment of truth—some part of us was good for nothing. And the hearing of those words struck hard, and there was pain and emptiness and sadness. I felt regret that I had not worked harder around the house or spent more time being less demanding, and that I was not more capable of taking care of myself. I realized then how precariously we lived and how necessary it was to be independent, not relying on anyone or anything.

Mom always harped on me to stay in school and get a good education. "Don't be like me. I'm nothing but a scrub lady," she would say. Her words cut like a jagged blade ripped across my skin. I felt both sadness and anger. Hearing those words made me want to run as far away as I could, not from her, but from our poverty and from our shame. I hated those words, in part because they were true, in part because they belied the truth of who my mother really was, of who I was. Yes, we were poor and brown and burdened. Yes, we wrestled with cultural and social perceptions that made us question the heart of who we were. But "dammit the hell anyway," as my mother used to say, we were not nothing! We carried the history of those Oneida warriors who enlisted in times of war and died in foreign lands. Our stories preserved the elders who survived the Depression by eating corn husk soup and wild berries and taught survival skills to their children. We represented traditional healers who rendered prayers and blessings, all while bearing the collective weight of government policies that sought to remove and relocate Indian tribes against their will. Most important, we were the family who forged a trail of survival all the way from Oneida to Utah, where we carved a life from a different land and a different culture.

I didn't want to be poor like my mother, to live in the kinds of houses we lived in, to scrape for every nickel we had, and to always be in want for something better. I wanted to push as far beyond her poverty as I could to accomplish the life I envisioned for myself. So I did just that. Over three decades of pushing boundaries, I eventually became the doctor of my boyhood dreams, and in the struggle to do so, I discovered a paradox: while striving to become less like Mother, I actually became more like her. I learned to redefine the boundaries that scripted my life, to become good for something, to push myself hard, right up close to the edges. And when I was finally there, finally at the clear edge of a boundary where both directions were visible, I would place one foot in front of the other and step across.

The Boundary Layer

THROUGHOUT HIGH SCHOOL my mother lectured me on the need to "get ahead." "You've got to get an education," she would say. Her stern lectures bordered on a scolding. She emphasized learning a trade or joining the Army to gain some kind of special skill. Those two choices formed the range of her experience and expectations. Her mind-set, which I regarded as based on the experiences of other Indian families who had left reservations, stressed a basic vocational approach to survival: learn a trade and enter the workforce. Becoming a successful Indian in a non-Indian world required families and students to develop a very different belief about their educational abilities, their future careers, and what it meant to live in mainstream America. Changing and overcoming a reservation paradigm was not easy.

With so many factors pushing the odds against higher education, it was difficult to understand how I managed to go to college, but I did manage. I was accepted at the University of Utah and enrolled in the summer quarter of 1969. The morning I left, my mother pressed an envelope into my hands. It held three hundred dollars—most of her bank savings. It helped pay for two quarters of college.

During orientation week, I checked "premed" on the intake forms. The checkmark determined my academic advisor, a chemistry professor who held a group advising session with twelve to fifteen premed students during the first week of class. I remember his first words: "Premed is a fantasy." He advised us to pick a major like chemistry or biology or engineering and gear ourselves toward a career in one of those fields. He warned that most of us would never see the inside of a medical school.

I chose biology as a default major because chemistry involved too much math and I had no interest in engineering. The biology department assigned yet another academic advisor, a botanist who did research in plant physiology. Rather than the frontal assault of the chemistry professor, the new advisor seemed more approachable and rather informal as he smoked his pipe while asking a few general questions: name, science courses taken in high school, future plans, and the like. He asked about my ethnic background. American Indian, I told him. Oncida tribe from Wisconsin. We chatted a bit about Native culture. He had a distant relative who had married an Indian woman and said I had quite a heritage. The advisor probed my math background and my grades in high school. He discovered my weakness in mathematics and asked me a point-blank question: "What would you like to do if you do not get into medical school?" Silence. I had never thought of that possibility. He waited for the answer. I finally gave it to him. "W-Well . . . ," I stammered. "Biology, I guess."

He pointed at me with the stem of his pipe. "Biology is not a career, it's an academic subject. Plant research is a career. Forestry is a career. Biology is not."

After looking at my class schedule, he said it was overloaded with yearlong sequence courses and I needed to drop two courses from either the chemistry, math, or biology series. He said the intensity was too much for the first year and arranged for me to see the American Indian student advisor the following day.

I learned from that advisor, a Navajo who held a master's degree in social work, that Native students did not go into the "hard sciences," as he called them. "We do better in social work and education," he said. Even though I had taken nearly every science class my high school offered, he felt I wasn't prepared for college-level science. He told me there was a huge dropout rate in premed regardless of ethnic background and that I should rethink my major, or at least make a backup plan. He asked if I had taken the interest inventory and career aptitude tests in high school. I had. I told him my scores indicated I should become a plumber or an "other." I took "other" to include becoming a doctor. He chuckled and said that he hadn't tested well either, then he looked at my class schedule and agreed with the biology advisor. He took a red pen to my schedule and crossed off math and chemistry. After leaving his office, I went to the registrar's office and dropped chemistry but kept the math and biology series.

The advisors were right. My freshman year quickly degenerated into a whirlwind of academic disasters and social distractions. I tried to manage two yearlong courses simultaneously but lacked the self-discipline to adhere to a rigorous study plan. The assigned math problems seemed a blur, as did the foreign accents of the graduate teaching assistants assigned to teach the problem sessions. The biology classes only reviewed what I had already learned in high school. The "hard sciences" became a drudge. I often loafed around and sloughed off on class assignments. There were parties to attend, ball games to see, and weekends to waste away.

Within a year I dropped my premed major just as my first advisor had predicted. And I felt the sting of confusion about who I was and what direction my future would take. If not medicine, then what? I bounced around for the better part of my sophomore year, changing my major from psychology to prelaw to music. Music lasted for three quarters, during which I studied theory and jazz composition. I had not mastered a musical instrument, so I had to take group piano lessons for two quarters. I learned to play every scale and, just to show off, I played one scale with my right hand and another with my left— four octaves, ascending and descending. It was my only musical talent. When it was clear that I didn't have a future in music, I decided to get practical and major in business. I started in the business school in my junior year.

That same year I started dating Collin Anne MacAskill, who had transferred from Allegheny College in Pennsylvania. Collin was the perfect combination of spunky and practical. She had a reasoned approach to life as a college student and paid attention to details and rules much more than I did. Her father had spent a career as a Marine officer and had deployed to three wars. Her brother was a Marine serving in Vietnam. She knew discipline and rules and protocol, but she also displayed a reserved sort of spontaneity that marked her as vivacious and willing to take risks. If that were not so, she would have never dated me. Disciplined as she was, she practiced her Christian faith in a manner that defied the more traditional religious norms of her Presbyterian upbringing. She involved herself in campus ministries that encouraged the growth of faith and compassion among students. It was attractive to me to see how she made faith such a central part of her life without making it overtly and harshly religious. Collin majored in recreational therapy and was a natural at helping people meet their needs for fun and companionship. That was her gift.

Our first date was during the tail end of my music studies. As a course assignment, I had to attend the Utah Symphony Orchestra and write a critical paper for theory class—free tickets compliments of the music department. I asked Collin if she would like to go, and she accepted. The seats were in the far back of the symphony hall, right behind a huge marble pillar. I asked if she wouldn't mind sitting behind the pillar, since I had to observe the musicians and write a paper. She rolled her eyes but agreed. Miraculously we had a second date, and more followed. We got married in 1972, during the spring of my fourth year of college.

In my final undergraduate year, I explored a military career as an alternative to business and medicine. I had several college friends who participated in either Air Force or Navy ROTC. They all talked enthusiastically about their military careers and the opportunities they had. I sought out the campus Marine recruiter and asked about a career in aviation. He started me on a path of screening interviews and application forms. I met all the qualifications and planned to finish college with a business degree, go straight to officer training, and then on to flight school. I would potentially go to Vietnam to fly fighter jets off an aircraft carrier.

My father-in-law, who had spent combat tours in the South Pacific, Korea, and Vietnam, advised me to consider what I would be risking for a military career and suggested that I might think about alternatives—consider other choices. He gave me pause. He was a Marine colonel; I was a college student married to his daughter. I figured he might know a bit more about the Marines and the current situation in Vietnam than I did. I trusted his advice and opted for a civilian business career. In the short term, that career turned out to be a part-time job at the Salt Lake City International Airport where I pumped jet fuel and parked corporate aircraft—minimum wage, no benefits. Collin and I lived in a twenty-by-twenty-foot basement apartment, paid one hundred dollars a month for rent, drove a used orange Plymouth Duster, and lived from paycheck to paycheck. We wanted something different, something more.

The University of Utah offered a master's degree program in human resource management that required only one year of coursework for those students who already had a business degree. It minimized the math and finance requirements of typical MBA programs and emphasized the people end of business. I enrolled in the fall and we budgeted our expenses to Collin's income. I worked in a student internship at the university and continued the airport job on alternate weekends. I completed the program in the summer of 1976. A business degree was practical, it would serve to provide a well-paying job, yet it was not the career that I wanted to frame my life. And as with the completion of my undergraduate degree, I stuffed my dream of becoming a doctor into a subliminal closet while I pursued the more practical aspects of starting a career. Whenever I dressed the part of a businessman, I would walk into that closet and see the dusty edges of my dream, that stubborn vision of me as a doctor. And I held two dreams of myself: one defined a practical survival; the other defined who I really wanted to become.

MASTER'S DEGREE in hand, I landed a marketing job at IBM and was offered a chance to relocate. Collin and I choose Anchorage, Alaska. In the fall of 1976 we traded in our Plymouth Duster for a new International Harvester Scout and drove the Alaska Highway to our new home. During our first year in Alaska we bought a house, a bush plane, and a camper. We spent weekends camping and fishing. In January 1978, our first son, Justin, was born. That summer we took him salmon fishing in a backpack baby carrier. We hiked and hunted, worked and dreamed.

As an integral part of IBM's training and business culture, I learned to write an annual marketing plan that listed all the steps required to accomplish my business and personal objectives for the coming year. Every year, at the top of my plan, I would write, "Go to medical school." Before my manager reviewed the plan, I scrapped it and wrote a different list with hard-core business objectives displacing my more personal goals. When I thought about what I was doing, I realized I was still unsettled about my future. The plans worked. I won numerous marketing awards during our family's three years in Alaska. My success at IBM drove me, but I still found myself wanting something different. And I knew exactly what that something was—the dream that I kept hidden and alive.

We relocated to Chicago in the late spring of 1979 in preparation for a marketing promotion. Within months I realized that my IBM career lacked the sense of promise that it held when I worked in Alaska. Darren, our second son, was born in September and my focus began shifting toward family and fatherhood responsibilities. Internally, I still had lingering thoughts of becoming a doctor, but they seemed so unrealistic and out of touch. I was at least ten years past the prime of entering medical school, and money and career opportunities were not things to be abandoned for a dream.

At age thirty, married, and with two children, I decided on the practical course. I would pursue further education and an academic career as an alternative to medicine. The educational part was also an incognito means of bolstering my academic credentials for a run at medical school if academia didn't work out. I didn't tell Collin the hidden part of my plan because I felt it might reveal I was still unsettled about my future, even though I had agreed with her that an academic career would make sense in providing a challenging outlet for me and stability for our family.

My advisor at the University of Minnesota was Professor Chuck

Manz, who researched and wrote about self-management. Professor Manz was young, energetic, and just enough of a maverick in pushing graduate students that he was a perfect match for me. He thought my proposal for research, a study of the physiology of stress and work performance, unique among the more typical business research proposals. With his guidance, the School of Business approved my rather non-traditional PhD proposal to integrate coursework in the School of Public Health within the College of Medicine. The college offered one particular course in the fall semester that I considered central to my plan, occupational medicine, taught by Professor Robert Veninga. It was designed for physicians and graduate students entering the field of public health.

After I presented my term paper, Professor Veninga called me into his office to discuss it. His first words were "Great paper." He had follow-up questions and generally made comments as to the importance of the original insight that it offered. Then he said something that jolted me.

"You should consider studying public health or medicine."

You should consider studying medicine. I needed those words. When I heard them, it seemed as if they enlarged their meaning as they traveled toward my brain. They reminded me of the Oneida healer's blessing I received as a child. I experienced an instantaneous awareness of a possible reality that nested itself in the word "medicine." My dreams about becoming a doctor became more than an undergraduate fantasy; they became transformed into image and movement and direction, and I felt connected to medicine once more. I tried to respond to Professor Veninga with the outward appearance of an objective and critical graduate student. Casually and almost nonchalantly, I acknowledged that I had, on occasion, considered the study of medicine. In my heart I felt like William Harvey himself had just opened the great doors of the renaissance medical school at the University of Padua, Italy, and said, "Please come in, we've been expecting you."

When I left Professor Veninga's office, I headed straight to the College of Business to talk with Professor Manz. I told him I wanted to switch directions and study medicine. He smiled and said he wasn't surprised and that I would be an excellent doctor. He offered to help by keeping me in the business program for another year as a teaching assistant. That single act of support gave me an endorsement to follow my dream. And like the comments of Professor Veninga, I needed that encouragement from Professor Manz. His support helped me understand that I would find my way to study medicine.

During the next two years, I studied the necessary science prerequisites for my application to medical school. I absorbed lectures in chemistry, physics, mathematics, and biochemistry, engaging the readings and the labs, often studying until after midnight. I would run my fingers over the pictures in the cell biology and biochemistry textbooks, mesmerized by the beauty of cellular structure and the intricacies of biochemical interactions.

On September 1, 1981, Collin gave birth to our daughter Jordan. She was born with a constriction in her aorta that required surgery. During Jordan's first two years, we spent numerous days each month in the offices of pediatricians and cardiologists. Our lives were anything but planned or predictable. We lived in a no-man's-land of uncertainty about Jordan's health and our future. She had her surgery at age two and a half and recovered without complications.

In the midst of that uproar of family stress, I continued my preparations for medical school while teaching at the University of Minnesota and at Bethel College in Saint Paul. Collin wondered how we could provide for our children if I left academics. She worried about the future and had questions about finances. I didn't have the answers. I thought perhaps I didn't need answers—only the confidence to get through. I assured her medical school would work out, that it was a now-or-never proposition.

We argued, she complained. We argued, I complained. We both felt angry and confused and out of control. Sometimes we screamed. Sometimes we cried. I felt she didn't understand my life's ambition. She felt I didn't understand or care about her needs. I told her I wanted more for the family. She said I wanted more for myself. Occasionally we gave each other the silent treatment. Sometimes we got on the same wavelength. We both felt a mixture of fear and hope as we muddled forward and backward, one stressful step at a time.

BEFORE I SENT out medical school applications, I visited the campus of the Mayo Medical School in Rochester, Minnesota. I met with the dean, Dr. Roy Rogers III, and we discussed my application. The only Roy Rogers I knew of was the one I had watched on television. I wondered if the dean was related but didn't dare ask. Dr. Rogers assured me I was competitive enough to make the first cut and was rather impressed that I made the extra effort to visit the medical school prior to applying. About a month later Mayo responded with a letter inviting me for an interview. Part of me marveled in disbelief; another part of me expected it. I set it up for late January. The morning of my interview, a blizzard hit and turned the roads to ice. The drive to Rochester from my home in Apple Valley, Minnesota, normally took little more than two hours. I left my house at 6:00 a.m. to allow enough time to get to Mayo. When I left the house, the wind chill was minus twenty degrees. When I arrived in Rochester at 9:30 a.m., it was minus thirty, cold enough to make my nostrils stick together when I breathed.

While I was on the road, one of the admissions staff members phoned my home to advise me not to travel and to reschedule the interview. Too late. I was already in their medical library warming up. I had my interview at 10:30, as scheduled. Dr. Rogers greeted me and I told him a blizzard could not keep me away from medical school. He chuckled and offered me coffee. The entire interview lasted almost an hour. I got extra time because the applicant scheduled after me canceled due to the weather.

Afterward, it took almost twenty minutes to clear the ice from my car and get it warmed up. As I traveled back to Apple Valley, I turned the radio on extra loud and drove perhaps a little too fast. Confident and a bit elated, I laughed and sang. "Hot damn! I'm goin' to Mayo."

Two weeks after my admissions interview, I received a letter from the Mayo Medical School. I took the envelope downstairs to my makeshift study to read it in private. I noted how thin the letter was, how light it felt in my hands. I had heard from other premed students that thin letters didn't contain the admission's "welcome packet" and were therefore rejections. I hesitated, tensed my shoulders, held my breath, and carefully slit the envelope open. I pulled out the letter and unfolded it. The first four words read, "Congratulations, we are pleased . . ." I breathed, said yes repeatedly, and finally sat down. I read the letter several times and focused on the first four words. My stack of MCAT books sat on the floor. I picked one up, fanned the pages, and laughed out loud; then I stood and shouted, "I'm in!" I would begin medical school in the fall of 1984. I had just entered the class of 1988 of the Mayo Medical School. And that was an awesome, yet almost frightening reality. I would finally become the physician that I had so often dreamed about.

THE DAY BEFORE classes began, I spent almost three hours exploring the halls of the Mayo Clinic and the adjacent Plummer Building, which held the medical library and the stacks of thousands of medical journals. At each lecture hall in the medical school, I sat in several different seats; first in the front row, then in the back, trying to find which ones gave me the best vantage point. In the student center, I checked to make sure my name was on a mail slot. It was. After a half hour I double-checked it. Still there. The anatomy building was surrounded by flower beds. I stepped over them and ran my hands over the walls, lingering as my fingers touched the weathered, tan bricks. I wanted to absorb anatomy through the walls like osmosis—let medical science flow through my skin and saturate my body, let knowledge become my oxygen.

As I continued to explore, I walked back to the Plummer Building and rode the elevator to the fifteenth floor, which housed the medical antiquities collection. I explained to the librarian that I was a new medical student and loved to read about William Harvey and the classical anatomists. Before I could ask, she volunteered to show me some original sketches from the earliest anatomy books in the collection.

We entered a humidity-controlled inner room where the librarian placed an ancient book on a large oak table. It was an original by Andreas Vesalius, *De humani corporis fabrica*. The fragile, slightly graying pages held printer's ink from the year 1543. The ink seemed to me only slightly faded; the smell of ancient paper drifted ever so slightly above the drawings. I gazed in silence as if in meditation. Almost imperceptibly, I nodded my head in affirmation. I was so overcome by the beauty and the historicity of the drawings, I struggled not to show emotion. The librarian said I could come back during the posted times; she even told me about an opportunity to study ancient books as part of an elective. As I left, I felt humbled by the study of medicine.

Anatomy was my favorite subject, as I guessed it would be. The course detailed every aspect of human structure, every bone, every organ, every cell, and their anatomical relationship to the whole body. It was one of the cornerstones of biomedical science. The anatomy professors, Drs. Cahill and Carmichael, did not assign lectures to graduate students but did all the didactic work themselves. They spent hours drawing magnified details of the human body with colored markers on whiteboards, often working through lunch. I tried to copy their drawings freehand in my notebooks. Dr. Cahill emphasized the ability to draw anatomical relationships from memory, arguing that a student who could sketch the details of anatomy was a student who understood the body, artistic skills aside.

Our medical school library housed numerous life-size and scaled-down models of the human body. I studied them all in detail, sometimes disassembling and then reassembling the models just to get the feel of the shape and size of the organs. Occasionally, while I was studying, I would remember the Visible Man of my boyhood days, the afternoons spent learning all the parts, taking them apart and putting them back together.

The pathology course included an optional research component that lasted six months. I took the option at the encouragement of one of the professors, Dr. Bahn, who used to say if doctors mastered the pathological basis of disease, they would be better prepared to diagnose and treat disease. I wanted exactly that. Pathology included duties on the autopsy service and in surgical pathology, where I accumulated hundreds of hours analyzing whole organs and their corresponding histological specimens. I studied diseases by system, organ, and cell and learned to determine causes of death at each level. I worked on a particularly difficult case that involved the autopsy of a teenager who was killed in a home fire. The teen had escaped the fire and alerted neighbors to contact the fire department, only to rush back into the burning house to help her mother escape. Both died of smoke inhalation. That was my first encounter with violent death and it shook me. I had seen other deaths in pathology, but this one was particularly tragic because it was so unnecessary.

To the degree that studying the biomedical sciences fascinated and engaged me, studying clinical medicine sobered my rather zealous approach to academics. Clinical medicine required a different kind of knowledge. It focused on real people and the diseases that threatened their lives and the lives of their families. Textbooks didn't describe the anguish patients felt and often transferred to their doctors. Patients came with fear and anger and tears; they wanted answers and hope and the promise of a cure. And the answers required more than mere recitations of facts about diseases and outcomes. Yes, they needed to yield the hard information about a diagnosis and a prognosis, but they also needed to show compassion in the telling and offer at least some encouragement.

The lessons on how to provide those answers didn't come from lectures; they came from hospital rooms and operating rooms and from talking through the tough times with patients and their families. Absent in that milieu was the excitement of the classroom and the laboratories. Of course, seeing a particular disease or its manifestations for the first time was always fascinating in its own way, but observing how disease and trauma made people suffer was itself a kind of vicarious suffering. To become an excellent doctor meant learning to carry that weight.

In clinical rotations, I honed my skills in taking histories and doing thorough physical exams. I spent extra hours in pediatrics, surgery, and internal medicine. I talked to patients about their diagnoses and prognoses. I watched them struggle, saw some heal, saw some die. Ultimately, what I learned about clinical practice was this: it was not so much the study of a different kind of medicine but more of a transformation into a different kind of person—a healer, a physician.

Over the three years of my clinical training, I learned to get close enough to patients to show empathy and compassion while remaining detached enough to move from one case to the next with the understanding that medical science could not save every patient. My first lesson in that regard came when Dr. Rhodes, a staff pediatrician, assigned me to follow the case of a small-framed, freckled ten-year-old girl with leukemia who wore a blue bandana to hide her chemo head. I spent hours with the patient and her parents and wrote copious notes in the chart. I read all the latest journal articles on leukemia and hounded the pediatric oncology fellow with questions. My treatment plans detailed the best course of clinical action. She seemed to be responding to treatment, but then a week into the case, a septic crisis hit. She died in the middle of the night. I was shocked by the reversal, feeling that I had at least some responsibility for the outcome, that I should have been able to prevent the untoward complications. I filtered the experience through my role as a father. I imagined how I would feel losing a child to cancer. And in that moment, I felt that being a father made me a more empathetic physician. When Dr. Rhodes saw how the death affected me, she said we had to consider our emotional responses in the context of all the patients we treated, not just the ones we lost; that we as doctors needed to be vigilant against succumbing to despair; and finally, that we were not our patients' friends or parents: we were their doctors.

During my initial clinical rotations as a medical student, I thought I would be the kind of doctor who always brought hope and a cure to the bedside. Sometimes that was true. At other times I was the doctor who brought only comfort, and that comfort had to suffice, both for my patients and for me. That was the reality of becoming a physician. It was humbling and frightening and heavy; it was promising and challenging and fulfilling.

— — —

By January of my first year at Mayo, Collin became pregnant. Her due date happened to coincide with my second-year obstetrics rotation, so when the time came, I asked her and my supervising obstetrician if I could deliver our baby. On September 22, 1985, her labor progressed rapidly and by mid-morning, nurses wheeled her into a delivery room. I scrubbed in and the obstetrician talked me through the entire delivery. Playing the roles of father, doctor, and husband left me a bit conflicted. I knew, as a husband, Collin needed me at the head of the bed. I wanted to receive our new baby together and hold her as a father. As a medical student, I wanted the clinical excitement and experience.

I was so busy with the birth, delivering the head, suctioning the baby's nose and mouth, and asking my wife for one more push, that when our baby was finally born I forgot to announce we had a girl. The obstetrician chuckled and made the announcement. I cut the cord, clamped it, and handed her off to the nurse. I remember shaking a bit, not from fear, but from joy as a new father. I felt pride as a doctor and a bit of guilt as a husband. I wanted to move between my roles transparently, as if there were no boundaries—to do them all concurrently. I'm not so sure I balanced those roles all that well. But on that day, with our new daughter, I was a doctor and a father and a husband—all three at once, best as I could be.

Justin and Darren, ages seven and six, and Jordan, age four, were excited for a new sister. The boys wanted to name her Jabba the Hutt, after the *Star Wars* character. Jordan picked a *My Little Pony* name. We settled on Katelyn Marie. We have pictures of all four together on the sofa days after her birth, Katelyn rather pink and wrinkled, Justin and Darren with rambunctious smiles, and Jordan hugging her new sister.

Collin homeschooled the children and kept us more or less organized and on track for family activities. Occasionally we went fishing or picnicking. The boys had piano lessons once a week and participated in the Awana Club at church. They loved the games and Bible stories and treats. Vacation Bible School was a big hit for the kids and it gave Collin a much-needed break.

A fair number of weekends Collin tended the kids alone because I had clinical rounds or studying. She tried to remind me that weekends were difficult and sometimes lonely, because while most families spent their weekend relaxing, too often she managed the kids alone and had to keep them entertained, disciplined, and fed while maintaining her own space and sanity. Just as I had lacked understanding for the difficulties my mother faced as a single parent, I did not completely understand the emotional and physical toll that medical school took on my wife, who, in many ways, functioned and struggled like a single parent.

COLLIN'S PARENTS AND my mother attended the Mayo Medical School graduation ceremonies in May 1988. Mom flew in from Salt Lake City wearing her fanciest tan cotton dress and her ceremonial turquois and silver squash-blossom necklace. Her shoes were brown leather flats that she had bought just for the occasion. It was her first trip on an airplane and she told me she wanted to look special for the trip. Her Indian boarding school education had qualified her to work as a housekeeper or a food-service worker. Her labors in those jobs continued past age seventy-five. She never learned to drive a car and always walked to work. She involved herself in her community. One year she won a blue ribbon at the Box Elder County Fair for a homemade cornhusk Indian doll she had entered. She made crazy quilts every winter, peach jam and dill pickles every summer. She brought me a jar of peach jam for a graduation present.

Commencement ceremonies were held in the Rochester Civic Auditorium. My family and in-laws sat in one of the front rows. After the commencement speech, the dean started calling names for the awarding of degrees. The attendees gave a round of applause. The graduates mostly smiled, but a few had tears welling up. My name was called somewhere near the middle, and I remember walking across the stage and glancing at my family as I went. My kids were smiling. Jordan waved. I waved back. My mother seemed rather somber. In the center of the stage were the dean, Dr. Franklin Knox, and associate deans of the medical school, Drs. Roy Rogers and Gerald Peterson. They presented my diploma, congratulated me, and shook my hand. And in that finite moment, on May 21, 1988, at age thirty-seven, I became the physician I had always wanted to become. Immediately before and after the official granting of my degree, I repeated to myself: *I finally made it. I finally made it.*

Afterward, in a private moment during the reception, Mom pulled me aside and pressed an antique silver and turquoise ring into my hand. With tears in her eyes, she said "God bless" in the Oneida language. She told me how proud she was and how sometimes she wanted to pinch herself just to make sure she wasn't in a dream. I smiled—said it *was* a dream.

Several times that day I opened the special folder that held my Mayo Medical School diploma. Printed after my name were the words "Doctor of Medicine." I paused in quiet reflection that I had become a doctor, that I was fortunate enough to have had my children and my wife help me with the journey, and that I had come so far from the Oneida Indian reservation where I had begun my life. I remembered my lawnmower ride with Jimmy and my first childhood encounter with doctors. I thought of the country doctor in Utah with the milky-white penicillin and the traditional Oneida healer who blessed my hands that they might do good things. I quietly promised myself that they would.

Part Two

_ _ _ _

FIGHT

61-November

O N THE FIRST DAY of Desert Storm in January 1991, television newscasts bristled with the luminescent green, night-vision images of ground targets on fire throughout Iraq. Buildings exploded from the attacks of cruise missiles and jet bombers. News reporters described the shock and awe as the air assault unfolded. I was on duty at the Finley Hospital in Dubuque, Iowa, and watched the news with the nurses in the break room. Charlene, who had been a young nurse during the Vietnam era, shook her head and said we didn't need another war; then she walked away to attend her patients. One of the male nurses, an Army reservist, told us how the Air Force was going to kick ass. I said he was probably right and continued to watch with a mixture of disbelief and belief, wondering if Desert Storm would become another Vietnam.

In the preceding months, I had received mass mailings from the National Guard advertising the benefits of military careers for doctors. They showed military doctors rappelling down mountainsides with medical equipment. Others showed combat hospitals, deployed trauma teams, medevac helicopters, and night-mission rescues. One of the brochures touted the virtues of a career in aviation medicine. It included training in the flight surgeon academy and promised a life of adventure. The gist of the messaging was that the military offered a medical practice that pushed boundaries. They were recruiting doctors with an eye toward living on the edge. As I read, I felt as if the military had wiretapped my thoughts and designed the brochures with exactly me in mind.

— — —

FOLLOWING MY POST—MEDICAL school internship at the Marshfield
Clinic in Wisconsin, our family had moved to Iowa, where I did an additional year of training at the University of Iowa Hospitals and then
started my private practice in emergency medicine in 1990. I joined
the emergency staff of Emergency Practice Associates and worked in
several hospitals in Iowa's larger cities, Des Moines, Dubuque, and
Waterloo, and in smaller communities as the need arose. I scheduled
as many as a dozen twenty-four-hour shifts a month and occasionally
threw in a few twelve-hour shifts. That number of shifts bordered
on excessive, but I scheduled them anyway because critical cases of
trauma and cardiac resuscitation engaged me like nothing else. And
when I wasn't working my ER shifts, I taught advanced cardiac life
support (ACLS) to other doctors in practice. Managing critical patients was my gift and I loved it and excelled at it. I became quick,
decisive, and knowledgeable; I built a reputation in the larger hospitals
as a "trauma dog."

Decisiveness and knowledge didn't automatically translate into
saving lives. Patients still died regardless of how fast I acted to stop
their bleeding or correct their cardiac arrhythmias. And when they
died, I often felt that just one more procedure or perhaps one more
unit of blood or a final dose of medicine could have made a difference.
When I called a code and pronounced the time of death, I felt like
somebody had cheated me out of completing a thousand-piece puzzle
by hiding the final critical pieces, except the enormity and emotional
impact of an unsuccessful resuscitation felt infinitely greater than the
momentary disappointment from a trivial game. Every patient who
died in the ER reminded me of the omnipresent risk of mortality.

The other aspect of treating critical patients was dealing with the
aftermath of tragedy. After a case, I counseled families and tried to explain how their loved ones had died. I saw family members fall apart,
physically and emotionally, as if suddenly ravaged by a Midwestern
tornado. I wanted to stand nearby and buffer them from their storm
of grief, but I could not. When they gathered themselves together to

leave the hospital, I lifted their tragedy and carried it with me as if it belonged to me, because in fact it did.

Despite the critical nature of emergency medicine, it had a rather mundane side. I frequently spent a majority of a shift diagnosing and treating common colds, minor cuts, bumps, and bruises, and doing preventive medicine. Quite a few patients came for nothing more than a medical work excuse. Minor fender-benders frequently clogged the ER. They required a "medical clearing" for insurance purposes, which, because of medical-legal issues, meant that a full gamut of X-rays and labs was ordered and a full exam documented. Those kinds of cases cut at the heart of the challenge and excitement in emergency medicine. They made me feel like my skills were being wasted. In any given month I accumulated cases that thrilled me and cases that bored me, and the boring cases abraded the entire ER experience. Some doctors left emergency medicine just for that reason. That was not an option for me. The Army and its opportunities seemed to offer a solution, especially to the vital connection to critical patients I needed so much.

The day after Desert Storm began I phoned the medical recruiter of the Iowa National Guard and asked if they needed ER docs. The recruiter, Major James Regur, assured me they did and arranged to meet me the next day at the Country Kitchen restaurant in Iowa City. He arrived just a bit after noon, dressed in his class A army-green uniform. We settled into a corner booth. The first thing I noticed was that he spoke with a fast, clipped pattern, like that of a high-strung person, yet his body language gave the impression of one in control. Major Regur was older than I expected and much thinner. He had thinning hair, an overly large hearing aid, and thick glasses. I wondered if he had ever carried a rifle. His black briefcase was stuffed with medical corps brochures like the ones I had received in the mail. He handed me several and began to explain the needs of the Iowa National Guard. He discussed benefits like paid medical conferences and retirement after twenty years of service and stressed that I had to pass a medical and physical exam. I told him no problem. He also said I needed an age waiver because I exceeded the maximum age for commissioning and that the waiver might slow the application down a bit.

"ER docs are in demand," he said. "If you have no medical problems and can run two miles and do twenty push-ups, we can start the application process soon as you're ready."

When I got home, I mentioned to Collin that I had started an initial discussion with the National Guard and that I was just looking at the "possibility" of joining. She stared me down and said it wasn't a good idea, that I didn't have the time, that it wasn't a good fit.

"Do you really need the military to do medicine?" she asked with just enough bite to make me defensive.

"No, but it's something I've always wanted."

She was disappointed that I hadn't talked with her before contacting a recruiter. I assured her everything was only preliminary. "Preliminary" was a word I used when I wanted to nullify any impression of making major family decisions without involving my wife. She knew better. So did I, but I said it anyway, because doing so served the purpose of allowing us both to feel as if we were not jumping headlong into unexplored territory.

By the time Major Regur had compiled all the various components of my application, Desert Storm was nearing an end, and I wound up deciding to put my application on hold. The major kept in touch and sent me information about special Army training and research opportunities in trauma and aviation medicine. I read the brochures several times. Every word and picture made military medicine seem so exciting, as if it were on the frontier of critical care and trauma research. Military doctors were a rare breed of doctor and that's what I wanted to be. In contrast, practicing civilian emergency medicine had become stale and predictable.

Collin knew my love-hate relationship with emergency medicine wore me down. Sometimes I would come home from a long shift and complain that I had done nothing but treat ear infections and colds and that I needed to work in a setting with more trauma. She had seen the Army recruiting brochures I left on the kitchen table, so when I told her in July 1992 that I wanted to explore the option of military medicine once more, she wasn't totally surprised.

"I know you're not totally happy with the ER," she said, after one of my shifts. "What are you thinking about the military?"

"I just want other options. Relocating to a trauma center doesn't seem realistic with our family."

"It's not," she responded.

"I think the National Guard might provide a challenge."

"But why do you always need a challenge?"

"I don't," I claimed, "but half my time is wasted in the ER. It's not exactly what I wanted."

She continued to reiterate her concerns about me fitting into a military bureaucracy and about how it would impact my time with our family. Her concern was that at my age I would be a late starter and would always be answering to officers ten to fifteen years younger. She saw that as more significant than the age gap I had experienced in medical school and told me that I would always be fighting against it. I responded that I would always be the older, new doctor no matter where I worked and that it made no difference to me. I needed more challenges in medicine and short of relocating to a large city where I could work in a major trauma center, I felt the Guard was a good part-time option. Collin also wondered out loud about the issue of military rank and how I would accept being senior in age and junior in rank. Not an issue, I told her. It didn't matter what issue she mentioned, I had an answer. Just short of exasperation, she told me to think about it hard before I did anything. I said I had.

I signed my application for the Iowa Army National Guard—age forty-two. After congratulating me, Major Regur set up a preliminary appointment for a screening interview with Lieutenant Colonel Kent Frieze, commander of the 1/113th Cavalry. The 1/113th drove tanks and flew older Cobras and Hueys. Some of the helicopters and their pilots had seen action in the jungles of Vietnam. The Cav needed a flight surgeon. The only thing I knew about the cavalry was that they fought against Indians and enlisted one tribe to scout against another tribe, and of course that Custer and the 7th Cavalry had been slaughtered at the Battle of the Little Big Horn.

Lieutenant Colonel Frieze had a large corner office in the Cavalry headquarters building of Camp Dodge in Des Moines. On the wall behind his desk hung a black Stetson with a gold-braided Cav hatband with his rank insignia pinned on the front. He was medium build and stocky, square-jawed—what I had expected of a cavalry officer.

"You're older than most applicants," he said. "Why do you want to join the National Guard now?"

Collin had asked that same question several times and I had responded confidently, yet now, when I faced it from a senior officer, I hesitated. Why did I really want to join the Guard? What did I have to do with soldiering? Was the military just another venue for trying to fill an unsatisfied need? Would I ever be satisfied in my career as a doctor?

"Well, I got a late start in medical school," I said. I gave him the short version of how I prepared for medical school and then redirected my answer toward aviation. "I had planned to join the Marines and become an aviator. My plans changed, but I've always thought about joining the military one day."

That part about *always* thinking about joining the military wasn't true. It just popped out like an inane and passing note of small talk that I failed to correct. I had only reconsidered joining because emergency medicine pulled me between the extremes of total satisfaction and total frustration. I didn't say that to Lieutenant Colonel Frieze. Rather, I muddled through an explanation of how being older didn't hold me back from becoming a doctor and that I had probably accomplished more than most applicants regardless of age. I let him know I wanted to take the Army combat trauma course and become a flight surgeon.

"We're always short of flight surgeons," he said. "You have to apply to the flight surgeon academy after a year of service. In the interim, you'll need to take your officer training courses. Your initial assignment will be as a field surgeon."

I was surprised. "I didn't realize I couldn't go directly to the flight surgeon course," I replied.

"You'll be first on the list after you finish your officer training and your initial assignment. Look at it like medical training," he said. "Training follows a hierarchy. Basics first, then advanced."

After twenty minutes of chitchat, Lieutenant Colonel Frieze gave me a direct look. "The job of the Army is to break things and kill people," he said abruptly. "You're a doctor. You okay with that?"

I had always thought my role as a military physician would focus on the care of the wounded, and never on the need to kill, yet without hesitation I said I was okay with it. Internally, I felt a nudge and a pause. The commander had put it so bluntly—the stated purpose of the military. I dismissed it. I left it hanging like a quirk of science.

MAJOR REGUR CALLED about a week later. My application had been approved. In late September 1992, Lieutenant Colonel Frieze administered the oath of a military officer and gave me a set of captain's bars. First assignment: the 1st Squadron of the 113th Cavalry Regiment.

I drilled in Des Moines or Waterloo one weekend per month. In the summer the entire regiment convoyed to Camp Ripley in Minnesota or Fort McCoy in Wisconsin. Training included range firing— mortars, pistols (the old Colt 45 and the newer 9mm), and the M16 assault rifle. I learned to throw grenades and drop mortar rounds— heard them thump, then hit downrange. Lofting mortar shells and firing at human silhouettes was odd in the sense that, for the first time, I saw the glaring irony of my life. A doctor training to become a soldier, a Native American in the modern cavalry whose roots extended all the way back to the Indian Wars. The branch insignia sewn on my uniform, its bold caduceus distinctive from any other branch of the military, told everybody, including me, that I was a medical corps officer. The designation set me apart as a soldier whose hands were trained to heal, yet in the cavalry those same hands were being trained in the art of war and the craft of killing. I contemplated how the two roles pulled against each other and how I needed to balance doctoring and soldiering and make them both work together.

That balancing act gave me pause, but it didn't prevent me from acquiring soldiering skills. I made my own ghillie suit by stuffing twigs and leaves and dried grass into the slits of my helmet cover and my camouflage jacket. My face and hands became a forest of camo paint: black, brown, and green. I ran the land navigation course with the best of the young Cav officers. I absorbed it all: the dirt, the smell, the tactics, and the unit camaraderie. I wanted to fit in. I *did* fit in. I saw the experience as another boundary that I had pushed against and crossed. It was another source of validation—another way of fulfilling that unrelenting need to become something more than I had been.

Following my first summer training camp, I requested airborne training thinking it might make me more of a soldier and a leader. Lieutenant Colonel Frieze denied the request and kept me focused on medicine and aviation. When a class position opened to attend the Combat Casualty Care Course (C4) at Camp Bullis, Texas, he approved my application immediately.

During the C4 course, I performed well enough to earn one of three recommendations for further training as a trauma instructor in the military. As a result, earlier than promised, during my initial field assignment, the Iowa Guard sent me to the flight surgeon course at Fort Rucker, Alabama. The course included lectures on the physiology of flight and the mechanisms of aviation-related injuries. The physician instructors taught from the vantage point of experience in Desert Storm or Vietnam, and whenever I could I peppered them with questions about combat trauma. The flight surgeon academy reminded me of medical school. Each new lecture fostered new interests in, maybe even a love for, all things medical and military. I viewed my new specialty as evidence that I had finally arrived at becoming the kind of doctor I had always dreamed of becoming.

As part of aviation operational training, I flew several hours in helicopter simulators to gain cockpit familiarization. The simulations rehearsed basic in-flight emergencies and included a scenario for landing. I crashed in two out of three trials and wanted to spend more time than was allotted. The instructors said the purpose was familiarization, not mastery. I talked them into one more hour of simulator training.

Even the fitness workouts were engaging. Before breakfast each day, I ran three miles, sometimes five. I spent an hour or more in the gym each day, pumping iron and punching the speed bag. I felt invigorated and renewed, fit and capable. When the flight surgeon class ran as a platoon, we sang a cadence: *"I don't know but I've been told . . . flight surgeons are mighty bold."* Most of the officers in our class were young, brash, and full of vigor. I was older but still full of vigor.

I captured every bit of the excitement packed in the academic and field training, reveling in the delusion among students and instructors that flight surgeons were a select group of Army doctors who deserved just a few more kudos from the ranks because we volunteered to practice medicine in the higher-risk environment of aviation operations. Our perception rested purely on pride in our specialty. It had no basis in fact or in the greater scheme of military medicine. The reality was that one kind of Army doctor held no greater or lesser significance than any other, and the doctor whose significance was greatest was the doctor whose skills matched the needs of a given patient at a given time.

The curriculum included high-altitude training, complete with an altitude chamber that simulated hypoxia. As part of the experience, trainees had to remove their oxygen masks in a rapid ascent to over 18,000 feet (simulated). I learned to experience the physiological changes and the early warning signs of oxygen deprivation and equipment failure. I tried to defy the hypoxic changes by taking shallow breaths. It didn't work. I felt the gradual onset of lip tingling and facial numbing, the fading of acute hearing, and the gradual confusion and dyscalculia. I wrote simple math problems in a notebook. 2+2= ___; 5-1=___. I couldn't solve them. I used my supplemental oxygen and recovered. Lesson learned. Recognize cognitive symptoms early. Correct problems quickly.

In all of the simulations and flight operations training, there was a pace and level of performance that distinguished military medicine from that of civilian practice. The medical principles held true and invariable in either case. Bleeding was bleeding, wounds were wounds; the treatments were the same. But military medicine added the dimension of performing under the pressure of combat where medical care was complicated by the military paradigm of battlefield triage and the need to return soldiers to duty as soon as practical. Triage allowed military doctors to withhold life-saving treatment based upon a soldier's likelihood of survival. In civilian emergency medicine, that decision was rarely, if ever, allowed.

Our class participated in a newly introduced training module, hyperbaric medicine. Many aspects of the training paralleled the science and medicine of naval deep-sea diving. As with all my encounters with new disciplines of medicine, I felt the need to explore the subject as if I were studying anatomy or physiology during the first weeks of medical school. The exploration not only satisfied a longing for more knowledge, it satisfied a deeper need to belong to something extraordinary. I was never satisfied with the ordinary. I had to become something and somebody beyond ordinary, a bold person who defied complexity and shaped it into my unique and ordered universe.

On March 22, 1993, an Army flight surgeon who had served in the Vietnam War delivered the graduation address to our flight surgeon class. The Vietcong had captured him when his helicopter went down on a rescue mission. He spent several years as a prisoner of war at the Hanoi Hilton. His daily prison routines included constant near starvation and the persistent brutality of the guards with their physical and mental torture. During his imprisonment, his captors hung him from his wrists and flogged him nearly to death because he ate a prison guard's cat to stay alive. As he described the details of his torture, I imagined myself as a captured soldier, and I knew I could never endure imprisonment. He told us how his fellow POWs developed a secret tap code and how they tapped out words on the prison walls to encourage each other or to say good night. They recited scriptures and prayed for each other and said "God bless." There were times when prisoners got a distant, unresponsive look in their eyes, and when they got that look, other prisoners tried to encourage them or sneak them food. The encouragement usually failed. The doctor described his eventual release from prison and how, over the years, he began to heal by turning from bitterness and hate. He said that his turning released him to live and love once more.

"I have a full life now," he said. "I've learned to forgive and to heal. The scars are still there, but they're less important." His peaceful manner gave strength to his message. Still, it was difficult for me to understand how a soldier could recover from years of torture and imprisonment, how a prisoner of war could come to the point of forgiveness. He reminded the graduating class that becoming a flight surgeon demanded more than acquiring a special set of skills; it demanded even more than a willingness to respond to an edict of war. He challenged us to think of our specialty as a commitment to provide healing and strength to fellow soldiers, whenever and wherever they needed a doctor the most—whether in a field hospital, in a medevac helicopter, or in a POW camp. He signed off by saying "God bless" in tap code: tap-tap, tap-tap—tap-tap, tap. As he finished his talk, the room was silent. Then it erupted in standing applause and tears.

Despite all I had heard about the inhumanity of war, I celebrated my new role. Yes, it meant struggling to balance the roles of a soldier and doctor, and if the need arose, pulling a trigger to kill. Yet within that struggle was something more powerful than war's inhumanity; it was the humanity of a military doctor bringing hope and healing to soldiers gripped by the certainties of war. And becoming a flight surgeon gave me the sense that I could do just that.

The commander of the academy called the graduates forward by name: "Captain Jon Kerstetter, Iowa National Guard." He pinned the silver wings of an Army flight surgeon on my uniform. My new orders read: "Captain Jon R. Kerstetter is awarded the U.S. Army Flight Surgeon Badge and hereby qualified as Military Occupational Specialty, 61N—Flight Surgeon."

OVER THE COURSE of several years, I was assigned an administrative headquarters position in the office of the state flight surgeon that

involved mostly flight physicals and monitoring the medical regulatory compliance of aviation units. I preferred the field. After a year in
the headquarters assignment, I received a promotion to major and was
reassigned to the 1/113th Cav. Lieutenant Colonel Dan Fix, a former
Marine who had fought in Vietnam, was the new unit commander. In
civilian life he ran a tire and oil company in Waterloo, Iowa. His executive officer was Captain Orr, a high-speed, low-drag Army Ranger
who loved training.

Commander Fix lived the doctrine "Train like you fight—fight
like you train" and he stressed that every officer should know every
other officer's role and be able to assume command if required. To
teach that lesson, he simulated broken communications, destruction
of the tactical operations tent, and downed helicopters. He faked his
own death and took various officers and NCOs out of action, then observed how other officers struggled with tactics and leadership. Captain Orr shifted to the commander position and I became his medical
advisor or executive officer. To push the medics, the commander had
me killed in a simulated firefight. It was eerie watching from the sidelines as the medics faced overwhelming numbers of wounded. The
commander honed us beyond our own specialized training and taught
us to adapt to a continuously changing battle. His training matrix
keyed officers for war, not just for summer training exercises.

"Think contingencies. Plan for everything you don't expect,"
Commander Fix insisted. "Train like you fight. Fight like you train.
Adapt and overcome."

"Yes, sir," we responded in after-action reviews. We did as com-
manded. I didn't know then that I would soon use that training in
response to a war without direct U.S. involvement, and that the skills
I learned, as critical as they were for field survival, would seemingly
serve no useful end in the face of overwhelming carnage.

War Zones

IN APRIL 1994, the Rwandan president and Hutu leader Juvénal Habyarimana was assassinated when a surface-to-air missile shot down his private jet near Kigali, Rwanda. During one hundred days following his death, armed Hutu militia retaliated and massacred an estimated eight hundred thousand Tutsis and moderate Hutus. In retaliation for the retaliation, the Tutsi-led Rwanda Patriotic Front overran the capital city of Kigali and vowed to cleanse Rwanda of all ethnic Hutus. Some news reports claimed up to two million refugees fled into Tanzania, Burundi, and Zaire (now the Democratic Republic of the Congo).

I read about the carnage in the newspapers and in the May 1994 edition of *Time* magazine. A correspondent quoted a missionary about the warring state of affairs in Rwanda. "There are no devils left in hell. They are all in Rwanda." Those eyewitness words alerted the world to the genocidal atrocities. Other news reports described the horrors with words like "innocent" and "child" and "corpse" in juxtaposition with "murder" and "rape" and "machete." In the reportage, brutality and death became synonymous with ethnic cleansing.

USA Today ran a front-page special report on the genocide. I was on duty at the Finley Hospital in Dubuque, Iowa, when I read it at lunch. It hit me that millions of innocent people had fled their homes in fear for their lives, many suffering from injuries and an epidemic of cholera. The carnage and inhumanity were unspeakable. In a sidebar column of the article was a list of international aid organizations that were preparing for a humanitarian response to the crises. There

was a call for professionals to volunteer for medical work in the refugee camps. I read the article twice, the sidebar probably five times. I
was intrigued by the intense nature of the crises and the possibility
of participating in a dangerous yet humanitarian effort. Earlier that
same day I had performed a trauma resuscitation on a five-year-old
girl involved in a car accident. The intervention was successful and
she survived her injuries. One of the staff surgeons asked me how it
felt to be involved in giving a child a second chance at life. When I
read the article about the Rwandan refugees, I wondered who was trying to give them a second chance and if my presence there could make
a difference.

By the end of my shift in the evening, I had phoned several of
the organizations on the list and asked if they needed doctors. One
of them wanted me to join their team within the following week. I
phoned Collin and told her about my day, about the *USA Today* article, and about my phone call. I told her I should go help. When I got
home, we discussed it.

"I think I have the right skills to help those people," I said with
confidence. "They need emergency doctors. This is something I could
do."

"But it's so dangerous. Doesn't the UN or the military have doctors who can go?" Collin had a serious frown that I usually interpreted
as "no."

"The UN *is* there, but they are using humanitarian groups to provide medical services. I don't understand how it all works, but I would
be on a rapid response team and work in the refugee camps."

"We can manage a month or so on our own, but I'm still worried
about safety," she said cautiously.

"The fighting has stopped," I pointed out. "They're supposed to be
in a recovery phase."

"I know, but it just seems too risky. What if you're hurt over there?"

"It's the same as if I were hurt over here. There are no guarantees."

We discussed how long I would be gone if I went and the logistics
of emergencies at home and how I would respond from Africa. I assured her all of those things would be made clear before I left and that

if she felt certain I should not go, then I would not, but that we would be missing a great opportunity to reach out to people who needed us. She tentatively agreed subject to getting more information. Over the next days I phoned the hotline set up by the International Red Cross. They referred me to the United Methodist Committee on Relief (UMCOR), a humanitarian group that provided medical care and relief for refugees worldwide. UMCOR gave me detailed information, which I discussed with Collin. She finally, but reluctantly, agreed that helping would be a good thing. I notified the ER staff at the hospital and they adjusted my shifts to allow for the time off. I also enlisted some local churches and charities to raise money for a shipment of medicine. Within a week I was on a plane to London to meet with the team from UMCOR. I was the only doctor in that particular first-response group.

We flew from London to Nairobi, Kenya, the staging site of the United Nations mission to Rwanda and the surrounding area refugee camps. From Nairobi we took a small two-engine prop plane to Bujumbura, Burundi, where we stayed one night in a hotel. From the open windows of our rooms, we could hear distant gunfire coming from the border of Zaire. In the morning we hired a private convoy of three vehicles to take us into Uvira, Zaire.

As soon as we passed the border checkpoint, I wondered if I had made a mistake and should have listened to Collin's warnings. Soldiers wearing tan uniforms and maroon berets lined the road, belts of ammunition slung over their shoulders. They wielded machetes and wooden-stock rifles, which they waved at our driver as they halted our convoy and demanded money for our passage. They threatened to confiscate our passports and our boxes of medicine. The convoy leader negotiated a payment, and after a tense hour we were finally allowed to pass. On the road into Uvira, we saw soldiers beating people with the butts of their rifles, demanding payment for passage. When we arrived at our final destination, a mission hospital less than thirty miles from Bujumbura, we were frazzled and worn, hot and scared.

I stayed in the home of a doctor named Wanume who had escaped the regime of Idi Amin in Uganda. Dr. Wanume established a mission outpost hospital with the support of the United Methodist ministries. His twenty-bed hospital was built of wood and white stucco and had one operating room and a five-bed section for cholera patients. Together, we treated war injures, tropical diseases, and delivered babies. We cautiously treated one patient dying of a hemorrhagic fever we thought was Ebola. An attached twelve-by-twelve-foot pharmacy had run out of medicine three weeks prior to my arrival, and I offered boxes of the medicine we had brought from the States. Wanume said it would keep him stocked for about a month. I gave him a book of current perspectives on infectious diseases, and he was so grateful he almost wept when he turned the pages.

"I have not had a medical book for five years. I left all my books in Uganda when I escaped," he lamented. "I shall read this book every day."

We stayed with Wanume for just two weeks before we moved north to Bukavu, Zaire. That had been our plan, to spend time supporting outpost doctors where we could, but also to spend time in areas that had no medical services. In the northern camps, and generally in most of the camps bordering Rwanda, tensions ran high. Hutu militia members leveled charges that Tutsi infiltrators were spying on refugees. They even accused aid workers of spying for the United Nations in order to bolster a hidden agenda. One group spread rumors that medical aid workers were doing experiments on Hutu refugees. There were daily incidents of violence, rape, and even murder. There were no adequate UN security forces to quell the violence, so aid workers proceeded cautiously to their respective camps.

We had been assigned to assist at a medical camp near the Panzi Refugee Camp, bordering Bukavu. Our first day at the camp started at 7:00 a.m. with a drive from the central part of Bukavu, where we stayed in a run-down hotel and guest houses. The drive took more than an hour. Mud and ruts from the constant rain made the road nearly impassable. Along the roadside, literally hundreds of children scampered to the sides of our vehicle, and our drivers swerved to avoid hitting several of them.

The scene on the way was nothing short of horrifying. Thousands of blue tarps, which the UN had distributed, one per refugee family, lined the road and the nearby fields. It looked like a sea of twelve-foot-by-twelve-foot shelters with campfires spread about, giving off a gray smoke that hung in the air. Some families didn't get tarps. Instead, they made do with sticks and pieces of wood and canvas. Between the rows of tarps and lean-to shacks I saw only mud and puddles and refuse. Some of the blue shelters had been trampled by the thousands of refugees. In many cases we saw naked children with open wounds standing near their mothers. We wanted to stop and help, give medicine and clean water, but if we did, the action risked setting off a chain of violence because we did not have enough to give everybody. We had been instructed to stay on the road and proceed to the camp at Panzi.

What I saw, I could have never prepared for. I was fully prepared for the practice of emergency and disaster medicine. In many ways, that kind of doctoring came easy to me. But Rwanda was far more than a disaster, even more than a genocide. Its near millions of refugees, its countless numbers of wounded and ill, and its malaise of camps and bodies scattered in the mud all coalesced into a heavy feeling that humankind had become lost and unredeemable. The greatest health risks were not germs or injuries or bleeding, but people. And that realization gave way to sadness and emptiness.

When we arrived at the medical camp, the scene was similar to what we had seen on the drive in. Hundreds of small tents filled the surrounding open land as far as we could see. Two large medical tents had been set up adjacent to a Catholic missionary grade school atop a slight hill with a graveled road. Our arrival created quite a stir of curious patients, some of whom had bandages on their legs and arms and heads. Some of them walked alongside and greeted us in Swahili or French. A few had makeshift crutches made from tree branches. Many of the wounded had faces devoid of any expression.

"Do you bring medicine?" one man said, his arms reaching toward me. "Do you bring food?"

"Yes, I have medicine," I responded tentatively, not knowing how

64

Jon Kerstetter

and if I could help these patients. The translator explained that we were the first medical team to arrive and the patients were desperate to see us.

I wanted to get into the medical tents to make an initial assessment, so I asked for the translator to accompany me. There was some discussion between him and a person who seemed to act as the informal spokesperson for the patients. They had not expected us to arrive that day and they said they needed time to prepare.

"I don't need any preparations," I said, urgency creeping into my voice. "I just want to see the patients and get an idea of how to proceed."

The spokesperson addressed me in fair to broken English. "Sir, I am Sergeant Nkunda. I am chief medic of the hospital. Welcome."

I was surprised that I was speaking to a soldier, much less in English.

"Sergeant, I am Major Jon Kerstetter of the National Guard. Where did you learn to speak English so well?"

"Fort Sam Houston, Texas" he said, grinning. "I had training there as a medic three years ago." He turned up the flap on his khaki shirt pocket. Sewn onto the underside was a U.S. Army Expert Field Medical Badge, earned by less than 10 percent of all Army medics.

I couldn't have been more surprised. He went on to explain that the Rwandan Army had sent their best medics to train at U.S. Army medical facilities under a training agreement. At the camp he had been doing emergency amputations and whatever else needed to be done as he waited for medical help to arrive. Apparently, I was that help. Doctors and medicine were in short supply or simply not available.

Nkunda showed me into the main tent. The smell of infection had saturated the air and it was nearly overwhelming. I could sense the despair that seemed to permeate the air as well. The tent had been set up by a UN crisis response team two weeks prior to my arrival. It had a dirt floor, no ventilation, and no separate area for contagious patients with cholera or tuberculosis. The camp provided no surgical facilities or pediatric beds. The water supply had been contaminated

by cholera. Sanitation facilities overflowed. The adjacent school building served as the operating room where Nkunda performed amputations. Wounded child soldiers and a mix of older civilians lay in rows
like stacked cordwood ready for burning. Some of the patients with
field amputations had infected stumps that lay open to the air. Flies
laid eggs in the necrotic tissues.

I was no stranger to field medicine through my training in the
Guard, but I had never seen the near-death certainty of refugees in
the aftermath of war. I had come prepared to make a difference, as
if I could just drop in and save lives. When I saw the conditions of
the camps, I considered my efforts weak and paltry at best and that
whatever I did there represented nothing more than a temporizing
measure before a bleak and tragic outcome.

On that first day I went from patient to patient with Nkunda. The
tents held close to three hundred injured and ill. I made a list of priorities. We needed to separate the cholera patients from the others immediately. The rest of the UMCOR team went to work on setting up
a cholera tent where infected patients could be isolated and treated. By
midday we had selected about twenty patients for isolation. I expected
half of them would die within a few days. And when that happened,
the rest of the patients feared being selected because it meant almost
certain death. Nkunda explained to them that if they stayed in the
main tent, everybody would die of cholera because of contamination.

That afternoon I operated on a boy who had been shot in the chest.
Infection had eaten away at his chest wall until it eroded through his
ribs and skin. I showed Nkunda how to drain the infected area by cutting into it and removing the dead tissue.

"I expect he'll be dead in a few days," I said to Nkunda. "We don't
have enough antibiotics to treat his infection."

"But at least we tried," Nkunda replied. He looked resigned to the
reality of our patients dying for lack of supplies.

I was surprised that the boy was still alive two days later, since we
had only a limited supply of antibiotics and not the appropriate ones
for his kind of infection. The team made arrangements to transfer

the boy to a different camp where a Swiss humanitarian group had pediatricians on their staff. We transferred him but never heard if he survived.

The same day, I treated an injured young Hutu woman whom Tutsi forces had shot as she carried water up the steep embankment from a nearby river. She had been sitting and sleeping on a two-foot-by-five-foot grass mat in the main tent for five days before I arrived. When she stretched her legs or tried to lie down, her feet settled on the dirt floor of the tent. She leaned her bare back against the center twelve-foot tent pole. Her breasts were exposed to the air. A ragged tan skirt covered her knees. She wore no shoes or sandals. Flies lit on her legs, arms, face, and chest—and on the baby in her lap. She did not brush them away. Systemic infection had set in. She had not received surgical intervention or antibiotics.

I smelled pus as I approached her mat. Sweat dripped from her face. It collected on her chest and ran into the wound on her breast. Her right arm hung limp and its motionless, swollen hand lay in her lap. She had a finger-size entry wound in her deltoid and a corresponding exit wound in her armpit. Between the entry and exit wounds lay a shattered humerus and a severed axillary artery. She had a secondary wound that pierced her chest wall and split a rib. The rib apparently changed the course of the bullet, causing it to travel through the base of her right breast, where it carved a tunnel and exited near her sternum, carrying with it fragments of bone, breast fat, and milk glands. I put my entire gloved hand into that tunnel to remove debris and pus. She felt no pain. Her breast was dead.

As I examined her right arm, she held her baby girl to her good breast with her other arm and rocked slightly. I had left my own children in the care of their mother, fully sheltered, safe, with ample food and extra money for weekend entertainment while I was gone. They would survive with barely a ripple in their routines and perhaps barely a notice that I was gone. The mother and child before me were hours to days away from their deaths. I became desperate to save them, to show them that I valued their lives.

The baby tried to suckle a parched nipple. It could not latch on and the mother could not make milk. She was dehydrated and lacked adequate nutrition. Her lips were cracked like the heels of her feet. I told her through my translators that she needed to have her arm amputated and her right breast removed because infection was killing her.

"How can I care for my baby with one arm and one breast," she asked. Her barely audible voice wavered. A translator told me she was afraid surgery could kill her, and she refused to die before her baby. "If I die first," she said, "I cannot give milk."

I explained that her breast and arm were already dead and that surgery was the only way to save her baby. She refused by simply and softly saying *hapana*, no, as she clutched her baby to her chest. I gave her as many oral and intravenous antibiotics as I could find. She died on her mat three days later, her feet coming to rest in the dirt, her head askew against the tent pole. A nearby patient had covered her body with a bloodstained blanket. We took her baby to a nearby pediatric camp where nurses bottle-fed her special formula. I did not have time to follow up. I presumed she died from malnutrition or dehydration. I hoped I was wrong. I also hoped I was right and that she died quickly.

In the days following the mother's death, I felt numb and incapable. The aftermath of genocide and its atrocities had torn limbs and lives, had killed fathers and mothers and left their babies starving and sick. I could not save them, the mothers or their babies, and that was a curse, watching them die, knowing I had the skills but not the power to heal, knowing that war had blown apart any reasonable chance that a doctor from Iowa could save an innocent mother from Rwanda. People died every day. The despair was palpable and I had to look beyond it or risk becoming useless. And that was the hardest part, to portray the strength of a doctor in the midst of a plague, to move with the wisdom and confidence that advanced the power of healing.

I performed amputations on several refugees whose legs had been severely injured and were infected. Some of them had already received field amputations, Civil War–style, performed by their own medics.

A few were missing limbs hacked off by crazed attackers. I performed the operations on a wooden table in the nearby grade school. Between taking photos, a Belgian photojournalist from the *Belgian Standard* batted flies away from the surgical incisions and instruments. Flashlights and sunlight served as the operating room lights. We didn't have an anesthesia machine or an anesthesiologist, so I administered intravenous anesthetics myself. When the patients began to stir or wake, I asked one of the team members or Nkunda to administer another dose. "Just squeeze half that syringe into the IV," I would say. After the patient stopped moving, I would continue. After the amputations, I gave each patient ten Tylenol tablets and told their tent mates to give them two tablets every four hours or so, or in between if they moaned in pain.

I had four cases of Army MREs (meals ready to eat) that the Iowa National Guard had sent with me. I handed them out to post-surgical patients to aid in their recovery: one surgery—one MRE. Two weeks after I arrived at the camp, a patient who was older than the other refugees, probably in his late forties, and who likely weighed less than one hundred pounds, asked me to amputate his arm in exchange for an MRE. I refused him both.

"An amputation must be medically necessary," I said, trying to sound objective and unemotional.

Using a mix of Swahili and English words, he told me it was. "*Doctare*, you cut." He held up his arm as if to offer it to me and drew an imaginary line across the middle of his right forearm with his left index finger. I told him I could not and turned away to attend other patients. The next day I saw him leaning against the back corner of the classroom where others had received amputations. He was staring out at the jungle. I knew he was on the verge of hopelessness. I felt guilty that I had done nothing of substance to help him, but I also knew that nothing I could give him would have enough substance to save him. I expected him to die like the boy with the chest infection, but when I saw him there alone, hungry, I decided to do something anyway. I sneaked him one MRE and a packet of multivitamins. He smiled and said, "*Asante sana*," Swahili for "Thank you very much."

— — —

AFRICA WAS MY first war zone experience. There would be more. I spent several months in two consecutive summers working in the Zenica Hospital in Bosnia, teaching emergency medicine and treating patients from the ongoing war. The injuries there were typical war wounds from small-arms fire, rocket-powered grenades, and mines. During the summer a group of five boys waded into the Bosna River for some summer fun. They were hit by an IED attached to a balloon floating downstream. The boy closest to the balloon bomb died of a head injury. Two other boys had shrapnel injuries to their chests and abdomens. The boys nearest the shore had penetrating injuries to their arms and faces. On other occasions, landmines injured or killed members of Bosnian families out gathering mushrooms or wood in the surrounding mountain meadows. The mines spared no age group and had a predilection for inflicting civilian injuries.

I made a similar trip to Albania in the late spring of 1999 and worked in collaboration with humanitarian organizations attending to Albanian refugees from Kosovo. At the peak of the refugee crises, the United Nations estimated the number of refugees at over six hundred thousand. Approximately two-thirds of them fled into Albania. I joined the team of World Medical Missions at the Hamallaj refugee camp about twelve miles north of Durres, Albania, next to the Adriatic Sea. In our makeshift clinic/hospital, which was nothing more than a twenty-man, green Army tent with a smaller supply tent attached, I examined patients on a plastic folding table. A camp generator supplied power to a string of overhead lights that, all added together, might have been the equivalent of a single 120-watt bulb.

Like the patients I saw in Africa and Bosnia, the patients at the Hamallaj camp sought refuge from ethnic cleansing. There was a pattern to the injuries; they were inflicted by armies, militias, and criminals with an apparent goal to kill and harm as many civilians as they could. The patients in the camp told of genocidal atrocities similar to what I had witnessed in Rwanda. Some refugees told me soldiers inserted long dirty needles into the legs of their victims and scraped their bones to cause pain and infection. In the first week of providing medical evaluations for over three hundred refugees, several of them told me their captors forced them to drink gasoline; others mentioned forced fistfights with their sons, and if they refused to fight, their sons would have been killed. Serbian attackers had raped women, young and old; some of the women had been mutilated by knives drawn across their faces and breasts.

The Kosovar refugees all related stories that I had heard or seen from other refugee camps since my time in Africa. None of them, the stories or the patients, surprised me. And though I felt sorrow for them, I also felt detached. It was a skill I had developed: remain detached in spirit without being distant in practice. It gave me an edge for treating patients I knew would die.

WHILE AT THE Hamallaj camp, I met several Albanian doctors from the University of Pristina in Pristina, Kosovo. They told us of their underground medical school for Albanian students and how hard it was to teach and practice medicine under constant threat from Serbian forces. Over the course of several months, the Hamallaj project director, Ken Isaacs, and other leadership from Samaritan's Purse and World Medical Missions agreed to collaborate with several faculty members from Johns Hopkins Medical School in a project to establish an emergency medicine teaching program at the University of Pristina. Essentially, we followed the Albanian doctors back to their university and joined with them in teaching medicine. By July, I was asked to join the project as the in-country director in Kosovo. I would have to spend three- to six-month blocks there, teaching and treating patients.

When I returned home, I talked with Collin about the project. The opportunity to work with the staff of Johns Hopkins on such an international scale held the promise of excitement and an opportunity to be a part of rebuilding an entire medical infrastructure where one had been decimated by war. Those kinds of opportunities were rare, and I had been asked to participate. Collin had seen how much the experience in Africa and Bosnia had enriched my professional life, and regardless of the hardship the trips brought on our own family, she was inclined to support the work because she saw that by doing so, we both played an important part in responding to a critical humanitarian need. In a large way it was an extension of living a practical faith that was not bound by distance or culture. The bottom line was that we made a difference in refugee camps and war zones, and as long as that was true, I felt inclined to go and Collin felt inclined to support that work. Beyond that, there was an attraction to disaster medicine that was undeniable. I liked the chaos and the edginess of what I was doing. Collin and my kids knew it, and they allowed me the freedom to practice that kind of medicine even though the time away sometimes made it tough at home.

At the end of July, I took a six-month leave from my Iowa emergency medicine practice to take the position in Kosovo. The six months stretched to two years, back and forth, home and Kosovo; I taught emergency medicine and worked with Ministry of Health officials to establish emergency medicine in Kosovo. Dr. Julian Lis, my immediate boss at Johns Hopkins, recruited visiting faculty from Johns Hopkins and nearby medical centers. I put them on a rotating lecture schedule. In our initial two years of the project, we established an emergency medicine curriculum in conjunction with other departments of anesthesia and surgery. I met with Republic of Kosova president Ibrahim Rugova in the late summer of 2001. He signed an executive order recognizing emergency medicine as an official medical specialty in Kosovo.

During the time spent in Africa, Bosnia, and Kosovo, I developed a heart for international and disaster medicine. There was a certain intrigue and toughness that came with working in dangerous missions that required a persistent focus on rapidly changing environments. Medical equipment and pharmaceuticals were often in short supply, and disaster medicine forced a reliance on the "thinking" aspects of medicine rather than the "technological" aspects of medicine. Part of the mystique of international practice was adapting to and overcoming such shortages, making do with whatever was available. And beyond all the intrigue and personal fulfillment, there were the patients. The work I did contributed to a sustainable program of international medicine, to be sure, but the patients I tried to help—the ones at the Panzi refugee camp and the ones in Bosnia and all those in Kosovo—changed me. They reminded me of my desire to heal, to be a part of something greater than medicine or science or myself. They were the reason I had become a doctor in the first place.

In all of my refugee camp and war experiences, I learned I needed those patients just as they needed me. Their need for a doctor fueled my need to be a doctor. Everything I did for them mattered, and as detached as I had to become for professional survival, I became attached to those patients; I was the doctor who gave hope and even laughter with medicine. I lifted patients' spirits and by doing so lifted my own. There was a feeling that unified us, patient and doctor, against whatever calamity was trying to destroy us, so in the end we all survived together.

Call-Up

AFTER 9/11, EVERY soldier, whether on active duty or in the Guard or Reserves, knew they were bound for war. The only thing they didn't know was the timing and destination of their deployments. I knew that Iowa's 109th Area Support Medical Battalion (ASMB) was staging for a call-up, so I volunteered for a reassignment from headquarters in Camp Dodge to the 109th because I wanted to participate in that first wave of deployments. I was fifty-three at the time and had been practicing medicine for fifteen years. I had been on first-response teams in Rwanda and Kosovo and had provided rapid and effective mass casualty intervention. That was my personal strength in the field, intervention that was quick, decisive, and responsive to a rapidly changing environment.

In January 2003, Iowa Army National Guard soldiers received alert letters announcing an imminent call-up. I showed mine to my wife and notified the hospitals where I worked. Collin reacted with a mix of emotions. I had difficulty understanding them all. She expressed what I interpreted as quiet acquiescence. I also thought she felt fear, but it wasn't really fear at all; it was more like what you might see when a person receives a terminal diagnosis and accepts it by showing love or strength instead of panic or fright. Collin and I talked about the mechanics of deployment: how long I would be gone, how to reach me for emergencies, and how she would be notified by the Army if I were injured or killed.

A myriad of predeployment details needed to be organized: financial details such as life insurance policies, bank account numbers, mortgage papers; simple things—titles to cars, lists of doctors and pastors, and family emergency contacts. We spent hours digging through files to find the needed information, and finding each valuable piece took on the proportion of a crisis. Yet none of it was a crisis; they were things that simply needed to be done without emotion or reaction, like painting the house or doing taxes. I didn't have a will, so we had to talk about the legal implications of my death. Surprisingly that didn't bother us. What did bother us, though, was the need to feel that we didn't feel, that we could detach ourselves from the impact of being torn apart by war and the possibility of never seeing each other again. And of those frightening things we hardly spoke. Instead, we tried to hold each other at night as we talked about our children and the need to love and support them during my deployment. At times we simply tried to power through the days knowing that our remaining time together was disappearing faster than our ability to grasp each day's meaning. Too often, we were short-tempered because time ran out and preparations did not go as planned. In part, we both acted like automatons, moving without thinking and reacting to the demands of the military just to get through the hours. And in all of our rushing, we tried to shield our children. I gave them only the basic facts about my deployment to Iraq and tried to minimize the risks of war—as if it were something I could hide.

I talked to Justin by phone. He was living in Chicago.

"There's a lot of moving parts in this deployment," I said. "I want to make sure you know I love you and appreciate you. I'm not asking you to take my place while I'm gone, but if you can look after your mom and keep in touch with her, I'd appreciate it. I need to make you aware of my will and legal stuff the Army has prepared."

"I understand," he replied businesslike. "How long are you going to be gone?"

"I can't say for sure, but something close to a year. I'll try to e-mail as often as I can, but phone calls might be limited. I am so proud of you and your brother and sisters. I love you all so much."

At home, I talked to Darren, Katelyn, and Jordan. Darren was working and taking classes at the community college. Jordan had graduated from the University of Northern Iowa, and Katelyn was still in high school. I asked each of them if they would help out while I was gone and they promised they would. I told them how much I loved them, and they said they knew and that they loved me too.

Jordan took it hardest. "Dad, I don't want you to go," she said with tears falling and her voice raised. "Why can't you just stay here and work in an Army hospital or something?"

I tried to reason. "It's not that simple, Jordan. I have certain responsibilities. Soldiers need me there."

"Don't soldiers need you here?"

"Oh, honey," I said, "they all need doctors, but I made a commitment when I joined the Army."

"It's not fair," she insisted as she stomped her foot. She was right. None of it was fair. Deployments weren't fair. The disruption of families was not fair. I had no reasonable arguments as to the fairness or legitimacy of combat or my involvement in it. I could only tell my children that I loved them and valued them and would try to return as soon as I could, and that the rest was up to God and the Army.

ON JANUARY 24, 2003, the 109th was ordered into federal active service. In the weeks following, Alpha Company and Headquarters Company of the 109th ASMB loaded onto a bus and drove to Camp Dodge for a week of soldier readiness processing (SRP), which included a week of administration checklists, legal and Red Cross briefings, predeployment medical and dental exams, and equipment and clothing distribution. In the medical lanes, dental technicians prepared a routine, forensic set of panoramic dental X-rays for each soldier. Medics drew blood samples for DNA tests to use in case our bodies needed identifying later. Army attorneys drafted wills and powers of attorney for each soldier family. Medical officers met with administrative officers to make sure their medical credentials and hospital privileges met the regulatory standards. Several times a day I phoned Collin to ask if she could find needed documents and fax them to Camp Dodge. She did her best to comply, but I could tell from her tired voice that she was frazzled.

Since I was new to the unit, I didn't know the other medical officers. It turned out that the other two doctors who had been reassigned to Alpha Company of the 109th were also new. On the first day of SRP, I met Majors Mike Brown and Tim Gibbons. Brown was a cardiothoracic surgeon from North Dakota and Gibbons was an orthopedic surgeon from Iowa. Not surprisingly, we hit it off right away, and as typical of doctors from different branches of medicine, we started giving each other lighthearted shit about our specialties. Brown stood over six feet tall and had the feet to match his frame. He had a bit of a lanky gait and dark brown hair that hadn't been cut in a while. My hair was just as long. I told him he looked like a woolly mammoth. He said I looked like a yak.

Major Gibbons had quite a remarkable collegiate wrestling career at Iowa State University. Brown and I joked that his low center of gravity and rather square head made us wonder about his ancestry.

"Hey, Gibbons," I joked. "Have 'em check your DNA for Neanderthal genes."

"We all have Neanderthal blood," he shot back, "especially you, being an ER doc and all—too much grunt and no follow-through."

At the end of the week I phoned Collin and asked if I could bring two colleagues home for a few days. We would be home in four hours and could she also fix dinner for us—a roast or something nice. She was silent at first and I figured I had pushed too hard; then she responded. Yes, it was okay. No on the roast. We could order pizza. I sensed her nervous tiredness through her worn voice and barely noticeable sighs. We had spent a week preparing for war, yet neither of us could fully understand the frustrations and fears and thoughts of the other.

During the week following the Camp Dodge SRP, the 109th marshaled at the National Guard armory in Iowa City for our final preparations and the loading of our vehicles and duffel bags. On Sunday, March 2, the soldiers assembled at the armory for the final time.

The mission was set. Form a convoy of military ambulances, troop transports, Humvees, and trucks of various sorts and sizes and head to Camp McCoy, Wisconsin, for pre-deployment. Outside the armory, sleet and intermittent rain battered the streets. Temperatures bounced around the mid-thirties. Families of the deploying soldiers lined the nearby streets of the armory as if waiting for a summer parade. They waved American flags and makeshift signs of support for the war and the soldiers. Many signs said "God bless" or "We love you." A few had the names of soldiers written in large bold letters. Children stood on the curbs and waved. Some of them cheered and smiled. A number of them clung to the sides of their parents. As our convoy rolled out the gates of the armory and past the crowd, I caught a last-minute glimpse of Collin waving a tearful goodbye. It was her birthday. She was fifty-three years old. My high school daughter, Katelyn, stood next to her and held her hand. I could see their faces tucked into their winter coats. I gave them a single wave, blew them a kiss, and turned my head around to watch them for as long as I could as my Humvee drove on. Seeing them huddled together in the cold, clutching each other, made me regret all the times in the past weeks I had rushed to get things done—times that contained no hint of love or patience or understanding. I had been too busy for war and now, in the literal final seconds of contact with my family, I had nothing left for them but a vanishing kiss blown through the cold and blustery air of a late-winter day in Iowa.

As the convoy proceeded out of town, it passed the headquarters of an Army Reserve unit. About thirty reservists lined the street and stood at attention as our convoy approached. They rendered a salute and held it as our vehicles passed. They weren't salutes of protocol, as when soldiers salute an officer; they were salutes that acknowledged fellow soldiers going off to war. To me, they signified the start of my particular slice of war, as if somebody were thumbing a stopwatch. Click—go to war. I didn't know then that nearly ten years later soldiers and their families would still be waiting for somebody to click "stop—go home."

When our convoy arrived at Fort McCoy, we broke into platoons and moved into the World War II–vintage barracks. The fort had once served as a cold-weather training facility. Nothing there resembled the Iraqi desert—not even close. The docs and other officers of the treatment platoon were assigned to the first floor of an older barracks. Cots with metal frames and thin, gray-striped mattresses sat against the walls, about four feet of space on either side. Major Brown brought a black plastic footlocker that he had stuffed with a few books, extra clothes and uniforms, a blanket, and just stuff he thought he needed. Gibbons and I (mostly) gave him crap about his extra stuff being non-essential.

Brown gave it right back. "Look at Kerstetter. Packed like he's going to a weekend conference."

"High-speed, low-drag," I replied. "You're taking enough crap for a vacation to Disneyworld."

Back and forth it went, all lighthearted—all the typical banter of doctors who possessed enough surgical and medical experience between them to start their own medical school or manage a national health care system. In a typical civilian week, Brown performed several cases of open-heart surgery and coronary artery bypass grafts. His expertise in chest trauma and cardiac critical care made him invaluable for soldiers with blast and ballistic injuries to the chest. Major Gibbons performed hip replacements, arthroscopic surgery, and orthopedic trauma surgery. Their expertise in general and specialized trauma skills brought a critical skill set to the 109th that most other National Guard medical support battalions lacked. These were not doctors looking to gain experience from a deployment; they brought their experience and expertise with them and hoped it would serve a vital purpose.

Most of the medics and admin specialists of the 109th tended toward younger and less experienced soldiers, but their senior NCO (noncommissioned officer) leadership had been in the Iowa National Guard for ten or more years. Some of the NCOs had deployed to Desert Storm. Among the medics, only a few had more than a few years of experience. Several had finished their medic training within the preceding year. They came from rural Iowa towns and from college towns like Iowa City. They played rock music on their iPods and watched DVDs on their laptops. Several had just started college at the University of Iowa or Kirkwood Community College. And they were mostly smart and fit. Two of the medics thought they could take on Major Gibbons in a wrestling match. He pinned them each in about ten seconds; then he wrestled them two-on-one and they went down in about thirty seconds. In all, the 109th was like most National Guard units. Its soldiers represented the likes and fancies of adults in their twenties and thirties. That was balanced by a much smaller, experienced group of citizen-soldiers in their forties with a few, like me, in their fifties. And at age fifty-three, I was the old man in our battalion.

During the four weeks of "train-up," every imaginable form of training took place: weapons qualification, self-defense, rescue operations, medical emergencies, patient evacuation, map reading, land navigation, equipment maintenance, radio communications, and convoy tactics. The training checklist also contained elements of combat strategy, team leadership, intelligence operations, and enemy tactics. Training did not end. Soldiers trained in the morning, at night, in the dark, in the cold—indoors and outdoors. We did portions of our desert warfare training in the snow that still lay in the heavily wooded acres of Fort McCoy.

Other preparations included mandatory briefings and lectures on sexual assault, military sexual trauma, and suicide prevention. Army staffers flown in from active Army bases disseminated hours upon hours of information on rules of engagement, the law of war, and the Geneva Conventions. Additional briefings included deadpan PowerPoint presentations about soldier ethos, and command concepts. The Code of Conduct briefings seemed the most serious and laid out the rules that governed a soldier's behavior in case they became a prisoner of war. The briefings were particularly troubling because they featured outdated video clips from the 1960s that showed overly dramatic actors providing only their name, rank, and identification numbers while being physically and psychologically tortured. Everybody knew that most soldiers eventually broke under torture, regardless of their personal ethics. Overtly, I gave assent to the Code. Internally, I feared becoming a prisoner of war and being tortured by an enemy or be-headed. In private discussions with other officers, I learned I was not alone in my fear. I held that fear close, as if it were a secret message I was dispatched to carry throughout the war, to be disclosed only to a covert operative in the dark of night when the war was over, and maybe not even then.

Later in the week the docs mustered all company medical person-nel for a training exercise on carrying and loading injured patients. Medics parked their ambulances in various positions in the snow and rigged the litter stanchions to carry four patients. The medics and docs all took turns trying to rig the ambulances. Most had never done an ambulance rigging in their Reserve or National Guard training; and the ones who had were rusty and out of practice.

We planned the loading exercise as a fifteen-minute block for each team of four to six. When teams actually ran the exercise, they needed closer to a half hour. During the delays and restarts, the mock patients waited conveniently on nearby patient litters. Nobody bled actual blood or lost real limbs. Our pretend patients wrapped themselves in drab-green Army blankets to keep warm. A few sipped hot coffee from oversize travel mugs.

The teams loaded patients with the same difficulty they encoun-tered in rigging the stanchions. The weight of the patients and the litter averaged 170 pounds; a few topped 200. Medics struggled to angle the litters into position and lock them in place. Their feet kept slipping. Team members jammed fingers, pinched hands, and bruised their arms. They fell down, dropped litters, and yelled in frustra-tion. The mock patients moaned and complained. A few of them were dumped in the snow. They brushed themselves off and climbed back onto their litters while mumbling about their mock injuries and their mock pain. As I watched, I shook my head and silently scoffed at the performance. *Bullshit.*

When it was my turn to load patients, I resolved to do better than the other teams. As my team proceeded to lift our patient, I forgot the coordinating step to turn the litter for loading. We stalled trying to figure out which way to turn. One of the medics slipped in the snow and dropped his corner of the litter, nearly dumping our patient. The team hollered in unison, which was about the only thing we did in unison. We struggled to maintain a coordinated lift to the ambulance. I pinched my hand between the litter and the stanchion. I bungled the loading. I wanted to show leadership and skill. Instead, I showed ineptitude. I felt tiny and limited and flawed—as if perhaps I was not a soldier at all, or at least not a very capable one. I got a vague feeling in my gut that I might never be ready for war, that perhaps the entire 109th might never be ready.

SimMan

TO MAKE TRAINING more realistic, we enlisted the Army's new-
est medical acquisition, a first-generation training simulator
called SimMan. SimMans were the descendants of the Resusci
Anne mannequins commonly used for CPR training. The concept
was enticing: train with a computer-operated simulator, essentially a
semi-robotic patient that provided real-time, lifelike feedback. Perform the appropriate steps of a trauma protocol, the fake patient survived; do the opposite, the patient died. The bonus for instructors and
trainees alike was that the simulator closely mimicked real biologi-
cal responses to interventions. That was not a small thing. Realistic
training in medicine, especially in trauma, was hard to attain short of
doing medical training in a trauma center where staff doctors monitored a trainee's every move. That was the kind of training I had done
to prepare for my career, and it was not easy to get.

Our physicians were of the first nationwide cohort of military doctors trained for combat medicine using computerized patient simulators. I thought it sort of cutting-edge to be using computerized
patients that cost more than an Army doctor's annual salary. Practicing on SimMan was far better than using a Resusci Anne mannequin
whose hard plastic skin didn't feel anything like real skin and whose
chest felt like a stiff mattress spring when compressed during CPR.

SimMans were different. Each simulator measured about six feet
tall and weighed 170 pounds, the presumed height and weight of an
average soldier-patient. They were all dressed out in Army DCUs
(desert camouflage uniforms), including desert boots and Kevlar
helmets. They had audible heartbeats and breathing sounds as well

as palpable pulses. Their pupils reacted to light or stayed wide open and fixed in response to a computer command. When I first saw our five SimMans on gurneys I was suspicious; I thought they looked too much like static Resusci Annes. But as I worked with them and their variety of detachable body parts, I began to appreciate how realistic simulator training could become. These were more than rubber and plastic; they felt and acted real and added a deeper level of seriousness to our role-playing trauma scenarios.

Training oversight was assigned to Gibbons, Brown, and me. We trained in collaboration with an Army Reserve Combat Support Hospital (CSH) from Wisconsin. The first day of my training, I spent a half day with simulator technicians learning about the computer programs and the interchangeable body parts. The training software included a menu of preconfigured scenarios that provided the full gamut of combat injuries. There was no lack of wounds from which to choose. A trauma instructor simply picked a set of injuries from the pull-down menu on a laptop computer and pressed the start button. The software then took control, and SimMan displayed the appropriate physical signs that corresponded to the selected trauma. His pulse galloped or stuttered. Simulated blood squirted from simulated wounds. His breathing would become slow and sporadic and agonal. A cardiac monitor provided critical vital-signs data. When the instructor had a scenario ready, he provided a brief one-line medical history and told the trainee to begin. The medic or physician trainees then began their initial trauma assessment and practiced their interventions. As they proceeded, the computer tracked their performance and kept a timed log of everything they did. The instructor could modify the physical responses by adjusting the computer controls. A tweak here or there could push SimMan from manageable, to critical, to dead—all within minutes.

If I needed to show more tissue damage or a more critical scenario, I simply interchanged one body part for another and chose an appropriate computer algorithm. SimMan mimicked the appropriate responses that corresponded to human injury and treatment, but unlike real soldiers he didn't moan or writhe in pain. He didn't ask if he was "going to make it" or ask his doctor to tell his parents that he loved them.

Brown, Gibbons, and I taught mandatory training scenarios that included ballistic wounds to the chest and abdomen, open and closed head injuries, traumatic amputations, and extensive full-thickness burns that covered over 50 percent of SimMan's body surface area. I regarded the simulated burns as a bit too artificial, because the burned plastic skin didn't look anything like real full-thickness burns with their char and oily soot. Other scenarios included multiple broken bones, a fractured pelvis, and various states of cardiac and respiratory arrest. To make things more challenging and push the trainees a bit, I severed both legs. I left the detached legs on the gurney and rigged a pump to squirt fake blood from the stumps; then I grabbed a green Army blanket and covered SimMan from the waist down. When trainees lifted the blanket I hit a computer button. Red water squirted onto the gurney and dripped on the floor. Trainees always got a stunned look on their faces and hesitated as they collected their thoughts.

I pushed the soldiers hard because I wanted everybody to run the simulations perfectly. I viewed their performance as an extension of my teaching and leadership. If *they* weren't perfect, *I* wasn't perfect, and in front of Brown and Gibbons and the other docs, anything less than perfection was simply not good enough.

I gave trainees only a minimal patient history or sometimes no history at all. I simply said "trauma patient—critical" or "patient—unknown injuries." I always added more simulated bleeding as the scenario progressed. I dialed up the heart rate to two or three times normal or slowed it to a standstill. As a subtle test, I dropped SimMan's core temperature to simulate a critical loss of body heat. I increased respirations to dangerous levels or simulated labored, agonal breathing. When the docs and medics tried to intubate SimMan in order to provide him with a "breathing tube," I clicked a button on the laptop that inflated a small air bladder situated beneath his hard rubber trachea, making emergency intubation nearly impossible. Some treatment protocols required an emergency cricothyroidotomy, a vari-

ant of a tracheotomy also known in trauma care as a "cric." Trainees had to make a midline surgical incision in SimMan's neck, cut an
opening in the underlying trachea without lacerating the carotid arteries, quickly insert an endotracheal tube, and then connect the tube
to an emergency source of oxygen. If done incorrectly, the procedure
could kill a patient.

If a trainee bungled the "cric" by doing it too slowly or not at
all, I clicked another computer button and pushed SimMan into an
unrecoverable, two-minute slide to his death. The cardiac monitors
sounded an alarm as his heart faltered in wild dysmorphic rhythms
and a flat bright line finally signaled a failed resuscitation. If SimMan
had had a computerized skin controller, his skin would have turned
pallid and damp.

Trainees got nervous, upset, and rattled. Most of them forgot to
perform critical steps in the resuscitation. Some of them underdosed
the simulator with critical medications. A few administered life-
threatening overdoses. Several punctured SimMan's lungs with a surgical trocar. One medic punctured SimMan's heart—pushed a trocar
right through the left ventricle. Some did not intervene fast enough
and he bled to death. One trainee cried when she failed to resusci-
tate her patient. Almost all trainees developed an uncontrollable hand
tremor, and when I saw them shake, I tweaked the computer to make
the simulation even harder, as if I were moving in for the kill.

The scenarios tested skill and speed. They usually ran for less
than ten minutes, during which we tracked everything: procedural
attempts and non-attempts, injections, incisions, every command, and
every question. Each trial. Every error. We monitored adherence to
trauma protocols and a trainee's ability to develop an efficient and
confident resuscitation rhythm—the ability to transition from patient
assessment, to medical intervention, to treatment monitoring, and
then to repeat the steps as necessary, without hesitation, and without
succumbing to the typical chaos of trauma resuscitations.

In the first week of simulator training, the training team tested
about ninety medical personnel. SimMan survived very few scenarios.
After two weeks of training, the plastic patient had a survival rate of

90 percent. He always died in about 10 percent of the cases, simulating an expected reality of trauma resuscitation.

Brown and I were fiercely competitive in a friendly sort of way. We tried to outperform each other on the SimMan. When it was my turn to test him, I dialed up the toughest cases. I set the starting point as a burned patient with hemorrhagic shock, an open chest wound, and agonal breathing—essentially three breaths away from dead. Brown responded rapidly and systematically. As the scenario required, he tried to perform an emergency intubation, and when he did, I tweaked the computer to make SimMan's trachea collapse or become obscured with simulated blood—anything to make intubation impossible.

"What the hell you doing?" he screeched.

I yelled back, "What the hell *you* doing?" Then I told him he had thirty seconds left and gave him a devilish grin.

He scurried to perform an emergency cric. I hid the scalpels so he had to use his pocketknife. "What did you do with the scalpels?" he barked in a squeaky high-pitched voice. I usually shrugged my shoulders or said they were destroyed in transit or hit by a bomb. When he finally cut SimMan's throat and put a tube in his trachea, he proceeded to correct the other life-threatening injuries. Insert a chest tube—done. CPR—check. Ligate a bleeding artery—a breeze. Technically, Brown's SimMan always survived, but I found ways to kill him off anyway—too much blood loss, hypothermia, or cardiac arrest.

When it was Brown's turn to test me, he pulled the same crap. "Okay, Doc, let's see what you've got," he chortled. He always killed my SimMan in retaliation.

When we were done with our scenarios, we simply hit the reset button on the computer. SimMan would be instantly and electronically resuscitated—alive and ready for another round.

Watching a patient simulator turn critical and die was strangely unnerving, even though everybody knew that SimMan could not be killed and would never actually be placed in a body bag. In the worst case, he might suffer a broken part or maybe some torn rubber skin— all of which we could replace from the parts warehouse within a matter of minutes. Everybody knew that SimMan's manufacturer parents would never get a letter from some commanding officer telling them he was a good soldier—that he had distinguished himself in battle and had served his nation with honor. I think what made the simulator training so unnerving was the understanding that, within weeks to months, some real soldier's life could very well depend upon how well resuscitation efforts were performed in the field and how quickly those efforts were put into play.

That understanding made the simulator training intense. Medics and docs got angry with themselves for botching a scenario. Like me, they wanted to show themselves as the kind of soldiers who could save lives in the rush of combat. Sometimes they got upset with the instructors, or with the SimMan computer, or with the Army—but mostly, they got upset with themselves. I tried to remind everybody that the simulator was a tool. "Learn from it," I said. "Make accurate observations, interpret the clinical findings, and then respond without hesitation."

I showed a PowerPoint presentation one night as sort of a relief valve from the SimMan training. It was a collection of photos I had taken during my work in Rwanda, Bosnia, and Kosovo. I assembled about seventy photos of patients from those war zones. I started the presentation by asking if everybody was confident from all the SimMan trauma training. A resounding Army "Hooah" filled the room. As each photo of a wounded patient hit the makeshift screen, the lighthearted banter of the classroom grew quieter.

The first pictures showed a teenage boy in Bosnia with half his chest blown open by a grenade. A dozen photos highlighted traumatic amputations and bones sticking out of limbs. One photo showed a young patient from Kosovo with a post-op infection that left his abdomen gaping and his intestines exposed to the air. His physicians had sewn empty intravenous bags over his open abdomen to keep heat and moisture in and flies and other contaminants out. One picture showed the boy's gaunt face. Several others showed various angles of his exposed and necrotic bowel. Another few showed the boy's head flexed downward, eyes wide open, as he watched a surgeon remove the plastic abdominal covering. I kept those pictures up on the screen longer than the others. I said nothing.

A few pictures of collateral children showed eyes fixed in an upward gaze so that only their white sclera and a small crescent of iris were visible. The photos revealed distorted faces, massive swelling, and the periorbital bruising that resulted from concussive blasts or blows to the head. The classroom grew eerily quiet when I showed the children.

The series of medical photos from Rwanda distressed everybody. They showed the Hutu woman I had treated who had been shot through the upper arm and breast. I explained her critical need for an amputation of her arm and breast. Soldiers, I explained, were not our only patients.

When the presentation was finished, I asked if anybody had questions. At first there were none. Then a medic raised her hand and asked what happened to the woman with the bullet through her breast. "Dead," I said. "It took three days. Her baby was taken to a pediatric camp." Lots of questions followed. Everybody wanted to know what kinds of medicine the different patients needed and what kinds of medical procedures could have saved them from their various injuries. Everybody took a deeper interest in the issue of medical logistics and supply, and in how to perform medical procedures in the field. Everybody wanted more SimMan training.

We continued to work on SimMan for a few more days, to the point where most of the trainees could manage all but the most complex of injuries. At times, after an intense training day, I wondered how the new simulator training would pan out in combat. In our training modules we tested a single scenario at a time. One medic or doctor stood at the ready, always leading a team of three or four well-equipped soldiers. The training objective focused on the rapid trauma resuscitation of complex injuries in a single patient. We ran other non-simulator exercises that trained soldiers in the assessment of multiple simultaneous patients. But in our simulator training, we never had the time or resources to use ten or twenty SimMans in a

CROSSINGS89

single scenario where half of them died of wounds, or where we had to drag them out of a kill zone before providing medical treatment. Our simulation training focused only on resuscitative algorithms. We did not simulate combat fatigue, or fear, or the risk of dying in a war zone. There were no wounded children or other collateral noncombatants. Missing from our simulations was agony and weeping and the real pain of a slow, torturous death.

I knew that SimMan added a powerful and realistic dimension to training. He gave us a tactical medical advantage that no soldiers, whether combat docs or patients, had possessed in wars prior to our war. But I also knew what he didn't give us, live soldiers who bleed from irregularly shaped holes as they gulped their final breaths, their bodies trashed from the violent inertia of war. We didn't get the smell of blood or charred flesh or shit from eviscerations. SimMan didn't stun our minds with images so horrific that we lost critical momentum and put our patients at risk of dying. That was the kind of combat experience that simulators failed to teach, however modern or computerized.

When I thought about SimMan, I was impressed with our scope of training, but I was also apprehensive because I knew that it was not the same as real war. A patient simulation was always a simulation, a war game, always a game. But we would not be playing games in combat or have the opportunity to hit a reset button.

THE WEEKEND BEFORE our departure, the battalion commander issued a forty-eight-hour weekend pass for one last family goodbye. Soldiers' families drove to Fort McCoy from their homes across the Midwest. The spouses who did not come were either working or simply could not endure another painful goodbye. For the spouses of a couple of soldiers I knew, the deployment served as the breaking point in their marriage. I phoned Collin and asked her to drive up for the weekend. She initially resisted, saying another goodbye was just too hard, but then she offered to come if I really needed her. I did.

Soldiers and their families flooded the local hotels around nearby

Sparta, Wisconsin. The hotels were of the "small but clean" variety. Families crammed into rooms that held only a single queen-size bed or two doubles. Some soldiers rented two rooms, one for their children and one for their spouses. On Saturday, the last day for shopping, many families hit the local retail discount stores. Everybody splurged on presents and snacks. The overflow lunch and dinner crowds at restaurants frazzled many of the soldiers and their spouses. Crowds and lines, waiting and frustration, seemed to predominate the weekend. Many soldiers made last-minute reviews of their Army-prepared wills and powers of attorney. Insurance documents, ongoing bills, and written instructions for what to do in case of emergencies stole valuable family time.

Despite all the last-minute details that needed finalizing, soldiers found time for their families. They found time for love—*made* time for love. One soldier's son brought a bike with a flat tire. The soldier fixed it in the hotel parking lot, and when he finished, his son rode it up and down the parking lot, his dad chasing behind. His kid grinned so wide that anybody watching could have counted all his teeth. Another soldier with a seven-year-old daughter made fifty-two smiley-faced crayon greeting cards that she could open, one each week while her mom was deployed. My wife brought a computer that needed fixing. I replaced a power supply—one hour and a few scraped knuckles. Families brought dozens of cookies and baked treats—enough to share with the entire battalion. Many soldiers wrote final love letters to their spouses, for opening after the send-off weekend—at home, in private.

After shopping and dining, it was back to the hotel. Collin and I reviewed some last-minute paperwork and some Red Cross information about emergencies. And we debated if we should watch a movie to kill time. We could hear movies blaring through the wall of the hotel rooms. I turned on the television and flicked through a list of movies. None seemed interesting, but we decided on one and watched it from the edge of the bed. And we didn't really watch it at all. We turned the volume down so we could talk. But we didn't talk much either, just some small talk and chitchat. We held hands and hugged and at some point Collin just started to cry and said how she loved me and how the kids would miss me. I cried with her, then we held each other and eventually made love like we did on our honeymoon. At one point during the night we managed to laugh about our marriage and our kids, and then we cried about the war and Collin said she never imagined being left alone during a deployment just as her mother had been during the Vietnam War. And I wanted to know how to comfort her and make the night less painful, but I didn't know how, so I just held her until we fell asleep.

The next morning in the parking lot, Collin gave me a wallet-size family photo. I promised to keep it on me at all times. I gave her one of my extra dog tags and a note that said I loved her and would pray for her every day. I told her I would e-mail her when I got to Iraq. Our chins quivered as we said goodbye. I didn't want to prolong the goodbye, so I kissed her quickly and walked away from her car. I met up with Gibbons in the parking lot and we drove back to Fort McCoy to load our duffel bags.

Camp New York

First Combat Tour, 2003

OUR BATTALION ARRIVED at Kuwait International Airport, midday, the first week of April 2003. In less than twenty-four hours we had traveled from Fort McCoy with its freezing rain to Camp Wolverine, Kuwait, where the outside air temperature hovered in excess of 100 degrees. When the aircrew opened the door of our leased DC-10, the Middle East heat infiltrated the cabin within seconds. Soldiers filed out of the aircraft and down the portable ramp. When I reached the door, I could see the heat waves rising off the hot tarmac. I uttered a drawn-out "Holy shit . . ." Everybody behind me wanted to get off and kept yelling at me to move it.

Brown, Gibbons, and I gathered near the bottom of the stairs. We slung our rucks on our backs and walked to the assembly point about a hundred yards off the flight line. With just that short exertion, I felt trickles of sweat running down my neck.

"Just shoot me now and get it over with," I said with sarcasm.

"I thought you were tough, Kerstetter," Brown poked. "It's called desert warfare. What'd you expect?"

Cold weather was one thing. At Fort McCoy, I dealt with it like all the other soldiers by using layers of thermal underwear and by limiting my exposure. But heat was impossible to escape. The air blowing on my face and hands felt like I was standing in front of a pizza oven. We had to keep our uniform sleeves down because that was protocol. I could already feel the wet tracks of sweat in my armpits. I commiserated with the other docs about the stinking heat as I dragged my equipment through loading areas and checkpoints. I was not alone in my complaining. Soldiers blamed the weather for their misery, and it seemed somehow appropriate, even cathartic. It wasn't so much that war was to blame for our troubles; no, it was the desert and its miserable heat. After fifteen minutes or so, Gibbons finally said, "Let's just power through it, Doc."

That was Gibbons's style, former champion collegiate wrestler— head down and power through it. No use complaining. And he was right. We needed to face the weather as we would any other uncontrollable variable. Deal with it head-on.

The battalion attended a mandatory briefing held by the Coalition Forces Land Component Command (CFLCC) staff, the equivalent of a corporate administrative headquarters remotely located from the front lines of battle. After a general's welcome speech, we heard briefings about force protection, the law of war, sexual assault, and fraternization—the exact same briefings that we had heard at Fort McCoy. It was a prime example of Army redundancy; hurry up and wait—do it again just to make sure it was done right. Army staffers emphasized personal safety and the proper escalation of military force. The idea of "proper" was that lethal force should come into play only when absolutely necessary in order to avoid collateral damage. If a soldier could shout or shove instead of shoot to enforce compliance, then the lesser force took priority. Gibbons and I looked at each other with raised eyebrows. Later, we discussed an unspoken soldier rule: when under attack or threat, shoot first, ask questions later. Escalation of force was one of those rules of engagement that many soldiers viewed as a quagmire of war ethics. Yes, there was a need to recognize different threat levels and respond accordingly, but there was also a need to avoid becoming a casualty.

After the briefings, we waited in more lines to double-check our next of kin, insurance beneficiaries, and payroll forms. As CFLCC admin specialists verified our identification, they logged us into a computer as having arrived in a combat zone. That registration set off a chain of personnel tracking files and the start of combat pay, an extra $225 per month, non-taxable. The official DOD combat pay start date meant this was it, the real thing—war, no turning back, no more rehearsals, no more simulated patients. The next patient would have real injuries, real blood, and real death.

The seriousness of what our medical battalion was about to engage in made me look forward to our mission. At the same time, it made me feel a bit apprehensive. Like Gibbons and Brown, I was eager to use my skills in combat, but I also felt the weight of those skills. Soldiers depended on us to save their lives and limbs—to use our experience, training, and judgment to alter combat outcomes. And that was unnerving. I felt prepared, yet an element of the unknown loomed against the tangible elements of training. When I looked around, I wondered if any of my colleagues or fellow soldiers would become my patients. I wished I could have had more time to prepare, gained more experience, developed greater insight into combat. As it turned out, feeling prepared involved more than confidence in the fact that one had trained well. It involved more of a gut sense of readiness not easy to come by.

We spent hours moving our gear to large canvas tents set up in rows and blocked off into hundreds of numbered sections. The billeting area took on the look of faceless prefab tenements held erect by taut ropes and metal stakes driven deep in the sand. The chemical treatment applied to the tents to prevent rot smelled vaguely like blue cheese. Despite the treatment, mildew and mold grew in the corners and seams. Soldiers shouted to hear each other over the constant rumble of nearby aircraft and diesel generators. A haze of fine dust settled on duffel bags and weapons.

When we weren't slinging duffel bags or settling in, we milled around the DFAC (Dining Facility) and the main intersections between tent rows. We traded opinions about the briefings and the rumors that began to swirl about our mission assignment. We were all going home within a week—no assignments. We were pegged for a mission at Camp Doha in Kuwait for a year pulling of "sick call" for soldiers transitioning in and out of theater. We might deploy to a camp in the northern sector of Kuwait to run a series of battalion medical aid stations. Nobody was going into Iraq. We were all on standby for further orders. One rumor circulated repeatedly that the war was over and we were heading home. That one bothered the docs the most, because, if true, it meant we had spent all our time in pre-deployment train-up for nothing.

Our battalion docs and medics mingled with soldiers from other units. We heard about the threat of chemical attacks and about equipment shortages.

"Don't expect a full resupply of meds or equipment," one British doctor warned. "The supply routes aren't even properly guarded."

Some medics described the kinds of injuries some of them had already seen in theater, soldiers with arms and legs traumatically amputated or ones who had their faces burned off. By far, the harshness of the desert predominated the talk.

"The sand is like moon dust in certain areas," several medics told us. "It comes through the cracks and seams of the tents."

Just after midnight, I walked to the DFAC with Brown and Gibbons to have coffee and just get away from the chaos of the tent village for a while. It seemed like an oasis of relative quiet and normalcy. The décor reminded me of a hometown café. To me, it conveyed that the Army wanted our last meal before combat and MREs to invoke memories of tranquility. Tired and worn from the trip and the unloading, we took a table in a corner and got our coffee. The breakfast bar looked so appealing, we decided to eat and kick back for a while. I served myself three single-serving boxes of Frosted Flakes and a cup of raisins. Gibbons ordered bacon, eggs, and toast. Brown had the granola and yogurt. He mocked Gibbons and me about the healthiness of our choices. We settled down into a back-and-forth about our families and our mealtimes at home. We all had several children each, so we started talking about them and their adjustments to our deployment. "Jordan thinks I'll get shot and wants to know why we have to fight a war," I said. "I told her I didn't have a good answer."

"My kids are too young to understand everything. They think I'm going to fight bad guys with a gun," said Gibbons.

Brown's children were young too, but he said he had tried to explain that Daddy had some important work to do for soldiers and that he would be home as soon as he could. In all our conversations, we found that much of the burden of explaining what we were doing and why we did it fell to our wives. That conversation was not easy. It invoked too many memories of good things at home, but also of strained relationships over our military careers. In a strange way, the conversations about our families gave us a resolve to do our missions well so we could return home quickly. It was striking how we had reacted to war, as if we had like-minded personalities or the same soldier-doctor DNA.

Thirty minutes after we sat down, a lieutenant from the headquarters company rushed in and banged a spoon on a metal tray. "One Hundred and Ninth, listen up," he said. "Finish your coffee and get your gear. We're heading north in one hour." He left us instructions to muster at a specified holding area, duffels in hand.

I chuckled and shook my head. "More hurry-up-and-wait bullshit."

Gibbons simply said, "Yup."

Brown asked the lieutenant where we were going. The answer was generic.

"Up north. We got orders."

Word from the battalion leadership soon circulated among the troops, confirming the lieutenant's news. We were heading north. North was good news. It meant leaving Camp Wolverine for a real mission. There was widespread excitement in the battalion that the rumors of going home or staying put were unfounded. Despite that excitement, questions continued about what exactly "north" meant. North, to northern Kuwait, near the border of Iraq? North, as in northern Iraq with the 101st Airborne? North to Baghdad? North to Kurdistan? Docs, medics, and support staff all asked questions aimed at verifying our mission parameters. Who were we supporting? Nobody knew. Was our assignment to a field hospital, to medical aid stations, or as replacements for medical staff in armor or infantry units already on station? Nothing. The scant information from the chain of command was laced with the uncertainty of words like "possibility," "depending on," and "it appears." The unsettling feelings of not knowing mission details only drove more questions. We had "north."

We wanted more. "Don't worry," the leadership told us. "You'll get what you need when you need it."

During the short ride to the holding area, I contemplated our battalion's arrival in Kuwait, how it reminded me of the jerky movement of broken gears on a faulty machine rather than the precise movement of a well-oiled army. I still wore evidence of that jerkiness. My desert combat boots did not fit and I kept turning my ankle. Deal with it. Wear extra socks. My ankle still turned, constantly reminding me of inefficient movement, first a boot, then a battalion.

At 0200 hours the entire battalion loaded into a convoy of rented minibuses that looked suspiciously like tourist buses. They held about thirty soldiers each. One of the medics started clowning around and pretended to be a tour guide. "Tickets—please have your tickets ready," he announced. He made his voice sound like a circus barker. Soldiers laughed with a sort of nervous laughter until one of the lieutenants finally told him to knock it off.

The image of riding into war in a rent-a-convoy was not what I had imagined about riding into war. In one sense, it seemed to ridicule the notion of a powerful army on the move. It gave the impression of something patched together and miscalculated. In another sense, it showed the leadership's ability to adapt. I remembered the words of Lieutenant Colonel Fix: "Adapt and overcome." I wanted to be flexible and recognized the absolute need for it, yet I felt that riding north into war on a tour bus seemed like a symptom of a deeper problem. The Army was a machine. I was merely a single cog or less.

The sides of the buses sported large, tinted sliding windows that maintenance workers had covered with cheap black curtains in the interest of security. They also disabled the overhead lights, presumably to prevent enemy lookouts from seeing our silhouettes. Sculpted seats covered with purple-striped velour held about one and a half soldiers per row. The rows were supposed to hold four passengers. Soldiers carried their weapons, ammo clips, tactical vests, and one small personal bag. Some of the gear snagged the seat corners and tore the fabric.

Straps and cords tangled in weapons. We were tired and pissed, hot and sweaty. A soldier near me punched a seatback with his fist while cursing Saddam. A few soldiers bitched about the buses, some about the Army in general. Others were speechless and subdued, as if some learned helplessness from a psychology rat experiment had overcome them and they had lost the will to fight back. They just moved unemotionally along, plopped down in their seats, and wiped the sweat from their expressionless faces. I grabbed an aisle seat in the middle of the bus. I kept telling myself to relax. Gibbons and I exchanged exasperated looks as he dropped into the seat directly across from me.

After an hour of loading, the drivers started the engines. Black exhaust blew from the tailpipes of the bus in front of us and into our bus. The air conditioner circulated hot, dusty air that covered our skin, noses, uniforms, and weapons. The ranking sergeant in the bus told the driver to turn off the blower. The driver, a foreign national, kept nodding in agreement, but did nothing. The sergeant finally reached over and turned off the air while repeating to the driver: off—on, off—on. The driver smiled and nodded.

The convoy finally started moving on some back-road route. Our driver followed directly behind the vehicle in front of him. That vehicle followed the vehicle in front of them—dark gray elephants, trunk to tail—all hoping that the lead elephant knew where the hell he was going. We took so many turns on side roads that it seemed we were lost in a maze. Nobody kept the black curtains closed. Not that it made any difference for stealth or security. Anybody five miles away could have seen our dust column rise above the twisting roads, even at night. Soldiers pulled neck gaiters over their faces, but they still breathed the dust into their noses and lungs. We listened to coughing and throat clearing and snot blowing during the entire trip.

The convoy moved so incredibly slow. I imagined that wherever north was I could have walked there faster, and certainly done so without the constant dust and the cramping that was beginning to settle in my legs and back. I had flown on plenty of C-130 flights with their tightly spaced webbed seats and had felt the stiffness of long flights, but in the rent-a-convoy, stiffness had long given way to cramping. Soldiers twisted, shifted, and adjusted. They tried to stand up to stretch their legs. After more than an hour of slow-churned dust and jostling roads and drinking from Camelbacks to stay hydrated, the soldiers needed a latrine break. The sergeant in charge radioed the convoy command with our request. Nothing doing. Keep moving.

A particularly rough stretch of road slowed the convoy to a walk. The buses lost their tight formation and the distance between each one stretched out so far that we could barely see the vehicle in front of us. Our driver veered too far off the road, then snaked back into line. We all began to sense that something was wrong and started to get nervous. We had had briefings about enemy insurgents who infiltrated the ranks masquerading as contract workers. A lieutenant shouted at the driver to stay on the road. The driver ignored his instructions or simply misunderstood them. He kept diverting from the convoy, weaving on and off the road, stalling momentarily, then jolting forward. Gibbons ordered one of the lieutenants to get a weapon on the driver. The lieutenant sat in the front row with his rifle on his lap and aimed at the driver. From the middle of the bus, I shouted, "If he breaks convoy, take the bastard out." I meant it. I didn't want our bus full of soldiers to show up on CNN as a newsflash. The driver may have understood that part. He quit moving off-road.

The soldiers had been hollering for an hour to stop for a break, so we radioed the convoy commander again. "No go on the latrine break. Keep moving north. Stay in the vehicles." One of the female soldiers sitting behind me started cursing and screaming about how she was getting sick and about how she might have an accident. She needed to stop—convoy or no convoy. We kept moving—another thirty minutes of negotiating potholes and stop-and-go busing. Finally, screaming in desperation, the soldier stood straight up in her seat and dropped her battle uniform trousers and her standard-issue underwear. Shaking and crying, she pissed into plastic cups, and onto her hands, and onto the velour seats. Whatever piss she managed to get into cups, she tossed out the window. Other soldiers started yelling and cursing about the goddamned Army and the bullshit convoy. Short of mutiny, the convoy commander ordered a ten-minute stop.

Soldiers dropped their uniforms in plain sight of each other. Nobody cared. Nobody watched. Nobody said anything. Everybody pissed—in a desert—heading north into war.

OUR CONVOY FINALLY arrived at Camp New York, northern Kuwait, about 0600. New York was one of several camps in northern Kuwait known as a *kabal* (Arabic for "fortress") established during Operation Desert Storm as defensive outposts and later converted to staging areas and live-fire ranges for military units on the move to Iraq. A few hours after our arrival, the battalion's leadership went off for a quick meeting with the camp commander, the "mayor." When they returned several hours later, they told us that the camp had no information about our arrival and that they could not accommodate us in the regular billeting area. Surplus tents had been set up near the camp perimeter for National Guard overflow. They were located on the perimeter road about a quarter mile from the Patriot missile batteries and a half mile from the burn pits where the camp's lowest-ranking soldiers had the duty of stirring fuel into sewage and burning the mixture. Adjacent to the burning sewage, piles of garbage smoldered and burned continuously. The smoke of those fires produced a stagnant haze that choked soldiers and burned their eyes. A desktop sign in one of the headquarters tents read, WELCOME TO CAMP NEW YORK.

The day after our arrival, we got our first bit of solid information about our mission status—in limbo. In the process of rapid deployment, the battalion had been separated from its equipment. Transport vehicles, ambulances, and medical supplies were somewhere on a ship heading toward a port in Kuwait. The battalion had arrived semi-ready for war without its vehicles and major equipment. The supply disconnect was the first of many. It plagued the early movements of the war when the Army moved faster than its own supply chain. In a medical crisis, the personal items in our duffels could never sustain us for even an hour of critical care. We were to wait until our equipment arrived before going anywhere.

In the interim, our battalion medical staff would relieve the Regular Army doctors and medics assigned to sick call duty at the camp medical aid station. The duty consisted mainly of taking care of the basic medical needs of soldiers, most of which could have been handled by medics. None of it required surgical expertise or emergency care. It was primarily routine stuff: sprains, minor cuts, coughs, diarrhea, aching joints, and sunburn. Sick call was not combat medicine; it was the kind of medicine that bored me in my civilian ER practice. I railed against the disconnect. I wanted to provide patient care that demanded the most of my skills. Gibbons, Brown, and I felt we would have been more useful assigned to an echelon III or IV facility (a fixed-base Army hospital or field hospital) where our skill sets could come into play. Critically wounded soldiers in Iraq needed us. We needed them, but our orders mandated that we perform sick call at Camp New York, thirty miles away from Iraq and the real war. The disparity between our medical skills and the mission needs drove us nearly insane.

Beyond the bullshit assignments, Camp New York typified an early Iraq War experience. The DFAC blew down several times a week. The large tent simply could not stand against the desert winds and the sandstorms. The camp leadership responded by setting up three medium-size mess tents. That worked about half the time. The mess staff always tried to prepare at least two hot meals per day. Fresh fruit was plentiful. Six ice cream freezers lined the edge of the mess tent. They ran off generators that kept them cold most of the time, but when the generators failed, the entire ice cream shipment melted within hours.

Hand-washing stations placed twenty yards from the DFAC entrance typically ran out of water or soap. A chipboard wooden floor loosely nailed together by government contractors barely kept us from sinking into the underlying sand as we ate. White plastic patio chairs often bent or broke from the weight of soldiers and their gear. Folding eight-foot picnic tables covered with the permadust of sand tilted and wobbled. Some of the tables collapsed during a meal, dumping trays of food on laps and feet. Soldiers tied ripcord around the table legs to reinforce them, then stood them back up. A mess sergeant tried to keep soldiers moving quickly. Chow down. No chatter. Move out. Make room for others.

And Camp New York had sand. Sand in the food, in the sleeping bags, in the latrines, in the sick call tents. Sand in underwear and socks and duffels. Sand in eyes and ears and nostrils and mouths. I felt sand on my teeth when I swiped my tongue. Soldiers coughed up sand in the morning after breathing it all night. The dust of sand made us look like light colored badgers. It blasted our goggles so that a single pair lasted about a week, sometimes two. During one sandstorm, I found a young soldier wandering around near my tent—head down, hands over his Kevlar helmet. I hollered at him to get inside the tent with me.

"Yes, sir," he said with relief.

"What are you doing out here?" I asked.

"Looking for my hooch, sir."

We used sand to our advantage. Soldiers filled empty buckets with sand and kept them in the workout tent—a makeshift gym with a single set of barbells. We worked out for fifteen minutes in our uniforms and sweat like we had spent an hour in a sauna. There were no showers in the tents, of course, so we planned our workout schedule to coincide with shower day. When we finished working out, we marched to the shower point, washed and rinsed, then put on a clean uniform. It was our way of getting back at the sand.

THE CHAPEL WAS located near the DFAC. It held approximately two hundred soldiers, three hundred if everybody crowded in, not nearly enough space for a camp of several thousand. On Sunday, or any day, soldiers could attend a worship service or vespers, or just go there to pray or attend one of the briefings on combat stress relief. I attended Easter sunrise service with Major Gibbons and Major Brown and a few of our physician assistants. The chaplain used the occasion to talk about the newness of life and about how the resurrection of Jesus meant that we all could aspire to that newness. The implications were that a new life required death, either spiritually or physically. Before the service, we had all talked about our families back home, how we missed them and what we did as a family for Easter. We talked about faith and its role in our lives. We all agreed that faith kept us centered as people and soldiers, but sometimes faith was difficult to hammer out in view of the fact that if the need arose, we had to pull a trigger and kill. The sermon reinforced the idea of faith and renewal, but all three of us acknowledged that renewal for us meant taking a new role as soldiers from our typical role as doctors. That remaking was another kind of dissonance that became evident at Camp New York. And it didn't necessarily drive us to lose faith; rather, it made us seek more grounding in faith, simply because the task of soldiering made it clear that we, like all other grunts, needed grounding in something more powerful than ourselves.

WITHIN TWO WEEKS of our battalion's arrival at Camp New York, the commander of the 30th Med Brigade, Colonel Don Gagliano, assigned me a position on his medical staff at Camp Virginia, about twenty miles away. His brigade was bound for Baghdad and he wanted a doctor with international experience in rebuilding medical infrastructure. He sent an inquiry to the units marshaled at the kabal camps to see if there might be somebody who fit the requirements. Our battalion commander told me about the need and suggested a meeting. That same day I was driven to Camp Virginia for an interview. The colonel was a physician who had spent a fair portion of his Army career as an eye surgeon but had taken on more administrative duties as a senior officer. As we talked, it was clear that he wanted to match the experience and skills of his officers with specific needs of the mission. He sought out those with expertise that he lacked and seemed at ease with acknowledging the need for other subject matter experts.

"I reviewed your file." He looked at me over his reading glasses while leaning back in his chair. "Interesting work in Kosovo. Tell me about it."

"That was with Johns Hopkins. We rebuilt the training infrastructure and started an emergency medicine residency. I was responsible for the teaching and its ongoing development," I responded.

"I need someone who can work with Iraqi doctors to do the same kinds of things. It would mean less clinical work. You up for that?"

I said I was. The colonel said he would cut orders for my transfer into the 30th Medical Brigade. I would work directly for him in the capacity of what he called a medical integration officer and forward surgeon. I didn't know all the details of what exactly that meant. Neither did he, but he assured me I would be a welcome addition to his team of doctors.

By the time I arrived back at Camp New York, the staff in our battalion office had already received orders for my transfer. The battalion commander told me to pack my duffels. "You leave tomorrow morning. It will be a good opportunity for you," he said. I wasn't sure. The exact nature of the mission wasn't clear, but it sounded certain to include heavy doses of work with Iraqi government officials and U.S. Army leadership. I had expected to work with Gibbons and Brown in a trauma center somewhere in Iraq, treating the wounded and arranging medevacs. When I told them about the transfer, they both agreed that working with the brigade commander would be great and told me to keep in touch.

Within weeks we all moved north, as promised. The 109th was assigned to support the 101st Airborne Division in the northern regions of Iraq. Gibbons and Brown were two of the battalion medical officers who managed a battalion aid station and performed only sick call duties. They worked missions that went to the task of "maintaining the fighting force." During the course of their deployments, Major Gibbons did not perform limb-saving orthopedic surgery, and Major Brown did not operate on any soldiers in need of a cardiothoracic surgeon. As they and the other medical officers of the 109th prepared for their work in the 101st Airborne, I moved north to Baghdad with the 30th Med Brigade for a different kind of medical mission. In the coming months I would find out just how radically different and life-changing my missions would be.

Forensics

ROM THE BEGINNING of my reassignment to the 30th Med Brigade in April, Colonel Gagliano assigned me tasks that focused more on medically related leadership issues than patient care. The colonel's West Point experience and additional training as an Army Ranger both gave him a rather distinct perspective about military assignments and their performance. There was no mission large or small, typical or atypical, that didn't get its due consideration when it came across his desk. If a mission required even a sliver of medical expertise for its execution, he assigned it to one of his officers and told them to get it done.

Colonel Gagliano attended daily staff meetings with the Army top brass, General Ricardo Sanchez, commanding general of the Coalition ground forces in Iraq, or the chief of staff, Brigadier General Hahn, or Major General John Gallinetti. When he was unable to attend, I attended for him. It was a bit unnerving at first. The generals had all served in other wars; they had all risen through the ranks in their careers; they all knew soldiering like I knew doctoring. I was a mid-career officer, a National Guard soldier with only summer training and weekend drills to hone my military skills. Despite feeling inadequate, I quickly adapted to the role of providing subject matter expertise to the generals and their staffs.

The operational issues and missions at that level of command involved more strategic decisions than tactical actions and were never purely medical in their scope. The missions often involved working with Iraqi leaders at the highest levels of their government and required coordination with U.S. officials in the Coalition Provisional

Authority. Sometimes the missions focused on high-value targets or personnel. To a larger degree than I found comfortable, the work that Colonel Gagliano did and the tasks he delegated to me required attention to political forces in play. I hated politics. It had no place in medicine, but as I would learn through my assignments, every task at that strategic and complex level of war seemed to have a political undercurrent.

ONE OF THOSE complex missions surfaced in late July. It started on Tuesday, July 22, 2003. Soldiers from the 101st Airborne and U.S. Special Forces attacked a house in Mosul, acting on a tip given to Coalition authorities by an Iraqi informant. According to the informant, the number two and number three targets on the U.S. list of the fifty-two most wanted of Saddam's regime were hiding there. The military used a deck of cards to prioritize high-value targets in Iraq. They dubbed Saddam Hussein as the ace of spades. Uday Hussein drew the ace of hearts and his brother, Qusay Hussein, was named the ace of clubs. The reward for information leading to the capture or death of Uday or Qusay was $15 million each.

In a mission to find, kill, or capture Uday and Qusay, U.S. forces engaged in a lengthy gun battle and a missile attack on the targets' hideaway. Soldiers finally entered the Mosul residence after hours of fighting. They found bodies presumed to be the Hussein brothers, a teenage son of Qusay, and an unnamed bodyguard. Once recovered, the remains were flown to a secure location in Baghdad. When I heard of their deaths, I responded like other officers, with a blend of celebration and relief. In a sidebar discussion in the operations center, I remarked to one of the aviation staff, "We finally got the bastards."

On the day of the attack, General Hahn called me into his office and said he had an important mission for me. "You know by now that Uday and Qusay Hussein were killed in Mosul. I need you to make a positive forensic identification and certify their death certificates. You have a meeting with Ambassadors Kennedy and McManaway. Drop everything else. This is of the highest priority."

The ambassadors were the senior leadership of the Coalition Provisional Authority (CPA) and answered directly to L. Paul Bremer, head of CPA. My first thoughts were panic. Those were immediately replaced with dread, not because I feared meeting with the leadership of CPA, but because I knew virtually nothing about forensics. Nothing. I had been trained to keep patients from the hands of pathologists. Now I was being asked to perform a forensic task and I felt out of touch with the mission and with the specialty. I couldn't pretend to offer advice on something I knew nothing about.

"That's not my specialty, sir," I responded cautiously.

General Hahn's answer was direct. "Doc, you're the medical officer on the staff. This is your mission. Keep Colonel Gagliano in the loop. Let me know what you need for the task."

Whenever General Hahn spoke to officers about critical missions, he shortened his sentences and put the emphasis on action. He always reminded officers that they worked at the pointed end of the spear. When he was in that mode of communication, there was little room for discussion. I hesitated to question the mission and thought it might be best to snap him a quick salute and simply get on with the task, yet I needed to make him aware that nobody in theater was actually qualified to do an autopsy.

"Sir, we don't have the appropriate assets in theater for a forensic evaluation," I said.

"You're taking point on this task. It's a critical mission," he said firmly. "Make it happen."

"Yes, sir."

I immediately called Colonel Gagliano to let him know about the assignment and suggested that he could intervene and take the mission himself. He said if General Hahn wanted me to take lead, then I needed to take it. I protested mildly, stating that I was too far out of my lane of expertise. What I really meant was I wanted out of a mission that focused on the dead. I wanted to spend my time in trauma care and emergency medicine, not on some politically expedient assignment.

"You've dealt with more dead patients than I have," he stated flatly.

"None of us have any forensic expertise and we don't have a pathologist in theater. Plan accordingly and stay on task. Keep me informed
and let me know what you need."

What I needed, I thought, was a different mission. I wanted nothing to do with Saddam's dead sons. Soldiers needed my expertise in
the field or in combat hospitals. The Army needed doctors who were
trained in managing trauma, yet I was assigned to care for two dead
men who had dedicated their lives to the murder, rape, and torture
of Iraqi citizens. The incongruity made me want to curse, but soldiers and officers were expected to adapt to the needs of the mission.
I didn't have the option of asking the general to get somebody else for
the job.

I HAD WORKED closely with Ambassadors Patrick Kennedy and Clay-
ton McManaway since the first days of my assignment to the 30th
Med Brigade in Baghdad. In our meeting, I explained my concern that
no Army doctors in theater, especially me, were qualified to perform
a forensic evaluation. Both ambassadors knew I had worked with the
Institute of Forensic Medicine in Baghdad (also known as the Medico-
Legal Institute) and wanted me to make contact with the institute's
director, Dr. Faik Bakr, so Iraqi pathologists could collaborate on the
identification. McManaway wanted a plan of action and he wanted it
then and there.

"Dr. Kerstetter," he said leaning forward, "give us your best advice
on how to proceed. We need to be sure on this. There are political
considerations that are time-sensitive."

The thought of doing medical missions out of political expediency
was, to me, something akin to politicians kissing babies, but Iraqi law
and custom required an immediate release of the dead for burial, and
local political pressures demanded our quick response.

"Sir," I said. "The best way to proceed is by flying a team here from
the Medical Examiner's Office at Dover Air Force Base. They have
response teams that can deploy worldwide for this kind of mission.
They're the recognized experts in forensics."

McManaway shook his head and responded forcefully. "That would take too long. If the Iraqis can make the identifications and certify the Iraqi death certificates, you can sign the military death certificates. Would that work?"

I knew it wouldn't and wondered how far I could push that point. I also knew the mission was sensitive. There would be zero tolerance for errors. I needed to be clear and decisive.

"If we were to shortcut professional forensic standards, it would be equivalent to malpractice," I replied carefully. "We simply cannot allow ourselves to become compromised. A forensic team should collaborate with the Iraqis on this case. If I called the medical examiner's office in Dover now, they could deploy a team and have them here inside of twenty-four hours."

"Doc, you're putting us in a difficult position here," Ambassador McManaway said sternly, his brows furrowed. Any delays in identifying the bodies risked a public rebuke by the disposed leadership of Iraq.

"Yes, sir. We *are* in a difficult position."

Both ambassadors looked at each other, then at me. I suspected I had crossed a line of acceptable dialogue.

"Wait here while we confer with Mr. Bremer on this," Ambassador McManaway finally said.

L. Paul Bremer was a direct presidential appointee who didn't necessarily see things the way Army leadership did. I grimaced, thinking I would be ordered to sign the death certificates despite my professional objections. But when the ambassadors came back, they said I needed to get on the phone and order the forensic team to fly to Baghdad.

"You're right, Doc," Ambassador Kennedy said. "Do this one by the book. We'll handle the political fallout. Let General Hahn know what we decided and get the Dover team here yesterday." I felt like I had escaped the grip of a lethal virus. I would not have to sign the death certificates after all.

I phoned the medical examiner's office at the Dover Air Force Base in Delaware at 6:00 p.m. The time difference made it Wednesday, 2:00 a.m., in Delaware. I asked the duty officer to patch me through to the medical examiner on call. The medical examiner was a colonel, I was a major.

"Sir, this is Major Kerstetter calling from Baghdad on behalf of General Hahn."

"Major who?"

"Dr. Kerstetter, sir. I work for General Hahn and General Sanchez."

There was a distinct pause on the line. "Go ahead."

"We have a situation that requires the forensic identification of high-value targets. I am requesting immediate assistance from one of your teams. Time is critical and I have full authorization from the general to make this request."

"When do you need us there?"

"Yesterday would have been great, but today would be fine. We need your team here without delay."

The colonel was quick and professional. "You can expect our departure within four hours. I will notify you directly."

THE DOVER TEAM arrived within twenty-four hours, as promised. I had already begun negotiations with Dr. Bakr for his participation with the forensic team. His help would be essential. Most of Iraq did not believe Uday and Qusay were dead. The rumor on the street was that we had killed their doubles or not killed them at all. Initially, military leadership thought that a combined statement by Iraqi and U.S. officials would quell any suspicions, but it became apparent that more verifiable evidence needed to be offered to the public. Our thinking was that Iraq's own forensic experts could make the identifications in conjunction with the forensic team from Dover and that would be enough. But Dr. Bakr was skittish about signing any death certificates for the Hussein brothers for fear that he might be assassinated or his family targeted for cooperating with the Americans. In an emergency meeting with him and several of his colleagues, I tried to appeal to their responsibilities as forensic experts representing the interests of Iraq.

"Dr. Bakr, this is an opportunity to inform the nation of Iraq that the Medico-Legal Institute will not be manipulated by threats or rumors. Your expertise is needed to work in collaboration with our forensic experts from Dover. Together, we'll be able to inform your citizens that the terror reign of Uday and Qusay has ended."

"The terror will continue. You don't know Iraq." Dr. Bakr shook his head as he answered. He was an older, balding, and soft-spoken physician who, I would later learn, had a leaning toward entrepreneurial ventures. When he wasn't performing his official duties as director of the institute, he ran a private clinic and a pharmacy. He had received some of his medical training in Europe, where he became fluent in English. And he *did* know Iraq. He could recite its cultural history all the way back to the beginning of civilization.

"True," I said. "I don't. But I do know we have ended a reason for that terror. And you can validate that reason for the citizens of Iraq. As a colleague, I ask you to work with me to make an accurate forensic identification. The Coalition authorities would look favorably on your cooperation."

"We will need help rebuilding the institute and we need security." He raised his eyebrows and paused.

Taking his cue, I said I was authorized to provide the institute with assistance for new equipment and a security detail.

"I must discuss this with my colleagues. We can meet tomorrow again."

"Tomorrow is out of the question. We must decide today, this afternoon," I responded firmly. "The forensic team from Dover is expecting you to participate. The ambassadors expect you to participate. Please, tell your colleagues we must proceed today."

I felt a risk in being firm. If I pushed too hard, he might resist, but my mission was clear, and getting his collaboration was not optional. The next hours of negotiation were critical to the success of that mission and I feared my influence was crumbling. Dr. Bakr was right. I didn't know Iraq or understand the expanded risks he and his colleagues would take in working with the U.S. Army. He explained to me that he would not work alone, but if his fellow pathologists were willing to work as a group, then he would work with our forensic team and encourage his colleagues to sign Iraqi death certificates.

I sat in Dr. Bakr's office as he phoned some of his top colleagues. He wanted twelve pathologists to represent the institute. The first three colleagues he phoned agreed to help. The next two refused. So it went, over more than an hour of calls and discussions, until he got his team of twelve who agreed to examine Uday and Qusay Hussein and attest to their deaths. By the time the negotiating was over, it was well past 8:00 p.m.

Early the following morning, I met Dr. Bakr and his colleagues at the institute. Two pathologists didn't show. We loaded everybody else into two large vans. Three heavily armed infantry vehicles took lead and tail positions in our small convoy. I had been advised by our intelligence officers to expect an attack on the route to our destination.

By the time the convoy of pathologists arrived at the secure site, the Dover team had already completed the autopsies. Forensic medical photos and X-rays had been taken. The forensic team assigned causes of death and reconstructed the faces of the dead to allow for easier facial recognition. DNA samples were being processed. The Iraqi pathologists were not disappointed that the autopsies were completed. Several of them told us they would not even allow themselves to touch the bodies of Uday and Qusay Hussein.

The forensic team from Dover presented their evidence as if presenting to a mortality conference of their scientific peers. After the photos and X-rays were presented, the entire group of Iraqi pathologists were invited to view the bodies in the autopsy tent. Dr. Bakr stood to go first and motioned to me to join him. Going first was a position of leadership and authority. In a sense, it was an honor to go first. During the entire presentation I had thought about the role I was playing in what would undoubtedly be viewed by some as a historic medical event, the autopsies of Iraq's two most heinous and volatile monsters. They were serial rapists, murderers, and criminals so violent that even Saddam Hussein had imprisoned Uday in reaction to several brutal murders. These were not men, but devils whose unrestrained violence and arbitrary brutality tore at the lives of even ordinary Iraqi citizens. Like Iraqis, I hated them and everything they stood for. I could smell their stench from the autopsy tent. It turned my mind as well as my stomach. As Dr. Bakr held out his hand for me to join him, I rose and stood by his side.

"Doctor, please forgive me," I said quietly. "I cannot join you. I will not allow myself to see the bodies. I hope you understand."

He looked at me and took my hand. I imagined that, in his role as a pathologist, he had taken the hands of many Iraqi families as he counseled them about the loss of their relatives. He said nothing for a moment, then spoke with an air of compassion.

"I understand completely."

With that, he turned and led his fellow pathologists into the autopsy tent.

I felt relieved that he had not insisted on my joining him. I felt that viewing the bodies would have been too much to bear, not in terms of forensics or medicine, but in terms of my own sanity, in terms of the images and memories I would carry forever. I had seen their X-rays and photos. I had done my duty as ordered, taken the responsibility, made the necessary forensic arrangements. That was enough. Uday and Qusay were dead, their identification certain. I wanted nothing more of the mission, nothing more of their deaths and their bodies and their legacies. I longed for the living—for patients who needed rescuing or blood or maybe even just the touch of a doctor to assure them. As in other times when missions had drained me, I thought of my children. As I considered the task of viewing the forensic evidence, I felt that my refusal to witness the bodies of Uday and Qusay Hussein was my way of protecting my family from the entangling influences of their evil.

The Iraqi pathologists stayed in the autopsy tent less than a half hour. When they returned, they all affirmed the deaths of Uday and Qusay. They talked as if they had witnessed something that brought great relief to them personally. Two of the pathologists said words to the effect that they were happy the murderers were dead. One started telling us about the sufferings of families that he knew personally, of rape and torture at the hands of Qusay Hussein. And in the middle of telling us about those families, his emotions grabbed him and he started to weep openly. The tent was silent. And if it were possible to sense the depth of pain that the Iraqi people suffered, I sensed it then. When I heard the Iraqi doctors talk about the cruelty they had witnessed over the years, I was glad that I had stood firm and refused to view the remains.

With the death certificates signed, I returned to headquarters to report to General Hahn and Ambassadors Kennedy and McManaway. They thanked me for a mission well done and the general asked me to join him in his office.

"Well done, Doc," he said. "I know this was not your idea of a medical mission, but it was a mission that had to be done and I knew I could trust you with it."

"Yes, sir. Thank you."

He gave me the slightest smile that quickly turned serious. "I need you on one more task related to this mission before you're finished."

"Sir?" My response wasn't the affirmative "sir" that I usually gave. It was the puzzled kind that came with a shade of apprehension. I dreaded the thought that the mission still wasn't over.

"You need to work with officials of the Iraqi Red Crescent Society and your Iraqi contacts at the Forensic Institute to transfer the remains to Tikrit. Saddam's family will take control of the bodies for their final disposition. Give them the death certificates and then have them sign a transfer form." His orders were not a discussion.

"When does this all take place, sir?"

"As soon as possible but no later than forty-eight hours. Nobody gets any rest until this mission is completed and we have delivered the remains. Again, if you need anything, let me know. Work the details out with Colonel Gagliano." And that was it; short and final.

I met with Colonel Gagliano that afternoon and we worked out a plan of transfer. Again, time was of the essence for tactical and political reasons. I called Dr. Bakr just before dinner. It was difficult to tell him exactly what I needed, since some of the details were classified. I merely said that I needed his help making contact with the family of Uday and Qusay in Tikrit.

It seemed the entire country of Iraq was buzzing about the death and disposition of the Hussein brothers. Rumors surfaced about attacks by Saddam loyalists to recover the bodies because they were being defiled by military doctors doing autopsies. Other rumors claimed that anti-Saddam fighters would undertake similar attacks to take the bodies for political purposes. U.S. military intelligence reported that once the photos of the Hussein brothers went public, the secure and secret location of the bodies would no longer be secret or secure. We should expect an attack from either or both of the opposing forces.

Dr. Bakr would not give me the names of his contacts in Tikrit who knew the Hussein family. He was blunt. "Too dangerous!"

He did, however, give me the name of a leader in the IRCS who could make contact.

"Thank you, Doctor," I said. "You have done enough."

I phoned the contact at the Red Crescent Society, Dr. Hakim, about 7:00 p.m. He had already been aware of the request to have the Hussein brothers delivered to Tikrit. The request had come from a Hussein family spokesman, an uncle of Saddam. I didn't know if Saddam had a real uncle or if the spokesman was a distant relative simply referred to as uncle. It didn't really matter to me. I was tired of the whole affair and wanted only to be done with it so I could return to my role as a doctor. To do that, I needed to make direct contact with a member of Saddam's family for the final disposition of Uday and Qusay. Short of talking with Saddam himself, an uncle would do just fine.

I talked to Dr. Hakim in general terms. The final handoff would occur under the highest levels of U.S. Army security and we would not tolerate any attempt to interfere with the transfer. He understood that and knew the transport of Uday and Qusay came with high stakes. Their deaths had spurred an escalation of fighting throughout Iraq. The proper disposition of their bodies might de-escalate tensions. If we let the transfer degenerate into a political fight or an outright battle, more Iraqis and soldiers would die and we would have failed our responsibilities.

At the end of our conversation, he gave me the name and phone number of the uncle. Dr. Hakim offered to phone the uncle first and introduce me as the U.S. military contact. He suggested I wait until 9:00 p.m. to make my call. In the interim, I would receive a phone call from another Red Crescent member, a doctor whom I had worked with before on a humanitarian assignment. She would also help facilitate the transfer. Her call came within fifteen minutes.

"Dr. Kerstetter. It appears we will again be working together. Let us hope it goes as planned," she said.

"All I ask is that you help me on the day of the transfer," I replied. "We will be at a secure site. I don't know where yet. The details will come later. Will you be there representing the interests of the Red Crescent?"

To my relief, her answer was affirmative. "Yes. I have made that commitment as a colleague. I will help."

"Then I think it will go well. Do you know the person I am to call from Saddam's family?"

"Yes. They will talk to you with respect. They know you are a doctor."

Before I called the uncle, I phoned Colonel Gagliano to let him know I had the contact and would be calling. He had made initial plans for the security of the transfer and the logistics. We would move the bodies from Baghdad International Airport to an undisclosed location in Tikrit in the early hours of the following morning. From there, we would fly them to the final destination and I would accompany the bodies. The colonel would fly in a separate helicopter to officiate the handoff. If all went as planned, we would be back in Baghdad that afternoon and have a nice dinner.

I told him I wasn't trained in all the cloak-and-dagger stuff but that I was on target and doing okay for an ER doctor. He laughed and agreed. "Keep doing what you're doing and update me as needed. Call me back after your Saddam call."

I had felt a bit out of my element at first, yet was growing confident with all the intrigue and the dark-of-night doings of the mission. I never imagined my professional duties as a soldier or a doctor would play a significant role in the final disposition of Uday and Qusay Hussein, who, before my deployment from Iowa to Iraq, were not even names I would have recognized.

On the hour, 9:00 p.m., I phoned the uncle. He answered promptly, but the connection was poor and the line dropped in the middle of our introductions. Was that a sign of how things would go? I called him back and said I was sorry for the poor connection. He understood. We exchanged names. He sounded hard. Not rude, yet with just enough stiffness to let me know he was trying to gain the upper hand. I wondered if I was speaking to a murderer like Saddam and his sons.

"I have the responsibility of transferring the remains of Uday and Qusay Hussein," I said, my own words rather stiff like his.

"I understand. You are a doctor. This is unusual," he replied.

"Well, perhaps not. I have worked with your Red Crescent Society and have excellent relations with several doctors there."

"Yes, I have heard. We need to arrange the exact time and place for transfer. It should be done quickly to minimize our exposure."

"I agree. We will plan on fifteen minutes or less. You or your representatives may have a copy of the death certificates and may view the bodies in a secure manner. We will provide all the logistics and security. I have already spoken to my colleagues in the Red Crescent Society and they have agreed to monitor the transfer as a neutral third party. Is that acceptable?"

"We demand to see the bodies before we make the transfer," he said firmly. "Our family prefers to take possession at the Tikrit airport."

"We cannot use the Tikrit airport," I cautioned him. "The security risks are too high and we will all be exposed." I pressed on. "After you view the bodies, you must sign a transfer document; then you may take possession. You will receive copies of the Army death certificates and the Iraqi death certificates. The identities have been verified by a team of forensic experts."

He answered abruptly. "We will not accept your military death certificate." I worried for a moment our call would deteriorate into a pissing match of international proportions.

"That's fine. It is there only as an official document. You have the Medico-Legal Institute's death certificates to use if you want them."

"We will verify for ourselves the identities."

"I understand. Let us plan for the transfer tomorrow morning if you are in agreement."

"I agree. Again, we prefer to transfer at the Tikrit airport."

"Again, Tikrit is not an option. I will call you as soon as I have a time and location."

When we finished our conversation, I was relieved that we had come to a reasoned agreement despite our mutual needs to be blunt and firm. I was also struck that he knew I was a doctor, but then, he had already been talking with my contact at the IRCS, so I should have expected that he had gathered intelligence about me. I was still his enemy. Still, the information that Saddam's relatives knew about me made me think of those *SPY vs SPY* cartoons in *Mad* magazine, albeit our contact was far more serious and dangerous.

By 9:30 p.m. I was back on the phone with an update for Colonel Gagliano. "The uncle wants to do it at the Tikrit airport but I said 'no deal.' I told him I would phone him later with the details."

"Perfect. We need to brief General Hahn by midnight."

The final mission details were put on General Hahn's desk at 2315 hours. We would fly two covert missions in the morning: one was a cover mission with a load of supplies; the other would carry the bodies. I was to accompany the transfer cases. Colonel Gagliano would fly in a separate helicopter to the location with a small Army delegation and the official death certificates. He would sign the transfer papers for the Army, and Saddam's representative would sign on behalf of their family. The phone call to my contact at the Red Crescent and to Saddam's family member would be made only within the final thirty minutes before our landing at the transfer point. That would allow enough time for their delegates to arrive without broadcasting our intentions too far in advance. Security would be tight; infantry and aviation attack assets would be alerted. Air cover would be provided at the site of the transfer. Mission start time was 0500.

I spent the night trying to sleep but couldn't. I kept rehearsing the mission details. What if Saddam's relative didn't show? What if he said the bodies weren't those of Uday and Qusay? How about the bodies? What if we left them behind in a last-minute frazzle to hurry the mission? Worst of all, what if we were attacked during the transfer? I lay in my bed staring at the walls and ceiling. I revisited clips of my childhood, the hikes in the mountains of Utah, my gathering leaves for a science project. Mom. I remembered her chubby face and her hand-sewn aprons, the pumpkin pies she made for Thanksgiving. My boyhood had been so uncomplicated when compared to my missions as a military physician in Iraq. My whole life had been one dream—to become a doctor. That dream never included the sons of Saddam Hussein. It never saw me as part doctor, part logistics officer, and part mediator between the strongest army in the world and the family of the most violent killers in the world. I had counted myself fortunate to have become a doctor. I wasn't sure how to count myself in the larger picture of Iraq. I supposed that if I performed my tasks well enough, then I would have served some greater good, but the task at hand seemed to have no place in the greater cause of medicine. My only solace was that if we pulled the mission off without further bloodshed, well at least it would be something positive.

My alarm blared at 0400. I had fallen asleep in my uniform. It stunk of the accumulated sweat and grime of three days of nonstop activity. At 0445, after a quick shower and change of uniform, I met Colonel Gagliano in the parking lot behind my office. I had packed an extra clip of ammo for my pistol just in case, but as I strapped it to my vest, I figured if things got as far as me needing to draw my weapon, I probably wasn't coming back alive.

Our convoy to the Baghdad airport was small: four vehicles, eight soldiers, two critical documents, and two medical officers. We met with the commander of the mortuary affairs unit. His soldiers had received the bodies during the night and prepared their transfer cases under protection of a security detail and guards. Uday and Qusay lay inside the cases. Colonel Gagliano verified the manifest and the contents. It was time for breakfast. We sat and talked about some aspects of the mission but then drifted off to talking about our families. That morphed into talking aloud about how Saddam's family would have reacted to the news of the gun battle in Mosul and how they would accept that the brothers were finally dead. The talk of them spoiled whatever positive things we had been saying about our families. And that was how it went with war. In one moment you recalled the good things of home, and in the next moment the things of war and its inhumanity would creep in and destroy a perfectly beautiful and peaceful memory.

War drew soldiers into its ugliness. My mission involving Uday and Qusay Hussein did exactly that; it drew me in and marked me as an inside participant. I would never be able to forget the proximity. And at least for me, that closeness was abhorrent. I wished I had never been assigned the task, wished that I had had the guts to refuse it. But I hadn't. I had taken it. I had puffed out my chest and prided myself in being asked to do the mission. Who else in the theater could have done it? Two officers. Colonel Don Gagliano and Major Jon Kerstetter. And what did that pride or sense of duty accomplish? Well, it did get the job done. But it also exposed me to things I could never escape—the ugly and evil things done in war. All those experiences and images would find a permanent residence in my life and memories. I didn't get to choose which missions I would remember and which I would forget. They would all claim an equal purchase.

As the mission start time approached, I wondered how I would react to the Hussein mission ten or twenty years down the road. Would I be haunted by it? Would I ever tell anybody about it? If I met the Saddam family at some café in London or Paris someday, would they hate me or thank me? Would they say, "We remember you. You were the doctor who gave us back our sons for burial." Would I tell them how I hated doing so?

The time wound down and the helicopters arrived. I met with the pilot in command of the Chinook that would transport the bodies.

He didn't know the mission details until I told him he was about to fly Uday and Qusay to a classified landing zone near Tikrit. I saluted Colonel Gagliano as I boarded my flight. He saluted me in return. During takeoff, I prayed for the safety of our flight and for the peaceful transition on the ground in Tikrit. The word "peaceful" stuck in my mouth like a dry piece of bread.

Exactly twenty minutes before our ETA near Tikrit, I told the pilot to radio a message to my contact in the Red Crescent. A communications unit had rigged up some way to transfer a radio call over cell phone channels so I could talk directly with my contacts. When the line was secure, I gave the location of our arrival and the time of our touchdown plus or minus two minutes. I asked my contact to repeat the information back to me.

"Yes," I said. "Affirmative. I will see you in twenty minutes."

I did the same with Saddam's uncle. He took the information and said he would meet me at the site with the Red Crescent members.

"Be aware that our security forces are in place," I cautioned him. "They will escort your vehicles for the final kilometers of your drive. Do not be alarmed. They are there for your protection."

"I understand. We will cooperate."

We landed ahead of everybody else by design. We wanted no surprises and needed to secure the landing site before the various delegates to the transfer arrived. Overhead, two Cobra gunships circled in a pattern that would spot and engage any potential attacks. A nearby perimeter was set up with infantry soldiers at the ready. The crew chief of the Chinook lowered the tailgate. Two mortuary transfer cases rested on the cargo floor, out of the sun, away from harm. The ground forces and the helicopters overhead gave the sense that we might be in for a battle and the extra tension of our mission added to that sense. If somebody got too edgy with a weapon, the mission could deteriorate into a fight.

Colonel Gagliano's helicopter touched down about five minutes after I arrived. We stood together near the back of the helicopter. We could see the transfer cases from where we stood. Off in the distance, we could see the dust trail of a convoy as it made its way to our isolated landing zone.

"They're coming," I said to Colonel Gagliano with a bit of nervousness. "Do you have the death certificates and the transfer forms?" I wanted to portray myself as calm and controlled. My voice may have betrayed me.

Smiling, he patted his map case. "Just waiting for a signature," he said. "Everything is going to be fine," he added. Watching him react to everything so calmly made me wonder what I would be like as a colonel.

Saddam's relatives finally arrived; two black Mercedes cars and two Red Crescent vans parked in the area that soldiers had marked out well away from the helicopters. Colonel Gagliano stayed with the bodies. I walked over to greet my contacts from both parties.

After a quick greeting with Dr. Hakim, he walked me over to the car of Saddam's uncle. As we approached, his bodyguards opened the door and a rather tall, dark-haired man in business attire got out. I expected him to look like the pictures of Saddam, maybe shorter with a pock-marked face and a limp. Dr. Hakim introduced us. The man greeted me but did not extend his hand. I took his cue and I reiterated the procedures that we would follow.

"Yes, yes," he said impatiently. "I understand. Let me see the bodies. I have also two other witnesses who need to see."

"You may view the bodies in the presence of the Red Crescent delegates, as we discussed," I responded. I was firm without being obstinate.

The uncle stared at me for a moment. I could see the tension in his face. Then he said, "Yes, as we agreed."

As we walked to the Chinook helicopter, it was like walking on the hottest sand or dirt in Iraq. Every step seemed hard and awkward and prolonged. Everything to that point had gone as planned. No glitches. Nothing forgotten. I wanted so much to get through the next minutes unscathed. I suspected the other parties wished the same. There was nothing to gain from misdeeds or last-minute demands.

The soldiers guarding the loading ramp of the Chinook stood at attention as we approached. Colonel Gagliano stepped from the helicopter to greet the small delegation. He had prepared some official Army statement that conveyed a simple fact—we had delivered the bodies of Uday and Qusay Hussein, and in collaboration with the Iraqi Red Crescent Society, the U.S. Army was transferring the identified remains to the representatives of the Hussein family. Members of the family were invited to review the identities as members of the Red Crescent Society observed.

With the assistance of several soldiers, the cases were opened and the family members viewed the bodies. They said nothing as they did so. I could hear my heart pumping. I felt a surge of nervous adrenaline. A drop of sweat fell into my eyes and stung, but I didn't move to wipe it. Colonel Gagliano stood nearby, not at attention but at parade rest, observing the observers. Finally, the man whom I knew as Saddam's uncle nodded his head.

"Yes," he said without flinching. "It is them."

As soon he said it, he turned and walked toward Colonel Gagliano, who escorted the entire delegation away from the helicopter to a field desk that had been set up to sign documents. Colonel Gagliano signed his part of the transfer form and then Saddam's uncle signed his part. The colonel asked if I wanted to also sign as a witness, but I told him I didn't think it necessary. I really meant I didn't want my name associated with the final documents.

When they were done with their formalities, I talked with the Red Crescent members about loading the transfer cases into their vans. They would maneuver to within fifty yards of the Chinook loading ramp. They preferred their own delegates to do the offloading from the helicopter. That was not acceptable. Our soldiers had to offload the cases, but then they could set them on a wheeled mortuary gurney so the bodies could be moved easily without anybody getting hurt. And that was what we did together, a medical officer of the U.S. Army, representatives of the Iraqi Red Crescent Society, and members of Saddam Hussein's family. The transfer cases were loaded into the vans

and Saddam's uncle and the bodies of Uday and Qusay Hussein were
driven off, leaving a wake of dust.

OVER THE FOLLOWING days, I heard less about Uday and Qusay
Hussein and more about other missions needing attention. Toward
the end of the week, I participated in the care of an Iraqi child with
leukemia. Her father had been caring for her, and when she became
too sick to eat, he appealed to one of the Army medical aid stations in
western Baghdad for help. They passed his request up the chain, and
when it hit Colonel Gagliano's desk, he said it would be a good way to
reach out to the citizens of Iraq. He tasked me to pick her up and make
arrangements for her treatment. We had no pediatricians or oncolo-
gists in our combat hospitals, so I made arrangements with an Italian
unit that had a pediatrician to serve humanitarian needs. They evaluated the child and decided to fly her and her mother to Italy for treatment. The father was so grateful that, in tears, he put his hands over
his heart and mumbled something I could not understand. I asked our
hospital translator to help me. As I watched the translator communi-
cate, I saw that the father had no thumbs.

"He thanks God for you," the translator said. "You cannot understand him because he has only half a tongue. He was tortured in jail
for stealing food to provide for his family. He says the man who ordered his tongue cut out and his thumbs cut off was Qusay Hussein,
son of Saddam Hussein."

"Tell him we will do everything we can for his daughter and that
I will pray for his daughter the way I pray for my own daughters. And
tell him I am the Army doctor who sealed Uday and Qusay in a coffin."

As she translated, the father smiled and took my hand and praised
God for the death of Qusay. And I understood then that my role as
a combat physician was more than the role of a doctor. Performing a
mission that I deemed repugnant seemed wasteful to me. Yet, to this
Iraqi father, the final disposition of two vile murderers held a meaning far deeper than I could have ever imagined. To him, the proof of
their death brought closure and perhaps the element of justice that

he needed. I had never calculated that value in my prior assessments of the mission. The grateful father gave me a different perspective. It was not my duty or right to determine the value and impact of a mission, no matter its parameters; it was my duty to perform my tasks with the professionalism and certitude of an officer and a physician.

Triage

— — —

FROM LATE SUMMER, the tempo of the war changed. The number of IED attacks escalated, especially in and around Baghdad. In response, soldiers welded scrap-metal plates scavenged from whatever sources they could find onto the most vulnerable parts of their vehicles. The enemy responded with shaped charges and multiple IEDs wired to explode as a chain reaction. The resulting casualties arrived at Combat Support Hospitals (CSH) by ground and air ambulance.

One of my tasks in the CJTF7 (Combined Joint Task Force 7) Headquarters was to track IED attacks, the numbers of casualties, and the medical responses. I gave weekly reports with an analysis to the task force chief of staff, Major General Jon Gallinetti. The general was a Marine Corps aviator who had flown fighter jets for most of his career. He was a big man, over six feet tall, and when I first met him his commanding presence made me shake just a bit. He was direct and succinct in the way he talked, composed as one of authority, with a voice that could easily carry across a large room. Anybody who worked with him was quick to recognize that he expected his officers and staff to have a precise and complete understanding of the ongoing battle situation and be able to offer reasoned summaries and contingencies when asked. Hardened or shaped as he was by the demands of his career as a Marine aviator and by the demands of his role as a general officer, he nevertheless showed compassion and thoughtfulness for the Marines and soldiers under his charge. He was equal parts tough and thoughtful, firm and compassionate. That made him the kind of leader Marines and soldiers wanted to follow.

During a particularly rough week in terms of casualties, the general asked me to arrange a visit to the CSH without making it a big deal. When general officers visited a field unit, it usually involved a certain protocol that tended to make that unit's officers start jumping through hoops to present their unit in a positive light. The general wanted none of that. He simply wanted to visit the casualties and encourage them and the hospital staff.

Later that week I arranged for a visit late at night. The general, his Marine protection detail, and I made the one-mile trip in our Humvees, checked in at the gate, and entered the hospital unannounced.

Hours earlier, numerous soldiers had been injured in multiple IED attacks throughout Baghdad. The survivors of those attacks created a backlog of patients who required emergency surgery. In the emergency room, surgeons, nurses, medics, and hospital staff moved from patient to patient at an exhausting pace. They stabilized patients and performed rapid trauma assessments, then transferred patients quickly to surgery in the adjacent operating rooms. Teams of surgeons worked to stop bleeding and repair injuries. Blood transfusions flowed at will and surgical clamps clicked as fast as bullets in a firefight. When one surgery was finished, another began immediately. One operating table held a soldier with multiple orthopedic injuries. In an adjacent room, surgeons removed shrapnel from a soldier's abdomen. If an observer had watched from the side, the whole scene might have resembled controlled chaos, but a deeper look would have revealed something more. The ER staff moved with their own theme and pace, with a kind of gracefulness that resembled an improvised modern dance. Nurses and medics transferred patients on the count of three. One, two, three—lift. The trauma team identified wounds, started transfusions, infused antibiotics, and initiated anesthesia, then carried patients off to the operating rooms where surgeons responded with their own kind of methodical precision: explore, clamp, cut, and tie. They all moved choreographed to the rhythm of saving a life or salvaging a limb.

General Gallinetti and I visited the ICU, where the head nurse, surprised by our presence, wanted to notify the hospital commander to accompany us. The general simply asked the nurse to give us a brief rundown on the patients. We stopped by each bedside long enough for the general to pay his respects and lay his hand on a patient's shoulder if possible, and if not then on the patient's blanket. He wished the few soldiers who were awake a quick recovery and acknowledged their service. During the visit, I could see the compassionate side of the general. His time at the hospital was not mere protocol, it was personal. To me, he seemed like a father or a doctor to those patients in addition to a general, and he reminded me that soldiers and Marines who needed to be tough also needed to show compassion in the line of duty. As I watched him among the dying and the wounded, he was as comfortable and professional in a combat hospital as he was in leading high-ranking officers in a combat headquarters.

We walked from the ICU down the hallway to the triage room. One patient lay in a bed, a young soldier, private first class. He had a ballistic head injury. His elbows were flexed tightly in spastic tension, drawing his forearms to his chest. His hands made stone-like fists and his fingers coiled together as if grabbing an imaginary rope attached to his sternum. He breathed in a slow, sporadic, and agonal pattern. He had no oxygen mask. An intravenous line fed a slow drip of saline and painkiller. He was what is known in military medicine as expectant.

Some of his fellow soldiers gathered at the foot of his bed. Except for the captain, they were all young like the patient, late teens and early twenties. A few of them had sustained injuries in the same IED attack and had already been treated and bandaged in the emergency room. They stood watch over the expectant patient. One soldier had a white fractal of body salt edging the collar of his uniform. One wept. One prayed. Another quietly said "Jesus" over and over, shaking his head from side to side. Yet another had no expression at all; he simply stared a blank stare into the empty space above the expectant patient's head. A young sergeant, hands shaking, stammered as he tried to explain what had happened. The captain in charge of the expectant soldier's unit told the general and me that this was their first soldier killed—then he corrected himself and said this was the first soldier in their unit assigned to triage. He told us that the soldier was a good soldier. The general nodded in agreement and the room was suddenly quiet.

The general laid his hand on the expectant soldier's leg—the leg whose strength I imagined was drifting like a shape-shifting cloud moving against a dark umber sky; strength retreating into a time before it carried a soldier into war. And I watched the drifting of a man back into the womb of his mother, drifting toward a time when a leg was not a leg, a body not a body—to a time when a soldier was only the laughing between two young lovers who could never imagine that a leg-body-man-soldier would one day lie expectant and that that soldier would be their son.

As I watched the soldiers at the foot of the bed, I noted their worn faces, their trembling mouths, their hollow-stare eyes. I watched them watch the shallow breathing, the intermittent spasm of seizured limbs, and the unnatural gray of expectant skin. I took clinical notes in my mind. I did this whenever I needed to separate myself from the emotional impact of seeing the critically wounded. I noted the soldiers, noted the patient. I noted all the things that needed to be noted: the size of the triage room, the frame of the bed, the tiles of the ceiling, and the dullness of the overhead light. I noted the taut draw of the white linen sheets and the shiny polished metal of the hospital fixtures. A single ceiling fan rotated slowly. The walls were off-white. There were no windows. The floor was spotless, the smell antiseptic. A drab-green wool Army blanket covered each bed. Three beds lay empty. I noted the absence of noise, the absence of nurses rushing to prepare surgical instruments, and the absence of teams of doctors urgently opening wounds and calling out orders. There was an absence of the hurried sounds and the hustle of soldiers in the combat emergency room one floor down. Nobody yelled "Medic" or "Doc." Nobody called for the chaplain. Medics did not cut off clothing or gather dressings. Ambulances and medevac helicopters did not arrive with bleeding soldiers.

— — —

MORE THAN FIFTEEN years prior, when I was a newly minted captain, I attended the two-week Combat Casualty Care Course at Camp Bullis, Texas. The course was designed to teach medical officers combat trauma care and field triage techniques. The capstone exercise included a half-day mass-casualty scenario complete with percussion grenades, smoke bombs, and simulated enemy forces closing on the casualty collection point. The objective was to give medical officers a realistic setting in which to perform triage decisions. About twenty moulaged patients mimicked battlefield casualties ranging from the minimally injured to those requiring immediate surgery. Each medical officer in training was given five minutes to perform the triage exercise and to prepare an appropriate medevac request. Providing treatment was not an option. The exercise focused exclusively on making triage decisions.

All the participants could have easily completed the role-play within the time limit. Nothing, of course, was ever that straightforward in Army training. There was always some built-in element of surprise to test how well trainees coped with chaos. At Camp Bullis the element of the unexpected was a simulated psychiatric patient threatening to commit suicide while brandishing an M16 rifle and holding a medic hostage. In order to maintain the element of surprise, trainers whisked the doctors who had finished their turns out the back of the triage tent.

My turn. I entered the tent at the shove of my evaluator. The mock "psych" patient was screaming and threatening to kill his hostage. Other medics were pleading with the patient to lay down his weapon and let the wounded get on a helicopter. I was to take charge and get control. I did. I approached the screaming patient with quick, confident steps. I got about halfway across the triage tent when he pointed his rifle directly at his hostage and yelled, "One more step and the medic is dead." I backed off slowly, turned sideways, and quietly pulled my pistol. In an abrupt and instantaneous movement, I reeled around and shot the psych patient with my blank ammunition. "Bang—you're dead!" I yelled. A nearby evaluator took his weapon and made him play dead. One out-of-control psycho eliminated. I finished the tri-age exercise within the five-minute time limit. My evaluator laughed. "Damn," he said.

I felt great. I had control.

In the after-action review, the other medical officers asked about my decision to shoot. "Time," I answered. "I only had five minutes, so I maximized my effectiveness by eliminating a threat. It's combat," I argued.

One fellow doc asked if I would really shoot a patient in combat. A debate ensued as to the ethics of my decision. Nobody else had shot the patient. Nobody else had finished the exercise in the allotted time. Some managed to talk the psych patient into giving up his weapon. Those physicians had taken nearly fifteen minutes to complete the exercise—minutes in which some of the simulated patients died a sim-ulated death. In the end we decided that my decision to shoot, while potentially serving a greater need, may have been a bit aggressive; but it was in fact my decision, and it met the needs of the mission.

Emergency War Surgery, the military's bible of war medicine, de-fines triage as the assignment of patients to four categories of treat-ment based on the severity of injuries: Minimal, Delayed, Immediate, and Expectant. Assignment to the expectant category means that a soldier has no likelihood of survival. Based on that single calculation, a physician decides to withhold medical treatment. On the surface, the ultimate cost of that decision is a soldier's life. One decision—one life, perhaps even several lives. But there are other costs not so easily cal-culated, like the emotional cost to survivors or the psychological toll on soldiers who make triage decisions. Textbook definitions are silent on how military physicians prepare for, or react to, the demands of making a triage decision. No chapter in a military textbook instructs combat physicians in the multidimensional complexity of decision making that serves to deny lifesaving interventions for soldiers. There are chapters on why triage decisions must be made and chapters on how to apply established medical criteria in making those decisions. However, what to do next, after making the triage decision—not cov-

ered. And that vacuum of knowledge leads to a feeling of exposure and
vulnerability, neither of which can be tolerated in war. That doesn't
suggest that the process fall to someone else or that the criteria used
to make those decisions should be discarded. There is no other way.
In the end, the practice of military triage obligates doctors, whose
principal duty is the saving of lives, to perform tasks that share in the
brutality and the ugliness of war—tasks that are tantamount to pulling a trigger on fellow soldiers.

In the triage room, with this one particular soldier, I clearly saw
the disparity between the simulated triage decisions of my training
and the real decisions of combat. And it occurred to me that wartime triage tended to hit more like the force of a bomb blast. In an
instant, fragments of stone and metal exploded through the air with
such velocity that when they hit a human target, even if the target was
not killed, it was stunned and bleeding and breathless. It was in that
context that military doctors made live-fire triage decisions and stood
against the ethical force of their consequences.

In the process of making notes about the expectant patient, I
paused and moved closer to the bed. I put my hand on the patient's leg,
just as the general had done. I laid it there, let it linger. From where
I stood, I stared directly into the expectant soldier's face. I watched
his breathing, a long sighed breath followed by an absence of movement, followed by three to four shallow breaths. I matched his breathing with my own. I timed the slowing pattern with my watch. I made
mental calculations, then looked away. Once again I noted the quiet of
the room and the whiteness of the walls. I noted the empty beds and
the ceiling and the antiseptic smell. Again I watched the expectant
soldier, who was oblivious to all of my watching.

I stood at the triage bedside thinking, If this were my son, I would
want soldiers to gather in his room, listen to his breathing. I would
want them to break stride from their war routines, perhaps to weep,
perhaps to pray. And if he called out for his dad, I would want them
to become a father to my son. Simply that—nothing more, nothing

less—procedures not written in Department of Defense manuals or war theory classes or triage exercises.

I finally moved to the head of the bed and placed my right hand on his chest. My hand rested there with barely any movement. I turned to the other soldiers, gave them an acknowledgment with a slight up-turned purse of my lips, then looked away. I lifted my hand to the patient's right shoulder, let my weight shift as if trying to hold him gently in place. I half kneeled, half bent—closed the distance between our bodies. I noted the fabric of his skullcap dressing and the blood that tainted its white cotton edges. I prayed for God to take him in that very instant. I whispered, so only he could hear, "You're a good soldier. You're finished here. It's okay to go home now." I saw the faces of my own sons in his. I was glad they were not soldiers.

I finished, stood up, and walked to the foot of the bed. One of the soldiers asked me if there wasn't something I could do. I said no. I meant no. I wanted my answer to be *yes*. I faced the captain and put my hand on his shoulder, told him that we were finished, that his soldier did not feel pain, that he would be gone soon, and that everybody had done everything they could. The tone of my voice was neither comforting nor encouraging, neither sorrowful nor hopeful. It was, as I remember, military and professional. The captain said "Yes, sir" to the things I said and the way I said them. And the things I said had their own pace and rhythm; they flowed like the movement of triage itself, shaped by the needs of survivors. After a few moments of silence, the general and I quietly left the triage room and the hospital.

I REMEMBERED THAT expectant soldier so often after our hospital visit. I knew I'd seen his name in his hospital chart or was told his name by his commander. I did not take the time to write it down anywhere—and that bothered me. It bothered me because as the weeks and months went by, he remained nameless like so many other soldier-patients I encountered. And that namelessness seemed like a form of abandonment for which I felt personally responsible. I understood, in a professional sense, that the patient was not abandoned, that his triage was purposeful, and that it provided the ascent to medical efficiency, which ultimately saved other soldiers' lives. But I also understood that the theory of triage quickly eroded when confronted with the raw, human act of sorting through wounded patients and assigning them to triage categories. In my mind, the theoretical and the practical waged a constant battle, so that whenever I participated in a triage decision, part of me said yes, and part of me said no.

Ballistic Maneuvers

MILITARY DOCTORS USUALLY stick to the practice of medicine, but they also train to engage and kill an enemy if the
need arises. In pre-deployment stateside weapons training,
I fired tight clusters, hitting right in the middle of a cardboard target's head or chest. If my aim was off, my shots tended to strike the
left cheek or left eye socket, or the left side of the thorax and a little
high—just below the collarbone. I tended to pull off center when I was
rushed.

At Fort Bliss, Texas, close-quarters combat training simulated
enemy encounters expected in Iraq—contact in confined spaces and
distances of less than ten yards or so. One range scenario involved two
groups of stand-up targets. The primary group contained two simulated Iraqis located twelve feet directly in front of me. The secondary
group, three insurgents, stood at my ten o'clock position, twelve yards
farther back. One insurgent had a red-checkered keffiyeh tied around
his neck. The instructor always briefed me. "Okay, Doc," he would
say. "Focus on the center of mass. Kill your targets." Then he gave
a quick sharp command. "Engage!" Without hesitation, I shot the
first two targets, ejected the spent clip, then reloaded a seven-round
magazine. If the instructor yelled "Alive!" I hit the first two cardboard
Iraqis again—one bullet each, just to make sure they were dead. I then
rushed five yards toward the secondary targets, squared my shoulders,
and opened fire. The goal was to fire the first lethal shot before the
enemy had time to respond.

The live-fire drills were rigorous and thrilling in a way that
medicine was not, especially in the way they mimicked combat risk.

Medical risk primarily flowed one way, toward the patients. Risk in confronting an enemy flowed both ways—toward the target and back toward the shooter. An enemy always fired back. Soldiers reduced that risk by killing targets. And their weapons training and live-fire drills taught just that: killing—precise, quick, and efficient killing. Some instructors freely used the word "kill" on the range. "Kill the target." "Kill them before they kill you." "Get the kill shot." "Think one-shot kills." Kill. Kill. Kill.

I performed all the firing drills with gusto, mentally and physically psyched up by the "kill or be killed" mantra. But after the drills were finished and I was back in the barracks thinking about my day, I sensed the abrading of one set of skills against the other: doctor skills versus soldier skills, healing versus killing skills. Yet I didn't think of the polar differences as an unsolvable conundrum. Killing was not optional, and I had no ethical issues about killing an enemy who attacked me or my patients. I fully recognized the need to master both sets of skills. Being a combat doctor required it. But emotionally the meaning of the word "kill" carried with it all the tangible weight and moral implications of doctors training to become killers in reserve, as if killing were but another medical instrument in a repertoire of skills designed to save lives. I reasoned that in one way killing did save lives, so, ultimately, knowing how to work a weapon was as useful as knowing how to work a scalpel or a field radio.

IN SO MANY ways, combat medicine mirrored the speed and risk of close-quarters combat. Wounds hemorrhaged or re-hemorrhaged without warning, abruptly turning a stable situation into a critical one that threatened patients' lives as surely as a bullet. Bacteria embedded in fractures and shrapnel wounds pushed patients toward septic shock. Brains swelled from blunt trauma or ballistic trauma. The swelling could make a soldier brain-dead or just dead—period. Doctors learned to react to those sudden turns as if they were shooting at pop-up targets on the range. They shifted instantaneously from one critical scenario to another, from one kind of wound to another, from one patient to several patients simultaneously, all the while focusing on the target of keeping patients alive. Interventions were rapid-fire. Quick, invasive procedures became routine. Treatment of casualties looked more like a tactical assault rather than medical intervention. Trauma resuscitations created their own violence of action, their own entry and exit wounds.

During midsummer 2003, my team and I recovered a patient from a missile attack. He had shrapnel wounds to his chest, arms, face, and head. A large segment of his frontal and temporal skull bones penetrated his brain. It looked like a brick or a pipe had struck him on the front and side of his head. Something had sliced off the right side of his face and his entire nose and upper lip. I swept pieces of tissue and teeth and blood from his mouth with my finger. The movement was swift and forceful, and the patient responded in pain. Normally, I would have sedated him, but I couldn't wait because he was choking on his own blood. I got a breathing tube into his trachea and attached it to an oxygen supply; then we loaded him in our ambulance and headed to the combat support hospital across the Tigris River. Surgeons worked on him for hours: chest, arms, face, and brain. I saw him in the ICU later in the evening. I wondered if he would survive the next several days. He did survive.

I loved the speed and electric feeling of emergency and combat medicine. Something in my personality or my genetic makeup seemed to align itself with the critical demands and the imminent danger of medical emergencies. They provided a sense of excitement that fulfilled a base craving in me—the need for danger and thrill and risk. Simply put, war engaged me. I wanted to be part of its raw, savage action. I drew meaning and satisfaction from facing its challenges and had a constant desire to engage. To infantry soldiers, that desire translated into the hunt for an enemy and the blood-rushing engagement of a firefight—into that rare and exclusive thrill of facing and surviving the lethality of war. To military doctors, that translation was as intense, but we didn't measure it in terms of the number of bullets fired or enemy killed; we measured it by the number of soldiers treated and lives saved, in the excitement of pitting medical skills and clinical speed against the life-threatening nature of combat injuries.

In the course of my duties, I had continued to work with Dr. Bakr after our collaboration in identifying Saddam Hussein's sons. We consulted with members of the International Committee of the Red Cross and the Iraqi Red Crescent Society to provide solutions for identifying victims buried in several mass graves in and around Baghdad. As we worked together, we developed a mutual and professional respect for each other's expertise.

During July, Dr. Bakr asked for military assistance to transfer unidentified human remains to a remote cemetery. The bodies had been recovered from the streets of Baghdad and were accumulating at the morgue. The institute lacked adequate cold storage and the summer heat accelerated the decay of the remains to the point where the stench of the dead permeated the nearby streets. The situation demanded an immediate public health solution.

I arranged for an on-site visit and arrived at the institute just after noon—two Humvees and a team of five soldiers. The team secured the vehicles and guarded the forensic building while Dr. Bakr and his staff gave me a tour of the facility so I could witness the problems firsthand. Iraqi looters had ravaged the forensic labs during the early weeks of the war destroying everything: scientific equipment, medical reference books, storage bins, gurneys, and exam tables. They ripped copper wiring from the walls and wood from the floors. The institute had been the Iraqi government's central facility for forensic pathology. The looters reduced its laboratories to shards of glass and chunks of plaster.

I asked Dr. Bakr about the unidentified bodies. He led me to an adjacent open courtyard. There, he opened the thick, bolted doors of two walk-in meat lockers and a single refrigeration truck. Stuffed inside were over a hundred rotting Iraqi bodies. Most were young men. What I saw struck me as forcibly as had the carnage in Rwanda. I understood the absolute waste of human life and the inhumanity of war.

The bodies lay on racks, uncovered. As I stared at a few bloated faces, a fly from the truck landed on my right cheek. I slapped at it so hard, I left a bruise on my face.

There was no electricity or gas for the generators used to cool the storage units. I took one shallow breath and the smell of decay choked me. I grew nauseous and edgy, sickened like never before in my medical practice. It wasn't just the smell that got to me; it was the sight of all those men, those young abandoned men. I felt overwhelmed, out of place. Everything I witnessed seemed to shout directly at me. *Look! Here are dead, decaying men. This is part of your war. You're an Army doctor. Fix this, deal with it, make it better: Heal it.* There would be no healing. There was far more to the institute's issue than the accumulation and decay of bodies. Humanity itself was decaying. The bodies were proof: I was the witness. I was part of the machinery that made it possible.

I wanted to run from the images and the smells and the institute. I turned to walk away and said I had seen enough, but Dr. Bakr told me there was more. I said curtly that I didn't need to see anymore. He kept reminding me about the lack of refrigeration and supplies. I demanded we move from the courtyard, insisting we were finished. "I don't need to see all this shit," I snapped. "I get it!" I could tell I had stunned him by my demeanor. He looked both hurt and surprised. And when I saw his expression, I felt disappointed in myself and guilty that I had acted so unprofessionally, so unlike a colleague.

On the walk back to Bakr's office, he took me on a detour to the autopsy room where he pointed out the horrid work conditions and lack of basic supplies. I pressed him to move to his office.

"Sir, please," he said almost plaintively. "Allow me just a few minutes. I must show you our work."

He impressed me as bordering on desperation. As I looked at the room before us, I realized if I were him, I would do the same.

"Okay, Dr. Bakr. A few minutes. Nothing more."

He explained that the autopsy room's air conditioner had needed repairing since the beginning of the war and that the supply of body bags and examination gloves never got refilled. The pathologists and technicians worked in stifling and horrid conditions. Dr. Bakr introduced me to the staff. Two pathologists and six technicians stopped what they were doing and stood attentively. Two overhead fans wobbled slowly, barely moving the stale putrid air of the morgue. The technicians wore black butyl rubber gloves, the kind you might see in a factory where workers handled chemicals. A few of them worked barehanded. They all wore gray butcher's aprons stained with body fluids and traces of blood. Sweat rolled down their foreheads and necks. I asked one of the pathologists how many autopsies they typically performed in a day. He told me four or six, but they could do more.

"Sir, you can bring generators and supplies?" one of them asked.

"I don't know. Maybe," I responded.

Dr. Bakr thanked me for the time I spent with the staff and concluded the autopsy tour. As we walked out, we passed a wooden table about the size of a card table. On it were two body parts, an arm with a mangled hand and a partial skull with matted hair still attached. I saw flies crawling in the hair and heard them buzzing as we walked by. I just wanted to get out of that rendition of hell with its morgue and truck and meat lockers and all their unrestrained horror.

We finished the morgue tour and walked back to his office where his staff had prepared an assortment of fresh-baked cookies, tea, coffee, and Fanta. A gesture of civility in the midst of human depravity. In the hustle to make things just right, one of the staff forgot the ice. Dr. Bakr clapped his hands twice sternly and ordered someone to get it. Outside, the sun's heat shimmered off roads and buildings. Within five minutes, a bucket of ice arrived and the staff served refreshments on large silver trays with white linen napkins neatly arranged in rows.

"Doctor, please enjoy," Dr. Bakr said to me.

I didn't know what to say. I had no mental capacity for tea and snacks. I hesitated, then thanked him without expression. Again, I felt guilty that I had talked to him so sternly in the courtyard. He was a colleague just trying to do his job and reach a practical solution to a real problem. I had disrespected his position and authority as the forensic director. But I wanted to finish my assessment and get out. I considered a polite excuse to leave, then thought it would be better to stay and let Dr. Bakr tell me about his plans.

"I'll have an orange Fanta, please, with ice," I said flatly.

As we discussed possible morgue solutions, it became apparent that the resources needed (ice, electricity, body bags, and disposable supplies) got bogged down in the supply chain or were never given the appropriate priority as a public health requirement. I started to get frustrated and angry, not at Dr. Bakr, but at my own superiors who had assigned me a task that went too far out of my area of expertise. The mission focused primarily on the mechanical aspects of disposing the dead—nothing more. As had been the case with the Hussein assignment, I wanted nothing to do with the dead. I could not help them. I could not fix the stench in the streets or the inhumanity of a meat-locker morgue. But Dr. Bakr had requested medical and forensic assistance from the U.S. Army. I represented that Army. Offering no solution or claiming no ability to help was not an option. I finally told Dr. Bakr that I would request a logistics team to transport the bodies to a temporary cemetery and that we could work together over the coming week to tag and catalogue the bodies. He mentioned the need to refurbish and resupply the institute. Yes, I would also put that need in my report.

"Thank you, my friend. Thank you. Inshallah," he said with a smile.

En route back to CJTF headquarters, my team had to stop at the perimeter checkpoint we called Assassin's Gate. A lane of four or five military vehicles waited for their security inspection. A dozen or more civilian trucks cluttered a separate lane. The soldiers working the inspection and security detail had to spend extra time searching the trucks and their Iraqi drivers. Weeks before, insurgents had attacked the checkpoint with a truck bomb and small-arms fire. I wanted to get my team cleared without delay and had some terse words with the lieutenant in command. I could tell I still carried the anger I felt at the institute.

After finally clearing the checkpoint, my driver and I took the main road back to my office. A dusty brown, two-ton truck had been following us. It was non-military with Iraqi markings. I tracked it in my rearview mirror for nearly a mile. The driver was approaching too close, too fast. His truck almost rammed my Humvee as we slowed at an intersection. I hollered at my driver to keep moving, but he misunderstood me and braked instead. The Iraqi truck skidded to a near collision. I jumped out of the Humvee, and advanced toward the driver.

It took me only seconds to run the short distance. Seconds for the driver to see me charging at him. Less than a dozen feet away, I chambered a round in my pistol and aimed my weapon at his chest. I fingered the edge of the trigger—felt the mechanical tension.

The driver was so stunned he sat in his truck like a rock—a large, hot desert rock. Over the next three to four minutes, I screamed and cursed and berated him.

"You piece of shit! Move one inch and I'll kill you! Hands above your head!"

I expected him to understand every word of my ranting, to know that he teetered on the edge of his death and that I was the soldier who could push him over. He sat in that truck, that goddamned brown Iraqi truck with its Arabic marking, arms up high and vulnerable. I saw his eyes twitch and dart. He shook and blubbered like a child confronted by an abusive father. He responded to my rants by saying "Yessir, Yessir, Yessir," to the point that it became almost comical. Some other soldiers had gathered nearby and were watching the confrontation. I could see them in my periphery and hear them laughing in the background. One of them shouted, "Get 'em, sir." I couldn't tell if they were laughing at me or the driver. I didn't laugh. Neither did the man in the truck.

The driver continued blinking and tears fell down his cheeks. I saw a tremor start in his lips and chin. Another blink followed; then there was a flurry of them, like the kind of blinking people do when fighting back a flood of emotion. To me, each blink released pieces of fear and cast them outward toward me. I had seen that fear before, seen those eyes, that blinking.

The driver made a move to salute me Iraqi-style, right hand fixed to his forehead, and in the time it took him to move his hand from the top of his head to his right eyebrow, I reacted. My fingertip felt the curve of steel, felt the trigger tension, sensed the pressure. I breathed controlled breaths. All my weapons training came to mind—the necessary speed of assault, the use of overwhelming force and violence of action, and my instructor's warning to neutralize threats quickly and completely.

A BLINK OF a human eye takes three to four tenths of a second. A soldier's reaction time to a threat should take about the same time. It's a reflex, threat memory, trigger memory. It requires no thinking, only a reaction—the pull of a trigger. A bullet fired from a stock 9mm pistol can travel ten yards in approximately seventeen to twenty thousandths of a second—about twenty times faster than a blink. The speed and mass of a weapon's projectile can produce enough ballistic energy to penetrate a target like a ten-pound sledgehammer crashing through an ornamental stained-glass window. Depending on whether that projectile is spinning on its central axis or tumbling end-over-end when it hits—whether the penetrated target is skin or bone or brain, a chest or a skull or an abdomen—the resulting injury pattern may be punctate or gaping, stellate or torn, with or without secondary cavitation or shearing effects. The shape and size of every ballistic injury is different, and it's all determined within the span of a blink.

In the heat of a life-threatening crisis, people often see their lives flash before their eyes. In the heat of that confrontation, I had flashes too, but they didn't replay the past, they played the future. One flash showed a dead Iraqi driver by the side of his truck, me standing over him, weapon in hand. In another flash I saw a truck bomber who might have hidden explosives under his seat or behind a door panel. He may have been collecting intelligence to use later for plotting an attack. Those flashes burst forth as if set off by a trigger. They appeared and disappeared, mixed in with glimpses of the driver. Details that I had not seen at first caught my attention. The driver's-side fender was missing. The truck was more greenish-brown than brown. The driver was a boy with dark curly hair and a faint mustache, a boy no older than my own sons back home in Iowa, a boy who looked just like my youngest son. Both of them had those youthful troublemaker eyes—eyes that dared me or defied me. Rambunctious eyes. I locked on the driver's eyes. A memory of my son flashed on the scene like a double exposure in a black-and-white photograph.

I remembered my son with his troublemaker's eyes as he sat in our kitchen in Iowa while I berated him for being off target in his high school grades. I screamed relentlessly to make a point. The point being how to survive in a world so demanding. He trembled and broke at my bellowed threats, and as he did, I suddenly heard my own terrible and unrestrained voice, as if it were a shockwave from a bomb. My son blinked back tears, but then they fell. At first just a few, and then a flow, then a whole quivering face full of them—and his voice broke like glass hitting cement. I could see his fear and pain as it fractured his silence, maybe even his spirit. Then a distance welled up between us and I walked away, sad and powerless.

THAT MEMORY OF my son contained its own kind of non-ballistic force, perhaps reason or love or civility. Whatever it was, however it worked, it made me hesitate just long enough to break my attention and halt a reaction. And in that moment of hesitation, I recalled how the confrontation with my son resolved to no good end and how it left me full of regret. I started to think about the impact of pulling a trigger. What good end would it serve? Did the driver, the boy, even understand that he was a threat? As I reasoned with myself, I felt more like a father and less like a soldier. I felt suspended above the war as if looking down at myself and the Iraqi boy and my son. I saw their blinking eyes, their tears, and their shaking. The tremors of one became the tremors of the other. And then I saw it with clarity; both boys were wild, unthinking teenagers who didn't know shit about fighting a war or give a crap about encountering a soldier lost in anger over a snafued mission and a hundred dead Iraqis rotting in a truck far across the city of Baghdad. They weren't the threat; *I* was the threat.

I moved my pistol ever so slightly off target. I relaxed my finger, released the tension. I looked at the boy. I thought of my son. I then understood that the driver and his truck had already gone through security screening at the gate, that soldiers had vetted him and looked through his truck and under his truck, that dogs had sniffed for bombs and found nothing. Most of all, I understood that the Iraqi driver was just like my son at home, careless about his driving and much too young to die. I moved my finger from the trigger, held it on the side of the pistol, breathed deeply, and lowered my voice. I holstered my weapon and hollered at the boy one more time.

"You ever do that again and I'll hunt you down and kick your ass. Now get the hell out of here." I motioned with my hands to make him back his truck up.

"Yessir, Yessir, he said. "U.S. Army good," he added as he grinned slightly and backed his truck up a few yards. He saluted me once more and I shook my head in relief. As I walked back to my vehicle, I realized how the memory of my son had turned reaction to reason and how imperceptibly close I had come to pulling a trigger—how imperceptibly close a boy had come to dying by the hand of a doctor.

The Crossing

I TOOK MENTAL NOTES whenever I crossed perimeters and check-points in Baghdad. It amazed me how moving beyond physical barriers made me feel vulnerable, yet at the same time powerful. I noted a definite sphincter tightening when moving from the known qualities of a forward operating base to all the unknown possibilities beyond the wire, to the prospect of making enemy contact. There was something provocative and empowering about a chance encounter with an enemy sniper or a roadside bomb. It wasn't necessarily that the contact provided the means to confront the real and tangible fear of death; it was more that it might provide external proof that I possessed all the toughness and skill that war demanded—psychological, physi-cal, and mental. Two of my medical colleagues had been shot in the first three months of our work in Baghdad. One of the docs returned fire and killed the enemy shooter. After his hospitalization, he told me the story of his encounter and I realized how much I wanted that kind of contact—not the part about getting shot, but the part about actively engaging the enemy.

Whenever I crossed physical barriers, it evoked a combat mind-set that defined not only my duties as a soldier and a doctor but also my emotional and psychological state, in essence, a sort of chest-pounding bravado anchored by the need to display a tough soldier prowess. That emotional morphing pushed me from a frame of mind of being at war to a deeper understanding of being in war, of being psychologically and soulfully involved. The distinction felt real, as if in one case I participated in war from the sidelines and in another case I partici-pated from the epicenter, shouldering all the substantial weight and complexity of having to perform the duties of both soldier and doctor concurrently. The hard truth of combat medicine was that not all limbs could be salvaged, not all lives saved. Soldiers knew it. Doctors knew it. They spoke little of it, except to say that everybody did the best they could and everything they could. In the aftermath, my fellow medical officers and I had little time for grief or sorrow. We coped as quickly as we could, then we went on to the next case or the next mission, usually stuffing our grief or anger into whatever hiding place we could find. Part of being in war meant owning the combat doctor role without showing weakness or letting grief overwhelm you.

Iraq had no shortage of barriers and lines to cross. The simplest were lines on maps that separated geography and combat responsibilities among divisions, battalions, and platoons. Each sector was marked as an area of responsibility for some officer's command—from lieutenant to general. If you crossed into the wrong sector or into somebody else's area of authority, a new kind of battle often broke out. One of my responsibilities at CJTF involved helping to arrange treatment for Iraqi children with combat-related injuries or untreated childhood illnesses. That created a conflict with commanders of the military hospitals whose missions necessarily focused on the treatment of casualties from U.S. and Coalition forces. Adding Iraqi patients to their patient load stressed the limits of the medical resources. Commanders argued that Iraqis had their own hospitals and needed to seek treatment at those facilities. True, Iraqis had their own hospitals. But also true was the fact that those hospitals often lacked adequate medical supplies. Many of the local hospitals needed massive infusions of doctors and nurses and equipment. A mandate from the Army brass directed that medical units provide appropriate medical care for civilian cases as a way forward in winning Iraqi hearts and minds. Limited medical resources called for reasoned priorities and a strategy for integrating collateral damage and humanitarian care into the military medical infrastructure. Consequently, medical leadership fought a war within a war, doctors fighting doctors, administrators fighting doctors.

Beyond the realm of psychological and administrative boundaries, there were plenty of physical lines to cross, barricades and cordons, checkpoints and security zones. U.S. and coalition forces constructed those lines with concrete Jersey barriers, Hesco barriers, and razor wire. The lines defined occupied zones around operating bases, supply routes, key buildings, and hospitals. They signaled off-limit warnings: STOP—DO NOT ENTER—DO NOT CROSS. At the Assassin's Gate entrance to the green zone in Baghdad, three zones of escalated firepower marked with white chevrons painted across the road formed barriers to protect soldiers from enemy intrusions. When insurgents tried to run those barriers with vehicle or human bombs, soldiers guarding the lines would aim and fire and kill. I was near the perimeter gate one day when a carload of Iraqis neglected the large, red-lettered signs written in Arabic: DO NOT ENTER WITHOUT MILITARY ESCORT. LETHAL FORCE AUTHORIZED. Maybe the driver got confused about which painted road lines not to cross. Perhaps the soldiers at the barriers distracted him with their yelling and screaming. The car might have carried insurgents transporting bombs. The possible scenarios didn't matter; crossing the lines mattered. Less than ten feet past the outer DO NOT CROSS line, soldiers fired on the car, killing the driver and front-seat passenger. The dead were brothers, mid-forties, family men, father and uncle to the child in the backseat. The child's mother, injured in the confrontation, covered her surviving five-year-old daughter with her own body. After the fact, soldiers and interpreters questioned the mother. They discovered she wanted to take her sick child to the Army hospital. She had heard there was a pediatrician there who could treat Iraqi children.

In 1989, Saddam drew lines of speed bumps in the concrete road under the Swords of Qadisiyah in Baghdad. He had the "triumphal arch" built to celebrate his self-proclaimed victory in the Iran-Iraq War. The helmets reportedly came from the heads of executed Iranian soldiers. Saddam ordered the headless helmets filled with cement and embedded in the road. Thousands of additional helmets lay in cargo nets attached to the bases of two 140-foot metal swords grasped by the forged-metal likenesses of Saddam's clenched fists. I drove over the speed bump helmets once in a Humvee—like driving over small boulders. I stopped the vehicle to see if they were real. I got down on my knees. Each helmet contained a bullet hole. I touched the edges; some were smooth, others jagged. A few of the holes had stellate edges that showed a tinge of rust. Several helmets contained two holes, entry and exit. Most holes were about the size of a fingertip. One was the size of my hand. As I ran my fingers over the holes, I imagined that the soldiers who once wore those helmets were not that much different from U.S. soldiers. They would have had families at home, perhaps wives and children, maybe even a dog or a garden. Their families and friends would have wanted them to lie in peace. Instead, their deaths were on permanent display as reminders of inhumanity. I was sorry that I had run over the helmets. I wanted to reverse my tracks, remove the dirt my tires had shed. It felt as if driving over the helmets represented a kind of insult to the lives of those soldiers, who, for the sheer barbarity of displaying war trophies, had been executed by Saddam Hussein.

BARRIERS IN THE sand and clear lines of authority gave soldiers a sense of control over their sectors of combat. But they quickly learned that mere lines did not allow them to control much of anything, not the geography of combat sectors, not the duration of firefights or the tempo of war—and certainly not the random line between those who survived and those who died. Ethical lines governing the rules of engagement sometimes failed to keep soldiers from moving toward unconscionable and unjustified war behavior. And when soldiers crossed those lines, they did so without much regard to the harshness and cruelty that lay on the other side. They crossed, enemy and Coalition alike, as if driving over whitewashed lines where one side contained a perfectly acceptable kind of war and the other side contained a war that pressed against the ribs of the world and made nations hate and wail and gnash their teeth against reason and civility.

Those moral crossings reduced war to an instrument of the unforgivable. One side crossed into Abu Ghraib. The other side crossed into the Canal Hotel bombing. One side—the torture of Iraqi citizens; the other side—the dragging of burned and mutilated American bodies through the streets of Fallujah. The crossing dragged minds and morals into the darkness of humanity where frayed and savage logic permitted beheading and torture and indiscriminate targeting. At the core of it, the crossing taught us how to hate with a deep, visceral, and unrelenting kind of hate, the kind that thrived on the hard and jolting edge of war, like the hard and jolting edges of the holes in the helmets under the Swords of Qadisiyah.

IDENTIFYING THE FINITE moment of that crossing was elusive, if it was in fact a singular moment. It wasn't something that played out like a superhero transformation where in one moment you were a mild-mannered kind of person, and in the next you were totally and radically changed. The crossing took hold on soldiers in different ways and different degrees. One soldier I knew wanted to make sure he killed an insurgent before his tour was over. The chance to kill became his main deployment objective. Several doctors pulled high-risk force protection duties as a way of increasing their probability of enemy contact. I was one of them. A few docs channeled their rage against God or faith or politics. In all of the crossings, whether doctors or infantry, armor or aviation, enlisted or officers, one thing embedded itself in the minds and spirits of the soldiers—hate. It was visible and hard. Some learned it gradually, insidiously, after the accumulation of too many battles or too many patients. Some learned it rather suddenly, often at the death of a fellow soldier and friend. The crossing changed them. It made them hate, even if they weren't hateful people by nature.

A large part of my own crossing occurred during the Canal Hotel bombing. The Canal Hotel housed the headquarters of the United Nations Special Commission under the leadership of Sergio Vieira de Mello, UN High Commissioner for Human Rights. On Tuesday, August 19, 2003, an Iraqi insurgent drove into the alley next to the hotel and detonated a truck bomb. The blast was heard across Baghdad. At the time, I was getting ready for a battle update briefing. Before entering CJTF headquarters, I paused near the steps to chat with one of the ops officers, just casual stuff about the August heat and the weather back home and a bit about our families. It was just before 1700 hours. We took casual puffs on our cigars as we talked. We both looked out at the parking lot watching soldiers come and go. I had just mentioned how quiet the day had been when we both heard the thunderous explosion across the Tigris River.

"Time to go to work," I said.

We turned and headed into the ops center. Within the next minutes and hours, details of the attack flooded in. A quick-response force was dispatched to the bombsite, where soldiers performed an initial assessment, then sent updates and requests to the officers in the operations center. Thirty minutes into the response, Colonel Gagliano came to my desk and asked me for an update. The only information I had at that early point was that the Canal Hotel had been bombed and the total numbers of injured and killed were unknown but certainly enough to initiate a hospital disaster response. In the final count, more than one hundred people were injured and twenty-two killed, including the high commissioner. A U.S. forensic team was flown to Iraq and assembled to identify the remains.

The bombing occurred on a Tuesday. During the initial crisis response, a tent near the mortuary affairs unit at the Baghdad International Airport was designated as a temporary morgue. On Wednesday, I accompanied Colonel Gagliano and Ambassador Kennedy to the morgue to help with identifications. The ambassador was interested in speeding up the process in response to Iraqi requests. The morgue was a large tent and had been equipped with three stainless steel worktables and boxes of exam gloves and supplies of body bags. Outside the tent were rows of aluminum transfer cases used to transport the bodies of war casualties back home. I counted at least fifty cases. Inside the morgue tent were two folding chairs for anybody who wanted to or had to sit down; otherwise, the only other items present were some large wooden tables on which incoming body bags were laid.

Human remains from the bombsite were brought to the morgue where soldiers offloaded them onto the wooden tables. When I walked into the morgue tent, I was almost overwhelmed by the sight of body bags and the iron smell of blood. If it had not been for the presence of Colonel Gagliano and Ambassador Kennedy, I think I would have left. I worked with the forensic team to sort body parts into different piles based on their likelihood of belonging to a single person. I would unzip a body bag, reach in with my gloved hands, and lift those pieces out. Some of the recovered pieces were as small as a pack of cigarettes, some as large as a whole leg or half a torso. We analyzed them by matching their edge fit and anatomy and moving the pieces around as if we were working a jigsaw puzzle. As I slid the remains across the stainless steel stable, the sharp edges of bones and the tiny rocks embedded in the tissues made a scratchy, metallic sound. I felt the sound in my teeth. I could smell the smoky residual of charred flesh. When I zipped a body bag closed, I felt the vibration of its zipper, and that was the last thing I felt or heard with each set of remains.

The whole task of fitting parts together for identification made me feel distant and inhuman, as if overtaken by a certain dread and hopelessness that all of human life was reduced to the emptiness of gritty sounds and the mechanical vibrations of a body bag zipper. I think those sounds and sensations were what got to me. Anger and hatred welled up in me in a way that I had never felt before—hard-edged, biting—and I directed it toward the truck bomber and a universal Iraqi enemy and at the horrific and tragic ways that people died in war.

As the team made identifications, most of the dead turned out to be Iraqi civilians who worked on reconstruction projects managed by the United Nations. They hadn't signed up for war. I had. Other soldiers had. Soldiers expected to become targets; it was the core principle of war. But targeting civilians violated that principle, wasted lives, and wrought suffering on those who could not fight back. I hated that insurgents and truck bombers could strap on a bomb or drive a vehicle loaded with explosives and detonate themselves without regard to who they killed. I also hated that war created collateral damage. Some of those explosions killed and maimed children and old people. I saw those cases even before the Canal Hotel bombing: a child with her face blown off, a ten-year-old with burns so severe that I viewed her death as merciful, an old man with one arm torn off at the elbow and shrapnel embedded in his eyes. Did those innocents ask for war? Did they pose a threat?

After two days of working in that temporary morgue, I developed a judgmental attitude that seemed to find reasons to hate Iraq and hate my enemy. Bleeding became more than a clinical status; it meant that Iraqi insurgents destroyed lives without regard for the ethics of war. The char of flesh represented not just a burn but evil that occupied every thought and action of the enemy. Even the way I spat took on a defiant and aggressive demeanor. I had a more vivid sense of mortality and a clearer sense of my personal vulnerability and my absolute need to fight. I was crossing. I could feel the tension, one side pulling against the other, an internal battle with its own unstoppable momentum, humanity versus inhumanity, healing versus killing, doctor versus soldier.

During that internal battle, a strange thing happened. Aside from my secret desire to run from the repulsiveness of piecing human bodies back together, I wanted to get as far away from Iraq as I could. I wanted to be near my children. I needed their presence to sustain me. I needed to touch their skin and see that they were safe. I thought of my kids so often during the Canal Hotel experience. They would just pop into my consciousness. While I was working on a body part, trying to make it fit together, Justin or Darren, Katelyn and Jordan, would just appear in my thoughts, sitting at the dinner table or going off to school, laughing at something I said. I wanted them to leave me alone, because it felt like they were watching too closely. I wanted to shield them from the things I saw, but they kept interrupting me, as if pulling me back from the inhumanity of the bombing. They were like a counterbalance to the emotional maelstrom of the work I was doing. While the Canal Hotel bombing pulled me closer to the horrible aspects of war, my children pulled me back toward the beauty and meaningfulness of fatherhood. Even in the midst of the hellishness of war, I could see, and perhaps escape back to, the love that grounded me as a person. I needed my family; they needed me. And that was sustaining and simple and uncompromising. It reminded me that I was their dad and I needed to go home.

— — —

THE CROSSING DEFINED a new way of reasoning, one that stood upon a kind of super-rational logic that allowed me and other soldiers to view our enemy as rabid animals, incapable of human emotion or decency, incapable of feeling loss or tragedy or the need to act within the parameters of the military profession. Embedded in that crossing was a mirror that reflected back all the inhumanity of war, and at times, if you dared linger in that reflection, you could see yourself rendered savage.

When I consider my own crossing, I can see now that it had less to do with the hardening of my combat skills and more to do with hardening of my soul. Before the crossing, I saw the enemy simply as soldiers in different uniforms, duty-bound to wage war, just as I was. After the crossing, I recast them as the contagion of evil and I grabbed onto hate like an extra weapon, a weapon with no end to its destructive power. When I was honest with myself, I had to admit that on several occasions hate drove me and I became the kind of person I never wanted to become. And in that unholy crossing, it was as if I was no longer a doctor and war became the larger part of my life.

Second Tour

ROM THE CANAL HOTEL bombing to mid-December, I worked more atypical missions. None were as unusual as the forensic work I did during the Hussein case. I did some work on a mass graves project in conjunction with a team of forensic anthropologists. Our goal was to preserve forensic evidence for potential war crimes tribunals against Saddam Hussein. I worked more clinical cases in a medical aid station I set up in CJTF headquarters. I treated a few heart attacks and arranged for the treatment of many Iraqi citizens harmed by combat. At Abu Ghraib, I did a clinical assessment and recommended the establishment of a field hospital there to accommodate the many detainees.

My tour was coming to an end in December, and Colonel Gagliano asked me if I would consider extending my tour. I said I would if he absolutely needed me for the mission, but he could see that I was tiring and he decided to let me redeploy home with Major Gibbons. The week before I left, General Gallinetti called me into his office.

"Doc, you've done a great job. You should consider a transfer to the Regular Army."

"Yes, sir. I am considering it. I love my work here. It's been an honor."

With that, we traded salutes and I left his office. I wanted to stay, but I needed to go.

Following days of paperwork for release from the theater, Gibbons and I made our way to Baghdad International Airport and scheduled a flight back home. The route back to the States took us from Baghdad to Fort Bliss, Texas, via Landstuhl, Germany. We flew in an Air Force

C-17 Globemaster with about a hundred other soldiers who were all trying to get home for Christmas. If flapping our arms would have helped our aircraft go faster, we would have done it.

The reverse SRP, equipment turn-in, and medical screenings at Fort Bliss took just a few days. In the medical section, mental health techs gave us a questionnaire with the obvious intent of screening for post-traumatic stress and psychological injuries. Answering the questions in the affirmative meant staying on at Fort Bliss for further psychological evaluation. One of the questions asked about witnessing combat injuries or death. Another asked about exposure to firefights and imminent danger. Did you handle human remains? Did you discharge your weapon? There were the mandatory questions about feelings of self-harm and suicide. Most soldiers operated by an unspoken rule that encouraged them to minimize their responses or outright lie when answering questions related to matters of PTSD. Doing otherwise risked being labeled weak or a nut job incapable of dealing with the normal stressors of combat. Many soldiers thought that label could end a military career. Like many other soldiers, I fudged my answers.

One of the briefings included guidance about the transition back to civilian life. An Army psychologist delivered a short lecture about how returning soldiers might react to situations at home. We would drive too fast, continue our vigilance for car bombers or snipers, let our suspicions about perceived threats run unchecked, and speak to our family using demands and military jargon. We might jump at sounds that we thought strange or too loud; some would even duck for cover or hit the dirt. For those with highly technical careers like medicine or engineering or aviation, we might find our civilian careers less engaging, even boring, when compared to our typical tasks of deployment.

When we finished with our reverse SRP, Gibbons and I flew to Fort McCoy, Wisconsin, where we stayed two days while the staff there arranged transportation back to our hometowns. We had come full circle, from training site to demobilization site. We had made the transition from National Guard doctors to active-duty combat physicians and back, and it felt to me like we had done something of great significance, yet it seemed that we had done something so temporary and perhaps even insignificant when viewed in the larger context of our medical profession. That mind-bending kind of reflection floated in and out of a greater awareness that we were home and had survived. And arriving back at Fort McCoy in winter also reminded us of how good it felt to feel the chill of Midwestern weather and, within a matter of hours, to feel the warmth of our homes.

I WENT BACK to work in the emergency room at the Des Moines VA hospital. It had not changed. The staff worked at a pace that I wanted to crank up ten notches. They were professional and kindhearted and they were happy to have me back, but they were not in combat mode, as I still was. The typical patients demanded little of my skills. Gone was the intensity of combat and the wide range of trauma cases and tough decisions. It felt like the challenge of emergency medicine had evaporated. If a case didn't involve trauma or bleeding, I didn't consider it a real emergency. I still responded to cardiac emergencies with speed and professional acumen, but even those cases became less challenging than they had been before I deployed. At the end of a typical ER shift, I felt like the whole experience of practicing medicine lacked importance and vitality. I missed the military camaraderie and the invigorating combat tempo that percolated through everything I had done in Iraq, whether clinical or nonclinical. My work became bland and I slid into someone distant and useless as a civilian doctor.

After three months of trying to cope with the drudgery of the emergency room and the VA hospital, I phoned the medical corps assignments branch at the National Guard Bureau in Washington, D.C. An assignments officer told me about immediate needs for ER docs and flight surgeons for missions in Iraq and Afghanistan. Without hesitation, I volunteered for a second tour to Iraq. The assignment was emergency medicine. Within a week I received orders to report back to Fort Bliss for my second deployment SRP. I told my wife and children that the Army needed me in Iraq because of a doctor shortage. The truth was I needed the Army with all its attendant medical complexity and the stimulation of combat.

Out of twelve doctors going through SRP at Fort Bliss, I was one of two who had deployed previously. The entire group were reservists or National Guard physicians assigned as replacements for doctors already deployed in theater. Most of them didn't even know to which unit they would be assigned. I knew I was going back to Iraq as an ER doctor, but nothing more. And not knowing my specific assignment left me with the same gut-churning uncertainty I had felt during my first tour when our battalion arrived at Camp Wolverine and Camp New York.

The Fort Bliss SRP continued for three weeks before the assignments branch gave our specific deployment orders. I would join a medical group supporting the 30th Heavy Brigade Combat Team at the forward operating base known as FOB Caldwell, named after Army Specialist Nathaniel A. Caldwell from Omaha, Nebraska, who was killed in action in May 2003. FOB Caldwell was also the site of the Kirkush Military Training Base, which trained the new Iraqi Army. The base was located just twenty clicks (about twelve miles) from the Iran-Iraq border. Prior to its occupation by the U.S. Army, the camp had been an abandoned Iraqi military facility that served as an outpost against Iranian incursions into Iraq.

If cities and bases in Iraq had opposites, Kirkush was the opposite of the geography and missions I had experienced in Baghdad during my first tour. Kirkush and FOB Caldwell had two things: sand and heat. Heat was not unique to Iraq, but the heat at Kirkush felt like it stuck in your lungs when you breathed and boiled your red blood cells. It was so remote from the mainstream Iraqi cities that it was not even connected to the national electrical grid, nor did it have a reliable water supply.

When I arrived at Caldwell in June 2004, it gave me a different perspective of physicians at war. I had expected nearly the same experience as I had had during my first tour, but my experience there was quite different. I spent most of my days treating common soldier injuries and illnesses, generally the kind of medical care that I didn't like because I felt it didn't challenge me enough. Sunburn and heat illness and even heatstroke predominated. There were too many staff physicians assigned to the camp and too little coordination to use their skills elsewhere. It seemed that we did as much review and training as seeing patients.

The bright spot at Caldwell was meeting Major Joe Morris, physician assistant and former Marine. We hit it off right away, having a sense of humor and professional demeanor, mid-career aspirations, and a prior deployment in common.

Joe mocked the Army slogan "An Army of One" relentlessly. As a former Marine, he found it comical. "I'm an army of one," he would quip. "I have one sock, one shoe that fits, and I can only see one patient a day. Takes more than one to fight a war. Even a hillbilly like me gets that."

"I'm putting you in for a transfer to the recruiting command," I responded.

"Join now. Get a free desert villa and a combat bonus," he blurted in his Kentucky accent through his toothy grin.

Joe and I were older than most of the other medical staff and I was the new "old man" in the unit. Joe had deployed in the months prior to my arrival and had formed a Hillbilly bluegrass band complete with a washtub bass player, a fiddler, and a percussionist who played a comb and spoons. He played the banjo and could talk with a country twang that made soldiers forget they were at war in the deserts of Iraq instead of back home training in the deserts of Texas.

When Joe and I pulled a shift together, we split our time between clinical cases and training medics. On two occasions while I was at Caldwell, we activated a trauma alert when medics brought a dozen injured soldiers to the hospital after a firefight. Joe and I dug shrapnel out of wounds and stitched lacerations on patients. A surgeon operated on one soldier with an abdominal wound. The other docs treated superficial wounds and fractures.

The medical commander had assigned Joe the additional duty of monitoring sewage disposal. His job was to keep it safe and in line with regulations. He was the mayor of the shithole, literally.

"Got some land for sale," he'd say. "Beachfront property. A developer's dream."

"You're a natural at managing shit," I would reply.

We would laugh and carry on about how this was his real mission in life. During a lull in our hospital shift one day, we came up with a harebrained idea for a scientific paper on the theory of how fecal bulk in large populations determined the movements of primitive societies and even armies. Some of the ideas we got from a spoof academic article, "The Origin of Feces," in the *Journal of Irreproducible Results*. We proposed that large populations produce enormous mountains of crap and that, once produced, the fecal mountains forced migrations and wars in a survival effort to find uncontaminated land. It was a nutty way of coping with a bizarre and yet essential assignment; fecal contamination of the water or food supply could decimate an entire battalion.

DURING THE STRETCH of three months from July through September 2004, the combat action in our sector in and around Kirkush, though slow and steady, never rose to the same fevered pitch as I had previously experienced in Baghdad. When the pace was slow and the days dragged, I, like other docs, wrestled with boredom and guarded against a critical attitude. Many days I wondered if my assignments were useful and if they counted for anything that helped the cause of wounded soldiers.

I finished my three-month assignment at Camp Caldwell near the end of September. A few days before I left, Joe and his hillbilly band performed a one-hour show for the entire camp. The show rivaled any show you might see in Nashville. Joe had everybody, including the brigadier general of the brigade, laughing and forgetting that we were at war. I never heard so much hootin' over country and bluegrass music. The general even gave the band a standing ovation. The next day the USO entertained the camp with a salsa band from Los Angeles and a group of NFL cheerleaders. Joe and I sat in the front row near the makeshift stage in the area behind the hospital, generally acting like crazy college kids shouting and cheering at a homecoming game. He dared me to dance with a cheerleader, so, as the next song began, I got up and started to dance. I held out my hands toward one of the cheerleaders and she hopped down on the plywood dance floor. Soldiers hooted and hollered as we spun and dipped and swayed to the Latin rhythm, she in her cheerleader uniform and me in my Army uniform. At the end of the song, we took a bow and she hugged me. All the soldiers stood and cheered, and it felt like I had danced on behalf of the entire hospital staff, because in a way I had. Every soldier wanted that dance, that single wild dance that made us feel alive and wrapped us in a rhythm having nothing to do with war, yet everything to do with war. When I sat down, Joe slapped me a high-five and laughed. "I knew you'd do it." He said it was great. It *was* great.

I LEFT CAMP Caldwell the next day in the early afternoon. I said my final goodbyes to the docs and medics. Joe gave me a small brown rock that he said was a petrified turd he had gathered from the sewage field. I promised to cherish it. He drove me to the Caldwell airfield, where I loaded my duffel bags into a Black Hawk helicopter and flew to LSA (Logistics Support Activity) Anaconda, also known as Balad Air Base, north of Baghdad. From there I caught a later flight on a C-130 to Camp Doha in northern Kuwait. Doha served as the Army's hub for soldiers deploying and redeploying to and from Iraq. Upon my arrival, I checked in at the demobilization office, where a personnel sergeant assigned me to a waitlist. It would be seven to ten days before I could leave.

I spent my downtime making calls home and writing letters to my kids. I worked out in the gym two hours each day and followed that by a fifteen-minute soaking in the shower. I would take a loofah brush and scrub my entire body several times as I watched the soapy water swirl into the drain. I imagined my skin sloughing cells saturated with dust and oil and the scent of combat that had accumulated over my time in Iraq. In the dressing room, I noticed the absence of the locker room hoopla and the snapping of towels often displayed by soldiers.

Instead, the mood was subdued, not necessarily down or depressed, but unrushed and tranquil, a mood I experienced myself and felt represented a mixture of wisdom and gratitude and luck at having survived a tour of duty when others had not. I recognized the same mood in the soldier who came to the gym the same time as I did every day. He was a senior NCO in an infantry unit stationed about twenty miles from Camp Caldwell and had been in Iraq for nearly a year. He was tall, black, and muscled, with over fifteen years in the Army Reserve. He spoke in a cadence that was not hurried or abrupt, and he moved in the same deliberate, unrushed manner. He told me that during his deployment, he'd seen several of his soldiers injured and one killed in a firefight. He always sat on a locker room bench after his shower and quietly sang a hymn as he dressed, "The Old Rugged Cross" or "Amazing Grace." Nobody interrupted him. Soldiers came and went. They were quiet and respectful, as if attending some kind of chapel service. As I listened to him, I focused on the words of the second stanza:

> *Through many dangers, toils, and snares*
> *I have already come.*
> *'Tis grace that brought me safe thus far*
> *And grace will lead me home.*

Hearing the words took me back to the toils of my first tour. The singing didn't pull me down, but instead was uplifting and affirming. It made me thankful that I was safe and on the way home.

The seventh day at Doha I received an e-mail from a captain at the medical assignments desk at the National Guard Bureau. He wanted to arrange a conference call to discuss my demobilization. That was a bit unusual, since his responsibilities didn't focus on getting doctors home but rather on getting them to the theater. When I called at the arranged time, the colonel in charge of assignments thanked me for my last tour and then told me I was needed for an additional mission as a flight surgeon in a helicopter attack unit. I asked when the tour would begin. The colonel hesitated. "Well, that's the thing, Doc, it's an immediate need. You have to turn around from Doha and go back to Iraq. The aviation unit is en route."

I paused long enough to make the silence uncomfortable. There was a combat superstition that said you didn't volunteer for missions when close to going home because it would likely be the mission that sent you back in a box. You were supposed to keep your head down and become invisible. I knew superstitions were just that, but I also knew of cases where they came true. I had already told my wife and kids I would be home in a week. What would I tell them about an extended deployment?

"So, are you asking me if I want to volunteer for the mission?" I asked.

Then there was a pause on his end. "Well . . . we don't have any other options here," the colonel said. "We've run out of time, Doc. There are literally no other flight surgeons available now. We have to assign the mission to you. You're in place and you have the experience. The orders were cut this morning."

I chuckled a bit at that. "So you basically called to give me the good news."

"Basically," said the colonel, returning the chuckle.

"Okay. Just send the orders and contact information, and give me a few days to talk to my family. I think you owe my wife a letter or a card."

I sat for about an hour, thinking about what it meant to return to Iraq, wondering how my wife and kids would react. Mentally and physically, I had been winding down and had set my expectations for a transition home. I was tired and excited to go home, but I had trained for a mission like this and felt a burst of pride at being assigned to do it. While at Caldwell, I felt I hadn't contributed much in terms of medical leadership. Colonel Gagliano and General Gallinetti had challenged me during my first tour to seek more opportunities for command and staff leadership. Most of the missions they had assigned me stretched my skills in nonclinical and leadership directions. In the week before leaving Caldwell, I had promised myself to be more available for complex missions and leadership positions and to enroll in the command and general staff course for mid-career officers. I just didn't think the promise would come into play so quickly.

The next day, Saturday, I phoned Collin and told her about my new orders. I started the conversation by saying how much I loved her and appreciated her, then dropped the bomb about my extended tour.

"I know you don't want to hear this, but my tour has been extended. I'm going to be here another six months or more." There was no good way of saying it, so I just tried to get it across without much emotion. Collin was silent when I finished. I wondered if the line disconnected. When she responded, her disappointment was evident.

"We had all counted on you to be home for Thanksgiving and Christmas. Doesn't the Army have other doctors?"

"I'm sorry," I said. "There's a shortage of flight surgeons."

She replied in a dry, unemotional voice that matched my own. "What do you want me to tell the kids?"

"I will call them and talk to them," I responded.

We talked about the details of the extension, as many as I could give her, and she told me she would change her plans for the holidays. She didn't cry, but I could tell her chin was quivering. Her conversation, or at least her words, didn't leave the impression that she was angry or hurt, but I supposed she was at least a bit of both.

"Please be careful," she said, emphasizing each word.

"I promise I will. You going to be okay?" When I said it, I knew it was a stupid question. Extended tours were never okay, not for soldiers or their families.

"I'll be fine," she answered. "It's just a little tougher than I expected." I could hear her quiet sniffles through her words.

"I know, honey. I appreciate you. Hang in there a bit longer. I love you."

"I love you too," she said.

Her voice cracked as we said goodbye. Years later, she would tell me that particular phone call was her lowest point in all my deployments and that she felt so alone and empty, as if I had abandoned her; but she also felt obligated to be stoic and supportive, even though garnering that support meant stretching her emotions near a breaking point. From her perspective, my extended deployment was like a dark hole without a bottom and there was no way of knowing if I would ever come back and what she would do if I didn't.

I phoned my children and told them the new plans. They all voiced their disappointment and were concerned about the back-to-back tours. As in my first tour, they all promised to watch after their mom as best they could and to pray for me and the other soldiers.

Jordan was especially upset. She cried and told me she was going to call the president or whoever was in charge of the Army.

"Oh, honey," I said. "I love you so much. You can call whoever you want and I will be proud if you do, but I still have to do the mission."

"Dad, let somebody else go! I don't want you to get hurt." Her voice cracked and she spoke faster and more forcefully than she usually did.

"I know, sweetheart. I promise I'll take care of myself."

"But you've done enough," she insisted.

I didn't answer. I just listened and let her cry. She had questions about where and how long I would be gone. I didn't have the answers. I told her how proud I was of her and that I needed her love and prayers. She promised to pray for me every day and to write and encourage her mother. As we talked, she became less upset, but when we finally said goodbye, I could tell she was choking back tears. I was too. I wished I could have said "I'll be home soon," but I knew that wasn't true. I also knew I was looking forward to my mission.

Glint of Winter

As ordered, I stayed at Doha and joined an Army National Guard aviation unit headed to northern Iraq. Within a few days of their arrival, we moved from Doha to Udairi Army Airfield, at Camp Buehring in northern Kuwait, where their Apache pilots did a series of range fire exercises. The pilots and gunners were excited about the prospects of finally using their flight and combat training. I was excited too, because my new mission was exclusively in the role of a combat flight surgeon, which I had spent the larger part of my military career preparing for. During the two weeks of training and range firing at Udairi, I made myself known among the pilots and staff and worked with my medics and section sergeant to prepare for forward operations. I was the only physician and flight surgeon assigned to the battalion and felt the need to excel at my assignment. At night, I spent extra time in the gym to get myself into peak condition. When I could, I reread the flight surgeon regs as well as pertinent chapters in the NATO handbook, *Emergency War Surgery*. I rehearsed medevac procedures and aviation ops with the battalion medics. The time at Udairi infused me with the kind of excitement that I had had as a young college graduate getting my first real job. There was passion and enthusiasm, and I demanded perfection of myself and my medics.

In the first week of October 2004, days before we left for Iraq, the Udairi chaplain held a special early-morning prayer service for units crossing the berm into Iraq. He offered the service several times a month and kept a log of all the units that attended. We had talked a few times, and he told me that for a voluntary service it was the most popular one, with the exception of Christmas Eve.

The chapel was simple: one large room with a plywood floor, hundreds of folding metal chairs, and a large map on the wall with colored pushpins that marked the locations of forward operating bases in Iraq. A table with free literature about faith and hope rested slightly off balance against the back wall. Gray metal bookshelves filled with Bibles and pocket-size New Testaments stood near the entrance. A single wooden lectern with a hand-carved cross on its front stood on a slightly raised platform.

A little before dawn, the chapel began to fill. As soldiers entered, they piled their weapons and Kevlar helmets at their feet. Soldiers released their load-bearing harnesses and their personal body armor from their shoulders. The unavoidable thud on the floor and the clanging on the metal chairs signaled the start of the service. It occurred to me that enemy soldiers probably held a religious service of their own sort, at the exact same time, with their own variety of weapons thumping on their own temporary wooden floor.

After leading the congregation in singing "Amazing Grace," the chaplain delivered a short sermon about courage and trusting God for all of our needs in the coming months ahead. He read from the 27th Psalm. "The Lord is my light and my salvation; whom shall I fear?" The fumbling and stirring of the congregation ceased immediately.

The chaplain emphasized these words: "The Lord is the stronghold of my life." The stronghold, he said, was a place, both physical and spiritual, where warriors could stand and maintain their strategic advantage in battle. He also read from the 23rd Psalm, lingering on the part where God anointed David with oil, a symbol of blessing and preparedness. The oil of anointing had a special meaning for soldiers. It set soldiers apart from all other people. The sermon included a historical reference to Spartan warriors who, when preparing for war, rubbed olive oil into their skin and hair as protection against the harsh environment of war and as a symbol of their readiness for battle.

As I listened, my mind drifted to other battle sermons I had heard during my first tour. I recalled the armory prayer in Iowa City on the eve of deployment, the prayers before boarding transport aircraft, and the prayers offered in makeshift chapels in tents. Military chaplains called on God to lead us into battle and keep us safe. Soldiers said "Amen" and made the sign of the cross knowing that everything they were about to do blatantly defied any notion of holiness or safety.

When I heard a chaplain pray for blessings as we embarked for war, I always hesitated yet I always said "Amen." I had no doubt that soldiers needed the stronghold of faith and that sometimes prayer was all you had to hold yourself together, but I also knew of soldiers who prayed and were injured or killed in battle. Blessings didn't always make sense when it came to going into battle. Beyond my own weakness in faith, I figured my enemy sought the same blessings as I did and prayed for strength and courage and victory in just the same way. Did they feel the stronghold of faith and the assurance of the anointing? Did they feel blessed?

When the chaplain finished, he asked if anybody wanted to stand and pray. A skinny infantry soldier stood and asked the chaplain permission to pray. It struck me as peculiar—asking permission to pray, but the soldier was young, eighteen or nineteen and a private, the lowest ranking soldier in the Army, so he probably felt intimidated. The chaplain encouraged him. The soldier prayed: "God, my battalion is crossing the berm tomorrow morning. Can you make it so we all get home in one piece? Amen." Two short sentences, then "Amen." Then silence. Nobody else stood to pray. The chaplain closed the service by leading in the Lord's Prayer. Soldiers gathered their weapons and left the chapel.

I lingered a moment thinking about the service. The unsophisticated prayer of a private in the U.S. Army had cut directly to the heart of the issue of faith at war—control. It was central to military doctrine and command. Somebody always maintained control. No matter how small the duty or the sector of battle, some soldier always held control over a mission or a geographic slice of war. Control equated to combat victory and individual survival.

When the soldier prayed for God to control the outcome of war, I saw it as asking God to deliver the blessing of control so we could all get home in one piece, in essence, a prayer for God to stack the odds in our favor and against the favor of our enemy. The prayer stopped me cold. It made me hesitate and doubt my faith. I wanted to believe in my heart that what the soldier was asking would come true, but I harbored a sort of practical cynicism that it would not. I had seen the countless body bags of several different wars, and I knew the outcome in Iraq was not going to turn out quite the way the private was asking. When I heard the prayer, I realized the simplicity of this soldier's trust in God, and I wished I could trust so simply and powerfully. I admired the soldier. I did not think for a moment that his faith was baseless or that it rendered him weak. Rather, I feared that I had let my own faith harden, that I was no longer capable of pure faith and trust. His prayer gave me the sense that I had come to rely more on my own military instincts and medical skills rather than on the strength of prayer and the power of faith. I stood near the front lines of a battle and saw two sides, the side demanding faith and the side demanding control. I wanted both, but it was hard for me to comprehend how God allowed one soldier to die and another to live, or that some should lose limbs or eyes or sanity and some should lose nothing. Everything I knew told me that war distributed pain and death more like a game of roulette—a dealer spins the wheel and a ball falls on your number.

A SOLDIER WITH a neck injury lay in a combat hospital during my first tour in Iraq. He had manned the 50Cal on point in a convoy proceeding west, near the Baghdad zoo. As his vehicle approached an overpass, he glanced to the sides of the concrete abutments to scan for threats. He caught a glint of sunlight that spanned across the road. It reminded him of how a nylon fishing line would catch a glint of the morning sun, as it did when his father took him fishing in Minnesota.

As the Humvee approached the overpass, it became clear that the glint was a trip wire stretched across the road to trigger an IED. In an act of last-second thinking, the soldier threw himself backward on the top of the Humvee. The wire caught him at the top of his sternum. It scythed the skin from his neck, starting from his clavicles, then upward to the point of his chin. It ripped his neck open so his trachea was exposed. A ground medevac delivered him to a field hospital where surgeons stopped his bleeding and repaired his neck.

The soldier told me that his grandmother prayed for him back home in Minnesota. He said how fortunate he was to have a grandma like that, and how prayer helped him survive. I agreed with him that it was good to have a praying grandma. I added that his training and his quick reaction time also helped save his life.

I often thought about that incident whenever I went to chapel. It brought to bear the notions of fate and faith, my beliefs about control and circumstance. To me, it defined the precarious balance between the certainty and uncertainty of war. You could prepare for all the contingencies and feel like you were ready for anything, and then in a single moment, fortuitously, a wire could take your head. In the balance between faith and control, quick reactions seemed to be the key to survival—reactions in skill and reactions in faith.

A FEW DAYS after the chapel service, the battalion's pilots flew the Apaches and Black Hawks to the Qayyarah West forward operating base in northern Iraq, near Mosul. The rest of the battalion flew on two flights of C-130s.

Qayyarah Airfield was located about two hundred miles north of Baghdad and thirty-five miles south of Mosul. Soldiers called it Q-West or Key West because its real name used too much guttural throat and tongue and they couldn't say it without hacking up a small loogie. Calling it Key West also played on the absolute contradiction in meaning and geography. Key West, Iraq, had as much similarity to the city in Florida as the "Hanoi Hilton" in Vietnam had to a real hotel.

Key West's only claim to fame was its status as one of Saddam's premier Air Force bases that housed Iraq's first Soviet-made MiG fighter aircraft. In the initial wave of air attacks, American bombers reduced the base and its runways to craters and rubble. Within months of the ground assault on Iraq, Army engineers rebuilt the cratered runways so Q-West could function as a staging base for forward combat operations. It was renamed FOB Endurance, and endure was exactly what soldiers did there. Despite the endearing play on words, it ranked right up there in the top ten shitholes in Iraq. I had flown there several times during my first tour in 2003 when it was little more than a bombed-out dustbowl.

By the time I got back to Key West during my extended second tour, the base had undergone a transformation that made it functional and perhaps even modern compared to what it was in 2003. Still, measured next to my first tour experiences, FOB Endurance left me longing for the more structured chaos of Baghdad. In addition to my specific feelings about Key West, I had formed definite opinions about desert warfare in general. The midsummer desert brought its intolerable scourge of heat that could suck oxygen and sweat from your body and leave you drained of energy and focus, but the winter desert brought its own kind of suck that was equally draining. Winter nights brought cold and rain. The temperatures varied so widely from day to night that the ground cycled back and forth between freezing and thawing. Tracks left by military vehicles changed from frozen ruts into cold mud that infiltrated soldiers' boots and every piece of equipment and every hooch. In the daytime, the ruts filled with the drizzle of winter rain, forming thousands of interconnected puddles. At night the entire pockmarked surface of the ground would freeze again.

Walking or running was not easy. Soldiers fell. They broke their ankles and dropped their weapons. In a few cases a fall caused an accidental weapon discharge that injured nearby soldiers and, in one case, killed a soldier. When soldiers drove vehicles over the frozen ruts, the constant jarring could even break teeth and cause compression fractures of vertebrae.

The winter light projected a creepy gray pall over vehicles and aircraft, buildings and earth, muting whatever natural color they contained so they all appeared as dull and smoky objects. In the early morning, fog hung in the air like a limp, dirty curtain in an abandoned house. It played tricks on the eyes of aviators and flight surgeons, fooling them into seeing things that weren't really there or into missing things that were real and dangerous. Horizons dissolved in winter's haze, as did wires and obstacles. Pilots fought the weather, trying to avoid crashing—a war within a war.

Beyond the physical demands of the winter, it played havoc with time, stretching and transforming it into unwieldy blocks—four, twelve, twenty-four hours—rendering each stagnant hour cold and unbearable. And in those stifling blocks, time became as much an enemy as any Iraqi insurgent. Soldiers became bored and agitated, wanting to engage a mission when none could be engaged. They moved at the pace of sedentary breathing, working their knives and weapons over and over, rehearing their protocols and procedures. They worked their bored and weathered minds or their dreams of home and pictures of their kids and spouses.

If soldiers couldn't work their minds or dreams, they worked their authority over specific pieces of war they were assigned. They argued among each other, even among themselves, often second-guessing their own actions or the actions of other soldiers. Some aviators argued over who got priority for attack missions. I argued with a doctor in another unit over use of the medivac helicopter. He wanted it under his control. "That," I said, "is bullshit." My platoon sergeant tried to argue with me about how to prep a rescue mission. I did a field inspection of his medic bag and when I found it packed without the surgical dressings I had ordered, I threw it twenty feet through the air. The contents went flying. I opened his bottle of Tylenol and poured the pills in the dirt. "This is a goddamned war, not a Boy Scout camp," I yelled. "Pain killers don't stop bleeding. Now get your shit together or reassign yourself to the DFAC."

IF WINTER BROUGHT extra challenges or just downright grief, it also brought an extra connection to home and family. Thanksgiving and Christmas were alive with packages: two loaves of banana bread from a ninety-year old volunteer from the VA hospital in Des Moines, Iowa;

four hundred individually wrapped monster cookies from a rural church of a friend; hundreds of cards from schoolkids asking about camels or snakes or spiders. Support groups sent hundreds of DVDs, bags of jerky, and tins of flavored coffee. Magazines came in all shapes and topics: biker magazines with centerfolds of Harleys and their half-naked riders, *Motor Trend, Food &Wine*, and *Reader's Digest*. Somebody thought it was a good idea to send a copy of *Better Homes and Gardens*.

Soldiers' children sent handmade Christmas cards and letters with smiley-face stickers. The soldiers pinned them to makeshift walls or to the sides of tents, or folded them neatly and kept them in their pockets, as if the cards were rare books or holy artifacts. They were. My kids sent handwritten letters and cards that I read over and over. I touched every word and every stray mark of ink with my fingertips. I smelled the paper. Held it close to my chest. When I could, I read the letters every night. I finally had to stop because the love hurt so much and I wanted to be with my family instead of with soldiers. That feeling made for guilt and sadness and loneliness, all wrapped up tight— like a Christmas package of its own. I would eventually spend three consecutive winters in Iraq, and each one would become harder than the one before it. During each one, the letters from my kids would become harder to read. They always brought me close to the edge of too much love in the midst of too much war. I wanted to touch love and smell it, wrap my arms around it, sit in a room with my wife and sons and daughters, and say nothing at all, just watch them breathe, watch them love.

The winter desert brought many good things; packages and cards from home, phone calls to loved ones, memories and reminders of what it meant to be human. The good things were hard and soft like the winter desert. They reminded us of the hardness of war; they reminded us of the softness of love. Soldiers tried to keep them both alive—war and love. And that was harder than fighting the war itself.

The Sound of a Zipper

O CTOBER AND NOVEMBER 2004 were hard months. Insurgent attacks and IED explosions mounted in all sectors of Iraq. Combat activity in the northern sectors around Mosul and Key West demanded a significant uptick in aviation missions. U.S. infantry and aviation forces engaged Iraqi insurgents in firefights in and around Mosul. Army medical assets responded by moving field units to provide quick access to emergency care.

In early November, Operation Phantom Fury (Second Battle of Fallujah) dominated combat action in southern Iraq. Insurgents had been steadily infiltrating Fallujah, and by November their estimated strength exceeded three thousand. Coalition forces initiated the attack on Fallujah on November 7. Within a week they routed the insurgents and captured nearly three-quarters of the city. Combat support hospitals and field medical units flexed to accommodate the influx of wounded Marines and soldiers.

On November 8, the second day of the Fallujah battle, I flew with one of my medics from Key West to FOB Anaconda, north of Baghdad, to transfer a patient to the Air Force Theater Hospital there. Our chopper flew off to refuel and as we waited near the ER for its return, a Marine helicopter landed. Three Navy corpsmen and a hospital crew unloaded four wounded Marines and carried them into the emergency triage area on litters. They left a trail of blood from the landing pad to the front door of the ER. My medic stepped over the fresh blood and followed it all the way to the edge of the landing zone. He said he'd never seen blood like that before. I said I had and told him to get off the trail because he was being disrespectful. He looked at me rather puzzled but did as I said. Later I told him the blood reminded me of the "Trail of Tears" where thousands of Cherokee Indians died in a forced march under the authority of the Indian Removal Act. He didn't know anything about that bit of history. As best I could, I told him about the government's use of the military to force tribes from their land. I explained how I viewed the hospital blood trail as a soldier's Trail of Tears and how it was holy ground.

While the Battle of Fallujah occupied southern Iraq, insurgents mounted attacks in the north during the first week of November in the Battle of Mosul. Coalition forces, as well as Kurdish Peshmerga fighters, responded to the attacks and by mid-November had secured Mosul from insurgents. During one of the missions in support of the northern offensive, an Apache gunship took small-arms fire and an armor-piercing bullet hit the cockpit. The Apache cockpits had a thick high-tech plastic panel located right in front of the pilot's face. The bullet pierced more than halfway through that panel before it stopped. The mechanics dug it out and gave it to the pilot as a good-luck charm. A week later the same pilot was flying a mission near Mosul; another bullet hit his helicopter on the left side. I was at Mosul flight ops with some other battalion officers when the pilot radioed that he was hit. The copilot took control of the aircraft and landed in the center of the runway. I drove out to midfield with four other soldiers and pulled the pilot out of the aircraft. Blood covered the front of his flight suit. Some medics brought a stretcher and four of us put him on it and ran toward the hospital on the edge of the tarmac. I had broken my foot the week before, so I could hardly run with the extra load. A flight ops lieutenant helped me. In the ER, I evaluated the pilot with the other hospital physicians. An armor-piercing round had struck the helicopter, entered through his left wrist, exited, scythed the skin of his belly without causing internal injury, and then finally lodged in the opposite side of the aircraft. The mechanics dug that bullet out too, and gave it to him.

Those two months gave me the kind of engagement for which soldiers and Army doctors trained. Rigorous action. Intensity of attack. Critical decisions and procedures. It was a time when I sensed deep fulfillment as a capable soldier and doctor entrusted by command to do the kinds of tasks that few other physicians outside of the military, and even some within the military, ever experience. It was a time when I felt utterly confident and sure of myself, even to the point of thinking I could do my particular tasks better than anybody else in the whole damn Army. It wasn't a feeling of arrogance but rather self-assurance from crossing a threshold that defined combat expertise. When I graduated from medical school, I had felt that same confidence, that same bold spirit of having crossed from one side of knowledge and achievement to the other side. That kind of crossing allowed me to look back and see that I had done something important, even critical, in my life. And that mattered to me more than all the demands of the mission and the hardship of being at war.

The operational tempo of November extended into December. Whatever respite I expected after the Battles of Fallujah and Mosul came only sporadically and in small doses. Aviators flew, physicians treated wounds, artillery batteries shelled, and infantry platoons fought throughout Iraq. In the midst of all that action, Thanksgiving was celebrated at every forward operating base. "Celebrate" was a tough word to use in the context of war. It referenced all the activities of home and family and made us acutely aware of our own fragility—quite the opposite of a reason to celebrate. Regardless, soldiers were thankful to be alive and without injury.

For the most part, Thanksgiving was a remarkable day. Battles still needed fighting and patients still needed doctors, but soldiers tweaked the mission assignments to allow almost everybody to have dinner together at one of the serving times. The Army had flown in turkeys and all the trimmings, and the DFAC staff spent the larger part of two days preparing. The large center serving table even sported an ice carving and music played in the background. I ate dinner with several of the pilots and my medics. We relaxed long enough to talk about our families and how we missed them. After dinner, I threw a football on the tarmac with a lieutenant named Michaels and a couple of the medics. Michaels was loved by everybody. He constantly studied his craft and his faith and his career with an eye toward improving everything he did. He possessed the kind of zeal that was rare. Even when he talked about boot camp he made it sound so exciting that soldiers thought they should go back because they might have missed something. When I talked to him he made me conscious of my commitment to the mission. We occasionally sat next to each other at chapel services.

I spent my evening writing letters home and reading a book a friend had sent, *The Valley of Vision*, a book of Puritan prayers. As I read it, I realized the Puritans prayed for everything without ceasing. I wondered if they would have found reasons to pray if they had been deployed to Iraq. The only thing I and other soldiers did without ceasing were missions.

Thanksgiving passed. In the span of a day or two, it had taken on the aura of just another day at war—a memorable day for sure, but a day gone missing on a calendar of memorable days. On December 9, in the late afternoon, I met with the chaplain to discuss the combat stress program and a patient who was referred to him for counseling. After the meeting I sent all the medics to dinner and stayed on call in the aid station for emergencies. At 1900 hours I left the aid station and went to my quarters. I was going to rest for a while, then go to the gym, but I fell asleep on my cot.

Sometime later I heard a loud rap on the door that jarred me from a light sleep.

"Doc! Open up! There's an emergency," someone shouted. "Doc!"

"Just a minute!" I shouted back as I made my way from my cot to the door. When I opened the door I saw one of the flight ops lieutenants. His face was drawn into a serious frown, his speech on the verge of panic.

"Sir, there's been an accident. We have aircraft down. The commander needs you in the TOC immediately."

The seriousness and near panic in the lieutenant's face told me that whatever was happening was not routine.

"How many casualties?"

"We're not sure yet, sir. The commander will brief you."

I gathered my medic bag and rushed to the ops center. On the way I stopped briefly at the medics' quarters and alerted them. I wanted them to be prepared for the worst of all possible missions. "You need to prep for a disaster response and multiple casualties," I ordered the NCO in charge.

In the TOC, I learned that a Black Hawk helicopter had collided with an Apache gunship over the FARP (Forward Area Refueling Point) at the Mosul airfield. The initial details were conflicting. We didn't know if the crash resulted from a fuel explosion or enemy fire. As the commander and his staff in flight ops communicated with personnel at Mosul, it became evident that there were at least two dead, Lieutenant Michaels and Captain Finch. "These are our soldiers," the commander said to the officers gathered. "Get a response team ready for a flight to Mosul."

When I heard his words, my gut tightened. The mission now took on more emotion than a routine launch and recovery. The battalion would have to face the deaths of fellow aviators and I knew that would shake some of the soldiers. I had seen multiple casualties from my first tour, but these casualties were the first for the battalion, and it happened within just two months after arrival in theater.

It was a cold night, and a light rain made the helicopters on the flight line look darker than usual. Aircraft crew scurried about, removing wheel chocks and going through their checklists. They moved precisely and deliberately yet with a contagion of speed. The crew chiefs flashed hand signals to the pilots for the engine start sequence and the deep *whoosh* of fuel ignition resonated throughout the flight line. The raspy whine of the jet engines flooded the scene as high-velocity exhaust hit the cold air. In less than a minute, rapidly accelerating rotor blades generated the familiar *whap whap whap* of a Black Hawk helicopter. As we approached our assigned aircraft, the crew chiefs snapped a quick salute. I grabbed the handhold on the side of the aircraft, pulled myself up and through the open doors and buckled in. I plugged my headset into the intercom panel.

"COM check. Doc is up on six."

"Doc, you're loud and clear. Monitor six for updates."

My medic and I secured our medic bags to the frames of the seats. We exchanged an affirmative thumbs-up. In a matter of seconds the helicopter rose to a hover, pitched slightly nose down, then began to fly forward with increasing speed and altitude. Elapsed time for takeoff—less than sixty seconds.

From my seat next to the door, I glanced at the disappearing runway. The intercom popped with short, clipped updates and aviator code talk about the weather at Mosul and the current situation there. Forward observers reported small-arms fire in the area. Rain obscured the runway visibility. Airport security forces had secured the crash site.

As we flew toward Mosul, I lost myself in the possible scenarios at the scene. Would we take fire? Crash like the helicopters at Mosul? How many soldiers could I handle at once? What if the crew members were burned or trapped in the wreckage? Momentarily, I forgot where the hospital was located, although I had been there many times. The scenarios got me stirred up and edgy. I coached myself into focusing on the known details: two aircraft down; two, possibly more killed; several injured, all presumably at the crash site or the hospital. I told myself to calm down and read the mission as it developed. I countered my emotions and the adrenaline by consciously tightening and then relaxing my arms and legs and taking deep breaths. I visualized my heart rate slowing and my muscles on standby.

"Doc . . . Doc . . . Come up on channel one. We're ten minutes out and the commander has an update for you."

I fumbled with the channel selector and checked myself back into reality. Focus. "Ghost Rider Five Zero up on one."

"FiveZero—ZeroThree. We confirm two KIA. Nine WIA with burns. You copy, Doc?"

"FiveZero copies two KIA, nine WIA."

The next ten minutes vanished like spent rounds of ammunition. I sensed the warping of time as if the laws of physics and flight no longer applied to our mission; time jumped like a coded message frequency hopping on secure radio channels. I clipped my speech, movements, and thoughts like I always did in a crisis. I could hear the rotor blades thunder against the air and feel their vibration against my body. As I anticipated what might lie ahead, I remembered throwing a baseball with my sons and going to a soccer game with my daughters. We were laughing and the sun was warm. I could hear the slap of a catcher's mitt and see the puff of dust from its pocket. Then the memory vanished.

The pilot keyed the intercom: "Five minutes to the crash site."

I felt for my medic bag and placed my hand on my weapon just to make sure it was secure. The situation on the ground was not a firefight. If it were, an Apache gunship would have engaged and we would have diverted to land elsewhere. There would be no need to fight or shoot or kill. Our only mission was to find the wounded and the dead and secure the crash site. The tension of the mission wasn't in the threat of enemy contact but in the enormity of dealing with soldiers who had been injured and killed—soldiers whom I knew and cared for.

I loosened my seat harness, thinking it gave me an edge for moving faster. It didn't. My medic did the same. One of the soldiers across from me closed his eyes and made the sign of the cross. Silently, I prayed for strength, although I wasn't sure that's what I needed. I needed a clear head and decisive actions.

The downed aircraft came into view as we maneuvered toward the tarmac at the end of the runway near the refueling point. I could see soldiers near the crash site and they appeared to form a loose perimeter. The wreckage smoldered and fragments of airframe were heaped together and smaller pieces were scattered about. It dawned on me that my role as a flight surgeon was one of putting fragments back together.

Our Black Hawk hovered briefly over the crash before we began our landing about midfield, halfway between the wreckage and the hospital at the far end of the runway. Gusts of wind buffeted the helicopter as we finally touched down. A crew chief flung the doors open. I grabbed my gear and crouched low as I cleared the rotors and ran toward the crash with the safety officer and my medic.

The helicopter rotors whipped a light rain at hurricane speeds and the drops stung my face. In the distance, away from the airfield, I could see illumination rounds against the overcast sky. As we approached the downed aircraft, the first impressions were shocking in a way that only war can truly display. Shards of metal and high-tech carbon fiber littered the scene. Aircraft wiring dangled from the wreckage. Pieces of aircraft lay blackened; some were molten, their lingering smoke still acrid. Slicks of burned oil contaminated the ground. The rotor blades from the Apache had fractured. One detached blade of a rotor had spun through the air and embedded itself thirty yards away in the sides of a Hesco barrier filled with sand. The fuel technicians standing outside at the time of the collision had felt the wind from the rotor as it flew over their heads and hit the barrier. The heat of the burning wreckage had cooked off rounds of ammunition from the Apache, and as we assessed the site, we wondered if any rounds might still explode.

I felt stunned as I evaluated the scene, as though I had never seen the remnants of a bomb explosion or an IED or a Humvee shredded and its occupants torn or burned. I had seen all that and more, but this bit of war was personal, it involved a helicopter I had flown in, one that held the bodies of soldiers I felt responsible for because I was their flight surgeon. I had always been able to react to trauma objectively, yet when I saw the wreckage all heaped up the way it was, the Apache frame upside down, smoldering fragments scattered about, I lost any professional objectivity I had. I considered myself more as a soldier who had lost two battle companions than an Army medical officer. I knew the dead personally. One was Lieutenant Michaels, who had thrown a football with me and the medics after Thanksgiving dinner. The other pilot, Captain Finch, was an older soldier with a family. We had talked and joked about our children together. I was in awe of his career as an instructor pilot and his leadership in the battalion. Both were the kind of aviators everyone respected for their skills and faith and leadership. Even though I wasn't close friends with them, I had looked up to them and they to me, and that counted as being close in the way that soldiers become friends in war. So, instead of professional objectivity, I felt sorrow and loss, two emotions that Army doctors needed to hold at a distance, especially in the immediacy of a crisis.

The airport fire control squad had contained the fires and secured the perimeter before we arrived. In the rush to control the crash site, airport security squads had removed the bodies of the two aviators in the Apache and put them in body bags. They also transported nine injured soldiers from the Black Hawk to the Army hospital at the airfield.

I needed to get to the hospital to interview the survivors and attend to their injuries. One of the airport security officers drove me. I checked in with the hospital commander and he took us to the hospital wing holding our wounded soldiers. They had all sustained noncritical burns and cuts, and had been treated by the ER staff of the hospital. I briefly examined each one and tried to reassure them they would be fine. They all knew about the fatalities and lay in their beds in various states of shock. Most of them were in their twenties, the same age as Lieutenant Michaels. And the crash shook them mentally and physically. Several of them sat on the edges of their beds staring in disbelief. Their physical wounds were minor; their emotional wounds deep. They had been as good as dead, crashing in their helicopter, and they knew it. One of them told me he felt a thud and heard the shearing of metal; then they went down. They all thought they might get trapped and burned alive. One of the crew chiefs told me how he got hung up in his harness and couldn't escape. His struggling turned to panic. The more he fought to free himself, the more his harness snared him. He figured he was going to die in an explosion, so he finally sat back in his seat, took some deep breaths, and prayed, "God, take me home." As he relaxed his body, the harness loosened and he managed to free himself and run from the crash. Seconds after, the helicopter exploded. As he spoke to me, his hands trembled.

I asked the hospital commander about the dead and he said they were outside in the back of the hospital, waiting for mortuary affairs to pick them up. There was no temporary morgue. I found the bodies outside the back door in body bags resting on litter stands, the Dumpsters not too far away. I felt a wave of anger that the hospital staff put them there near the refuse, but I decided to choke it back because I saw how it would make things worse for our survivors and me. I needed a sense of calm, not anger.

I had learned the identities of those killed by the process of elimination and from the information on the flight plans, but I had not seen their remains. I asked the commander if I could cross-check the mission assignments and flight logs to make the identifications, then I could sign death certificates. But he wanted me to get positive identification, which could not be done by simply cross-checking the flight logs. "We need physical confirmation," he ordered.

"Yes, sir" was all I said in reply. I said it professionally, respectfully, and dutifully, but I also said it with dread.

I stalled the exam for maybe ten minutes, then finally approached the litter stands where the body bags rested. I could smell the residuals of smoke that clung to the fabric. I saw the large zippers of each bag and the way the raindrops mixed with soot and made tiny rivulets that ran down the sides of the zippers. I looked away—first at the sky, then at the nearby Dumpsters, then finally at the bags. The drizzle of rain was intermittent and cold.

I BEGAN MY exam with a full-length pull of the zippers. I pinched the large tab between my thumb and index finger, grasped it firmly, and made one long pull. That was the toughest part for me. The opening triggered a wild cascade of emotions and fear. I could feel my heart beating faster; I felt a choke in my neck. I started anticipating the broken pieces I would see. As I pulled, the zipper teeth made a metallic *voop* that changed pitch along the length of the bag. The bags opened slightly and I had to pull the edges apart to get a better view. At first, it seemed like I saw nothing—at least, nothing that actually registered. Then in the same way that the crash site had stunned me, the broken bodies stunned me. It was like a violent rupture of all that had made sense in my life. I lost all reference to everything I had mastered as a physician. I was not a physician, not even a soldier, only a man confronted with things that even God might turn from seeing. I gasped once, hesitated, then forced myself to observe each fragment. I couldn't immediately comprehend what I saw. (Even when I finished the exam and closed the zippers, I wasn't sure of what I had seen.)

I surveyed all the body parts, then returned to each part separately, then to the parts of parts. I wanted to rush the exam, but knew if I did, I would have accomplished nothing, so I slowed myself down and took small, shallow breaths. I moved my hands and fingers deliberately and cautiously. The truth was I couldn't move fast. I felt caught in one of those nightmares where something evil chases you but you can only run in slow motion. The nightmare surrounded me. There was no escape. In the identifications for the Canal Hotel bombing where the task focused more on forensics, I was able to give myself at least a modicum of escape with my clinical distance and objectivity, but in this case, that distance was lost the moment I grabbed the zipper and pulled. Knowing the dead brought me too close emotionally, and as I proceeded with the exam, their personalities began to emerge from the memories I had of them. In any other professional setting, I would have excused myself from the case. That was not an option for me. As their flight surgeon, I had carried some responsibility for keeping them alive during their tour, and now that they were dead, I carried the full responsibility for their proper identification.

I looked away several times, then refocused on the exam. I ran my fingers down the inside edges of the body bags and touched the fragments of bodies. A wet dusting of soot covered the backs of my hands. Melted body fat collected in beads and stuck to the fabric of the human remains pouch. I saw patches of skin, their edges curled like the peeled edges of paint sloughed from the walls of a burning house. There were remnants of charred muscles. Bones protruded through limbs; their shafts looked like splintered sticks of wood. The legs of one body were partially denuded. In the other body, a broken femur jabbed the sides of the bag. The burned-away leather of a boot revealed blackened nubs of toes. One foot was missing. Another one faced backward, attached to an ankle by a string of tendon. Blackened ribs outlined the thorax, which vaguely approximated the shape of a person. I couldn't immediately discern the torn stump of a neck. I carefully touched its edges: nothing came to mind. I saw no tongue—no mouth—no face.

I stopped. I sensed I had been drifting. I saw and felt nothing in particular, only the vague, amorphous shapes that lay in a bag of vinyl.

I lacked a firm sense of clinical findings. I looked away, then back at the remains inside the bags. My eyes jumped from one piece of human remains to another in no particular order—because there *was* no particular order. My hands started moving slowly in the air, retracing where they had been. I talked to myself. *Slow down. Use your training. Make your observations from what you see. You're a flight surgeon. Make yourself do this.*

I began again with my mind fixed on the protocol of a military aircraft accident investigation. When I was done, I wrote notes on a pad.

2 Dec 2004, Time 2345
POST-MORTEM EXAM.

Two human remains pouches are tagged and labeled; one set marked as A, the other as B.

Portions of limbs are missing. Traumatic disarticulation of the left arm of A. Right hand of B is missing. Left foot of B is rotated 180 degrees.

Widespread burn damage and traumatic evisceration is noted.

Head of A is unavailable for examination secondary to decapitation. Head of B demonstrates a partial decapitation. The brain is absent the skull.

Remains are unidentifiable. DNA tests required for definitive I.D.

An intact aviator watch remains in place on the left wrist of A.

Exam concluded. Nothing follows.

The words "nothing follows" got to me. I stared off into the night, into a dark fragment of time. I looked back at the remnants of bodies. The face of a watch told me a soldier's identity. I wrote two names on tags and pulled two zippers closed. I heard their nubbed, metallic, closing sounds.

— — —

A DAY LATER, when the nine injured soldiers were flown back to Key West, I interviewed them all at length and signed an aviation medical form grounding the crew from flight duties until they were well enough to fly again. They didn't like it and I didn't like it, but the regs demanded it. Within a week I could sign an up slip after an abbreviated flight physical and they would be flying again, back to a busy war. I thought about things that would follow us in the wake of that crash, in the life-defining moments of war: some soldiers would go home with ugly physical scars or deep emotional wounds, a few more might not go home at all, and most would be followed by the blessing and curse of surviving it all. As for me, I would carry the memories of a flight surgeon trying to bring healing to soldiers, whenever and wherever they needed me most.

Globemaster

ONE NIGHT THE first week of January 2006, during my third tour, I heard a warning signal from the base medical facility while walking from the library back to my quarters. It was an alert for an incoming medevac. I was alone on an open patch of dirt about a half mile from the hospital and could see the helicopter on approach to the landing pad. I thought we were receiving overflow from a nearby hospital in southern Iraq, so I ran toward the hospital. Udairi, despite all the advantages and roads of a fixed military facility, still had large areas of raw desert ground with holes and rocks and semi-buried remnants of steel rebar. Footpaths led from one major building to another, but many soldiers took direct shortcuts over the sand and dirt. When I heard the alert, I took a shortcut running without caution, reminiscent of the time I ran toward the FARP at Mosul. I could feel my boots give way just enough to throw me off. My feet and legs flexed and tightened to keep my balance. I should have used a pathway, walked instead of run, should have used practiced judgment instead of hurried judgment. But I was caught up in the moment, in the specter of a medical emergency.

I had run probably fifty yards when my right foot gave way as it hit the sand full stride. I heard a snap. I felt a lightning bolt of pain. My running momentum launched me through the air. In Army training, instructors taught me to bring my arms to my chest when falling and to roll with the impact. I had practiced falling—mastered the art of hitting the ground unscathed. None of that seemed to matter at Udairi. A single thought flashed as I flew through the air: *This is going to hurt.* I hit the ground with my arms outstretched and flailing. My left shoulder dislocated on impact and my right ankle either dislocated or broke. And there was pain, the star-seeing, breath-taking kind of pain that floods your body at the breaking of a bone or the tearing of a joint.

I lay on the ground for probably five minutes—enough time to catch my breath and wriggle to a sitting position. I cussed at myself, checked my ankle. No protruding bones. Perhaps not broken. I could not move my arm; when I wiggled my fingers and flexed my wrist, the pain in my shoulder made me nauseated. I sat in the dirt for a few minutes more, then decided not to wait for help. I grabbed my left elbow with my right hand, slowly elevated it above my head, took a deep breath, and rotated it laterally outward. Most of the severe pain stopped abruptly when the shoulder popped back into place. I wiped my brow of sweat, got to my feet, and tried to limp toward the hospital. The pain was too much. I just stood in the dirt, wanting to kick myself for being stupid and rushing out of control. The hospital had plenty of doctors and I wasn't even assigned there. I just wanted to participate in something critical, a venue where I could feel important.

I tried bearing weight on my foot and managed about ten yards in five minutes before I stopped and just said "Dammit." It occurred to me to sit down, but I thought doing so would minimize the likelihood of soldiers spotting me. So I stood and stared and waited. The stars, the night sky, the hospital and the tents off in the distance, all became surreal fixtures in a picture of waiting. I focused my attention on the pain, then shifted it to the hospital, then to the stars, and then back to my pain, all the while thinking how asinine it had been to run without caution where caution was essential.

A few soldiers and a lieutenant from flight ops finally drove near enough that I could flag them down. They got me into their vehicle and to the hospital. The docs and medics were still busy with the patients in the medevac. I didn't want to disrupt the staff, so I asked the lieutenant to help me to the bench outside the front door. My pain had softened a bit and I supposed I could have sat there for a while, but if I were offered a pain shot, I might have asked for a megadose.

"Sir, we should probably get you inside so a medic can look you over," he said.

"I'm fine out here. Just let me sit here until they're finished with their emergency. I'll go in when it calms down a bit."

"Sir, we can't just leave you out here." He was bold for a lieutenant, and I liked that about him. "You're supposed to check in."

"I'm a doctor. I'll be fine," I responded. "You need to get where you were going. I can wait here. If you want, just let the medics know I'm out here, but tell them I'm all right."

"Okay, sir, but we really should have someone stay with you."

"Really, I'm fine," I insisted. "But you're probably right."

One of the lieutenant's men drew the short straw and sat with me on the bench as we waited.

A hospital corpsman came out some twenty minutes later and helped me inside to a gurney. When he removed my boot, my ankle was swollen to twice its normal size and the pain in it and my shoulder was more than I would have allowed a patient to bear without giving them a shot. When the ER doctor evaluated me, she was concerned that I had broken both my ankle and my shoulder. The X-rays showed a displacement of the bones in my ankle and an abnormality in the shoulder. She fitted me with a boot cast and shoulder sling, then gave me a shot for pain.

"I'm going to send you for an orthopedic evaluation at Arifjan to-morrow," she said. "You need at least a CT or MRI and an orthopod to look at you."

"I don't have time to be injured."

"Nobody does. We'll make the time," she responded as if giving me an order.

I stared at her briefly. She stared back with the kind of clinical look that meant she was the doctor and I was the patient, regardless of rank or position. And that was the hardest part of being an injured doctor; I had to allow myself to assume the role of a patient. It was unsettling letting other doctors take control.

The next day my lieutenant and I flew to the naval hospital at Ar-ifjan, Kuwait, where an orthopedic surgeon examined me and ordered an MRI of my shoulder. The MRI showed the cartilage of the glenoid fossa broken into three pieces and the rotator cuff torn in two different spots. Two ankle bones were fractured and one of the tendons had snapped. He said I would need surgery on both and that they were operations that needed orthopedic subspecialists at Landstuhl or a hospital in the States. He wanted to transfer me to the Air Force CASF (contingency aeromedical staging facility) at Ali Al Salem Air Base in Kuwait for a medical evacuation.

"I can't leave now," I said. "I'm the only flight surgeon in theater. My replacement isn't due for another month."

"Well, you can't walk with a busted ankle, and your left arm will keep dislocating without surgery. You could delay a few weeks, but a month is pushing it." He seemed surprised that I resisted, yet staying in theater with an injury was not without precedent nor atypical. Sometimes it just had to be done.

"There's just no way I can leave without a replacement. It's not possible," I replied.

"Okay, sir," he agreed reluctantly. "Let's tape your ankle. You'll have to wear the rocker boot everywhere, even on missions. We'll stabilize your shoulder with an immobilizer. You can't lift and you can't run."

The doctor gave my lieutenant an order to make sure I came back if there were any problems. I thanked the surgeon and he filled out a medevac form authorizing my transfer. I had signed the same forms for many other soldiers over the span of three tours in Iraq and done so without realizing the full impact that single medical decision made on soldiers. A medevac order set into motion a chain reaction that transformed a soldier into patient—and that special category, "patient," spoke volumes as to the abilities and future of an otherwise willing and able fighter. Purposeful and necessary in its intent, a medical evacuation always caused an untimely separation of soldiers from their missions and from the unit to which they belonged. It was a dual-edged sword. From my new patient perspective, I felt grateful that medical officers made those decisions, but I also felt the weight of knowing that a surgical medevac was de facto proof that I was vulnerable and hurt.

THE FLIGHT BACK to Udairi was odd emotionally because for the first time in all my deployments I felt stripped of my rank and influence. Being designated a medevac patient made me dependent on other military doctors and on the medical system. I had always been in a position where others depended on me as a doctor; now circumstances had flipped that dependency, and the implications loomed large. Initially, I tried to pretend my injuries were little more than a nuisance. I was a doctor. I couldn't be hurt. But my colleagues at Arifjan classified me as a medevac patient, and that changed everything. It deflated my notions of a self-sustaining flight surgeon still capable of performing missions. Despite knowing better, I wanted to minimize the fact that my injuries diminished my usefulness as a soldier.

My shoulder immobilizer proved useless. It slid and flopped around, and mostly I slung it over the back of my chair. While at lunch with the commander and other pilots the day after returning to Udairi, I reached for the salt and my shoulder dislocated again. I let out a yelp. The commander asked if I needed a doctor. "Kinda," I answered. He knew about my fall and my evaluation at Arifjan, but we hadn't yet discussed the details. We met after lunch and I told him the plan.

"We'll do whatever we can to get your replacement here faster," the commander assured me. "Have your lieutenant help you as much as you need. I didn't realize it was that serious."

"I didn't either, but the orthopedic surgeon said it's complicated. I'll survive until the new doc shows up; then I can be his first patient." I chuckled a bit.

My replacement, a colonel and state flight surgeon from the Ohio National Guard, arrived the first week of February. I briefed him about my own case and he signed the flight surgeon authorization for my medical evacuation. His training on the computerized flight surgeon entry system and transmittals to Fort Rucker were light, so I spent a week overlapping duties to get him familiarized. During that time I received official notification that I had been promoted to the rank of lieutenant colonel.

A section lieutenant and two medics were detailed to fly with me to Arifjan. The commander gave them orders to assist me as needed. I told him I didn't need assistance, but my own replacement flight surgeon had overruled me.

From Arifjan, I would go to the CASF at Ali Al Salem in Kuwait no later than 1400 hours that day and stay in medical hold for two days while awaiting my evac flight to Fort Bliss, Texas, via Landstuhl, Germany. That was typical for a medevac. Ambulatory patients arrived a day or two before their scheduled flight and post-op patients or critical-care patients arrived the day of the flight, sometimes within hours of the departure time. The timing allowed the CASF doctors and nurses to stage the patients according to their needs and triage categories.

Paperwork in hand, my small entourage drove me to Arifjan. I diverted them to the PX where we sat for coffee and donuts. I offered the lieutenant some final instructions about managing the flight surgeon's office and we talked about his career. I don't think my words gave him any profound insights, but that short time together meant something to me, a chance to impart some hard-earned wisdom about medicine and careerism in the military. He listened intently and acknowledged each point I made with a hearty "Yes, sir." Halfway through our coffee, I wondered if I might have already crossed into that gray zone between relevance and insignificance.

Afterward, we drove to the flight line and boarded a flight for Ali Al Salem. That short hop would become my last mission aboard a Black Hawk helicopter, the last one as a flight surgeon in the U.S. Army Medical Corps. We left at 1300 hours and touched down about 1330. Before I left the tarmac for the CASF, I watched my fellow soldiers take off and head back to Udairi. Watching them leave gave me a mixed bag of emotions. I felt alone as if I had no colleagues in the military. I felt somewhat pissed that I had been careless and, as a re-

sult, injured. I also felt relieved that I was getting the medical attention I needed. In all, I felt conflicted: I wanted to stay; I needed to go.

The medevac flight to Landstuhl was scheduled for Sunday. I spent
Friday and Saturday at the CASF mostly sleeping, reading, and observing the staff as they checked patients and prepared for the medevac
flight. Their mission, like mine, focused on aviation medicine, but they
prepped an entire hospital full of patients, whereas I rarely prepped
more than one or two at a time. Watching them was like watching
ants build a nest. The docs, nurses, and medics worked with one objective, move the group (the ambulatory, the critical, the post-op) to
the next echelon of medical care and do it without complications.

On Sunday morning I woke to the sensation of a medic gently shaking my bed. "Sir, wake-up call. Time to get ready—zero five-thirty,
sir." I slowly rose to the edge of my bed by grabbing his outstretched
hand. My shoulder and ankle hurt. "What time is it?" I asked. He repeated: "Zero five-thirty, sir. The medevac arrived about an hour ago.
A C-17 Globemaster—real nice." He assured me that we had plenty of
time to get ready.

Ten minutes after the wake-up in the CASF, all the patients were
getting dressed—some with slight grimaces, others with no obvious difficulty. My arm sling had tangled in the middle of the night.
My ankle throbbed because I could not keep it elevated. A young Air
Force medic helped me get my arm situated and secure. He started
helping me with my walking cast. I told him I could handle it and he
politely told me he had orders to help.

I was a lieutenant colonel and flight surgeon. The medic was an
airman not yet promoted to sergeant. I looked at him, paused, and
yielded. He checked the skin on my ankle, gently feeling for swelling.
He asked if it hurt. It hurt. Then he grabbed my long white orthopedic stockings, eyed them, and discarded them. "Too dirty," he said.
He broke out a fresh new pair. I joked that I wore a pair of socks for
two months straight during my second deployment, and we smiled
and laughed together.

"Can't do that here, sir," he said, still smiling. Carefully he put the new compression stockings on my feet and then smoothed out the last of a few wrinkles around my right ankle. "I wanna make sure we don't get any friction rubs," he said. I nodded in agreement. He grabbed the walking-boot cast and carefully put it on my foot, then cinched all six black Velcro straps, but not too tightly. He double-checked the fit by having me stand, then ran his fingers around the edges of the boot where it might cause pressure points. His smile made me grin. "How's that feel, sir?"

"Feels good," I replied, grateful for his concern.

After breakfast at the DFAC across the street, I shuffled back to the CASF. As I reached the doors, I looked back toward Iraq one last time. The morning light cast shades of orange over the buildings of Ali Al Salem. A hand-painted sign pounded in the sand read simply: DFAC. When I glanced at it, I remembered the DFAC at FOB Marez, near Mosul. In December 2004, a suicide bomber attacked it, killing twenty-two people, soldiers and civilians, and wounding more than sixty others. In another incident an insurgent using a cell phone GPS targeted our DFAC at Key West. His coordinates were wrong and we escaped harm.

My eyes shifted to the line of patients returning from breakfast. They looked like ducks with broken wings, waddling back and forth across a busy war. I caught myself chuckling at the procession. Sometimes, for no reason at all, war made you laugh or say bizarre things, like you were an actor in a theater of the absurd. I commented once to my medics that a dog tag embedded in a dead soldier's throat was "interesting." During my tour at Caldwell, my roommate fell on his ass while climbing out of bed during an RPG attack. I laughed. During the first tour, Gibbons, the former champion collegiate wrestler from Iowa, had a nightmare. He rolled out of his cot and grabbed the soldier next to him, rousing half the company in the tent. I laughed at the commotion. Some of the other soldiers started laughing too, while others yelled to keep it quiet. Gibbons fell back to sleep as quickly as he had awakened.

As I sat and waited on my bed, a half dozen medical staff quickly attended a new patient with IED injuries who had arrived from one of the field hospitals. As I watched, the CASF turned bone quiet. Medics transferred the patient to a waiting gurney in the center row next to the other post-op patients. I could tell he had received aggressive treatment and that the distinction between his death and his life had been a very thin line—or maybe not even a line at all.

He was sedated. His face puffed out from shrapnel lacerations. His left leg was amputated above the knee. Clear plastic tubes, monitor wires, and catheters connected him to medicine, fluids, and machines. A cardiac monitor traced his heartbeat and other vital signs. The Air Force flight surgeon checked the tangle of lines and the array of monitors, rechecked his dressings, and listened to his breathing.

I felt useless as I watched from my bed, as if my injuries had erased my credentials and forced me to stand in a corner, observing only, unable to contribute. I wanted to move to the side of his bed and explore his wounds, stitch him up, gather dressings, and administer antibiotics. I possessed knowledge and desire and skill. To me, the final patient in the CASF became the universal patient and I became the universal doctor, yet all I could do was watch from the edge—nothing more.

I GRADUALLY LOOKED away from the new arrival and glanced around the CASF. Everybody who could was looking at the last patient and then looking away. There were quilts on the walls above each bed that volunteers had sent. I wanted to take one off the wall and cover the final patient as if to say, "This will keep you safe. Hide under here. The quilt will protect you from war."

A flight nurse finally came to my bed to confirm my name on the flight manifest.

"Kerstetter, Jon R., Lieutenant Colonel."

"Yes, that's me. I'm a doctor too," I interjected.

"Yes, sir," she continued without hesitation. "Let me reposition your arm sling. I'm going to add an elastic wrap around your chest so there's no chance of movement or dislocation during flight. We need to get one more set of vitals. We scheduled you for a pain shot before the flight. Are you ready, sir?"

I answered quietly, more nodding my head than speaking the words. "Yes, I'm ready," I lied. I imagined myself continuing in my flight surgeon's mission, making critical decisions, attending to the needs of soldiers. No matter, the flight was ready even if I was not.

THE PATIENTS RODE to the boarding area via ambulances and buses. A short ride to the airfield and there on the tarmac the Globemaster came into view. Large. Gray. Beautiful. "Real nice," just as my medic had said. If it was possible to feel love for an aircraft, then I felt love for the C-17 Globemaster. I admired its perfect size and shape, its wing camber, and its talon-like undercarriage. When I watched one take off, I stared at its outline against the sky. I loved how the Globemaster carried me to war, how it hauled me around in theater, how it brought water and food and medical supplies. I loved that it lifted the wounded out of war.

I viewed military aircraft as the icons of power. They attacked enemy positions, transported supplies, evacuated patients, spied during the night, and delivered troops. I saw them as tactical extensions of the minds and bodies of soldiers and military doctors, as extensions of me. Often during my tours, just before sunrise, I walked the flight line where the aircraft were lined up parallel to the runway, wheels chocked, perfectly aligned just waiting for a mission. The morning sunlight painted shifting colors on their frames. I let my eyes linger on the dark, olive drab and gray-green metal skins of aircraft, on the malted browns and the dirty tans of vehicles edging the flight line, and on the dusty white of stenciled numbers and warnings. I could identify each aircraft by its silhouette and the patterns of its colors and by its chipped paint and oily stains. I watched the aircraft crews as they performed their maintenance tasks and their morning preflight checklists. They advanced methodically toward completing a mission launch or engine replacement or aircraft configuration. Occasionally, I walked up to the side of a helicopter and just touched it for no reason at all, moving my hands across its warm skin, feeling the rivets and seams. The scent of JP-8 jet fuel mixed with hints of turbine oil, and flight line dust often lingered in the air over the runway. I breathed it in, that scent of aircraft and side-mounted rockets, the scent of war. It drew me in nearer to the mind of battle. The ritual functioned like a liturgy of sorts. When I was finished, I felt restored in my soldier faith and restored as a military doctor. The experience made me bold to the point that I laid claim to an aircraft. This is my helicopter. No other doc in the entire Army has this aircraft. It belongs to me. It's my office. It's where I go to war.

ON THE TARMAC, the flight medics assisted the patients up the loading ramp. A medic greeted me and took me to my assigned seat, right side, midsection of the aircraft, about six feet from the center row of litters.

The ambulatory loaded first, post-op patients last. The arrangement mirrored the beds in the CASF, ambulatory patients on the sides, critical and post-op patients in the center row.

The center-row patients were each loaded with packets of their medical records, op notes, and orders for the flight. The packets usually rode on the litter in a zippered waterproof pouch placed between the patient's legs. If the patient had no legs, the pouch rode at the foot of the litter. The nurses quickly flipped through the packets and ran a checklist. They cross-checked names with patients' wristbands. The usual post-surgical array of clear plastic intravenous tubes and monitor wires connected the patients to machines and medicine. White surgical gauze and beige elastic bandages clung to heads and limbs and abdomens. Oxygen flowed via dual-pronged nasal tubes or light-green plastic masks cinched around heads and faces. These were the kinds of patients that I had sent on medevac flights over my three tours in the Iraq War, the ones who occasionally asked if they were going to make it—to whom I always replied in the affirmative.

The soldier who arrived last in the CASF was finally loaded. When the loadmaster got his litter clamped into place, the patient began to wake. I suspected all the moving and jarring from the transfer roused him. He started to move his arms and head, then he mouthed some words to his nurse through his oxygen mask. His right arm started to flail, and he pulled the mask from his mouth and nose so it lay off-center, feeding oxygen to his cheek. He raised his head enough to glance toward his feet. His nurse signaled a medic to help. They held his arms and repositioned his oxygen mask, then she bent over and placed her ear close to his mouth. She cradled his hands in both of hers. He managed a garbled question. The nurse replied with a single word: "Yes."

The flight nurse continued to stroke the patient's forehead. She hailed the flight surgeon with a wave of her other hand. He shifted to the center row and checked the patient's monitor. I could tell from his lips that he said "morphine." He held up two fingers: two milligrams. He added additional orders. I imagined fentanyl or some other narcotic that made a patient unconscious. The morphine worked quickly, like a medical coup de grâce. The patient slept again and the nurse leaned over him and continued to hold his hand and stroke his forehead. I saw that a lot in the field hospitals, nurses holding the hands of fully sedated, critical patients, stroking their foreheads and sometimes whispering to them even as they slept. I did it on occasion—wished I had done it more.

ONCE ALL THE patients boarded, the loadmaster raised the loading ramp. It closed with a thud that shook the aircraft. The crew performed one last check of seatbelts. The engines started with a low, throaty growl that made the seats vibrate. After a few minutes the aircraft began its taxi to the runway. As we taxied, most of the patients just sat and stared across the cargo bay to the other side, staring in unison with the jostling of the runway.

The Globemaster finally taxied into position at the end of the runway and waited briefly for takeoff clearance. The four jet engines powered up and we began to roll. Within seconds the thrust pushed us sideways in our seats, and we held on to the sides of the seat frames. The C-17 made an uncomfortably steep combat assent. We were airborne.

The flight to Landstuhl was approximately five hours, during which the flight nurses and docs made frequent rounds checking on their patients. If I didn't know I was on a medevac flight, I could have been fooled into thinking I was still on the ground at the CASF. Nurses administered medications and gave shots; they hustled to their next patient, checked vital signs, listened to patients, and made progress notes on medevac charts.

Most of the patients looked around the aircraft, and when we caught the eyes of other soldiers, we quickly looked at our boots or off to the side. I tried not to stare at other patients, especially those in the center row, but it was difficult to avoid. The wounds and dressings and casts and wraps seemed to mesmerize the rest of us. Some bandages held a tinge of blood and some bulged from underlying gauze. I was relieved that I was not in the center row of patients. And I felt guilty for feeling relieved.

A young soldier with an eye injury sat in the seat to my left. I looked—tried not to stare. I made a clinical assessment: soldier in his early twenties, shrapnel injury to the face, puncture wound to the eye, probable loss of eyesight—soldier frightened and alone. His cornea looked dull. I assumed shrapnel had penetrated his eye. The black eye patch he was supposed to be wearing hung down around his neck. I don't know why he wasn't wearing it. I didn't ask. Maybe the pressure caused pain. Maybe the patch reminded him that he had a blind eye. Maybe it made him self-conscious or embarrassed or made him feel less like a soldier.

About two hours into the flight, I leaned over and asked him if he needed anything. He said he was fine. A bit later, I finally got enough courage to ask him what happened. He said an IED had showered his face with shrapnel and that he already had one operation to remove fragments from his face and eye. He told me how lucky he was that shrapnel didn't hit his brain, but that he had to have eye surgery to keep him from going blind.

"The doctors say I'll be okay with another operation," he said. "What happened to you, sir?"

I told him my story. He responded with a low-toned, elongated, "Oh . . . ," and then looked at his boots.

As we talked, I got a better look at his eye. It looked dead. I wondered if his doctor had really told him he was going to be okay. What I noticed more than his eye and his facial injuries was his mood. He kept staring at his boots. He planted his elbows on his knees, and his hands formed fists where he rested his forehead. Sometimes he shifted and cupped his chin in the palm of one hand and let the other hand fall between his legs. He stared that thousand-yard stare depicted in black-and-white photos of shell-shocked infantrymen in World War I. When he looked down, he looked like he was trying to adjust his eyes to the light in order to see the floor more clearly. He finally leaned back into the webbing of his seat, fixed a blanket over his shoulder, and rested his head on it and slept the rest of the flight to Landstuhl.

Watching him, I tried to imagine what he might be feeling—or fearing. I knew in a clinical sense that he might become one of those soldiers treated for post-injury depression and PTSD. I wondered if he would become one of the soldiers whose war experience would end in suicide. Whenever I encountered depression or suicide in the field, it always made me wonder where psychological injuries began. I drew no conclusions, but as I looked around the Globemaster, it seemed as though that seed might take hold during a medevac flight.

DURING THE REST of that flight, I wondered what kind of complications we all might have. And I noted how tired I had become in my tours as a military doctor, especially during my last deployment. I had learned to distance myself from the casualties I had seen, but now I was one of them. Clinical distance had always helped me face the challenges of war, but it couldn't help me face my own injuries. How could I distance myself from myself? There was a final thing: I had become a patient, one of the many numbers of soldiers who thought injuries were for others but not for them. I didn't realize that my injuries would change my life so abruptly, and I began to understand how war and its consequences extended far beyond a theater of combat.

Part Three

— — — —

ADAPT

Awake

— — —

The first thing I saw was the light. Blue. White. Intense. It reminded me of the light I had seen from an Alaskan glacier as shoulders of ice fractured and slid into the ocean. My family and I watched from a boat off a glacial bay. I responded with awe at the depth of the blue-white color and the massive icy waves. The crests of those waves moved outward toward a horizon that seemed dreamlike, ethereal, as if they were beckoning me to drift with them wherever they decided to go.

A strange partial gravity embraced my body. I closed my eyes and drifted. . . .

I heard the voices of Collin and each of my children. Their words traveled above the surface of those icy waves, strong as the blue of glaciers, soft as the weight of dust. They called my name. They sounded far away, like a distant wave breaking on the face of a rock.

My right leg tried to move—nothing. Bend it, shake it, kick it—nothing. My toes blundered about near the bottom of the bed. I couldn't sense exactly where they were or in which direction they were pointed. I lifted my head to see them. I saw a foot and a leg, all real yet unreal—attached yet unattached. The skin of my right arm tingled in spots and felt dead in others. My right hand flopped at my side. Its fingers poked without finesse and groped at the doughy consistency of my thigh. A large black hole obscured the right side of everything I looked at. I blinked repeatedly. The hole remained.

I recognized Collin and the kids but I couldn't say their names. I wanted to call to them. They were saying things I didn't understand, to each other and to me. They gathered near and touched my arm and my head. Their touch felt fuzzy, like anesthesia.

Something was off, but nothing specific came to mind. I focused on my right leg and skin. I remembered that I was a doctor, so I tried to sit up and diagnose myself. I managed to flail about with my left arm. A nurse tucked it back under the sheet. I furrowed my brow as if I were growling at her. Collin stroked my arm and I was able to turn my head toward her. As I turned, I saw the light again; its glacial blue saturated the room. A cool puff of air hit my face. It smelled like plastic. Something on my nose made me stir. I opened my eyes and saw a hand trying to smother me with a mask. I tried to yell but nothing came out. A nurse said to take some deep breaths. I did, then drifted.

I was watching an old silent movie with jittery frames that flashed and disappeared before I had time to catch their meaning. I drifted toward a hospital tent in Baghdad. A young Army doctor called my name as he shook my arm and asked me to wiggle my toes. I recognized his voice but his face belonged to somebody else. He called me "Mister" instead of "Sir" or "Doctor." I mumbled some unintelligible mush. He interrupted. Told me surgery went just fine. His words conveyed nothing useful, tangible, or real. He tapped my leg, then turned and walked away. I wanted to call him back, say a terse word, maybe two, but the words just circled my tongue and fell to the sides of my mouth. They clung to the inside edges of my teeth, where they hunkered down, entrenched and irretrievable. My thoughts teetered and fell like a drunken soldier on weekend leave. I wanted to speak, yearned to speak, just a single small word—but nothing.

Drifting in Iraq, I felt the buffeting of a helicopter. Something jolted me. My wife stood by my bedside, speaking. I heard her voice but not her words. A nurse positioned a pillow under my legs. She asked me to wiggle my toes. My toes had become detached. I faded . . . recovered . . . faded. I drove through Baghdad in a Humvee. Mortars exploded in the distance. The smell of medicinal alcohol hit me. A field hospital appeared. I awoke. Collin said, ". . . home."

I tried to speak again—nothing. I looked at my leg that was not a leg and closed my eyes, afraid without knowing why. My mind wandered back to Iraq. The walls of my tent flapped back and forth in a desert storm and the dust choked me. I heard a nurse say "Breathe." My not-leg leg, my drifting toes, and my dough-like skin all coalesced into a single amorphous appendage. Muscle dissolved into bone, bone into skin, skin into air. My right buttock flipped itself inside out and rested, concave, on the bed. My ankle became a knee, my knee a toe. My knee-toe wanted to wiggle but had no mind to wiggle. My calf pretended to be a thigh and my thigh wanted to try its skill at bending, right in the middle where it had no joint. My right hand and fingers flailed against my thigh, touching without touching. My left hand reached across my trunk and rubbed my chest, face, and arm. My right shoulder was missing, as was the right half of my face. The hair on my head separated itself, real on the left, fake on the right. I looked at Darren and Justin. They were missing parts of their faces. That bothered me more than anything. I closed my eyes for a moment, then opened them. Their half faces remained.

My mouth seemed to be fighting a mapless war. I ordered my tongue and lips to speak, but they formed only broken approximations of speech. Words crawled along the length of their neurons, unconcerned that they should find my mouth. Unlike my crazy leg, my words did not coalesce. They scattered and hid. They ran from my brain. I started to get pissed, then drifted back to sleep and back to my war. Each time I awoke, I gained a little more sense of where and who I was. Collin looked more real. Justin, Darren, and Katelyn all smiled and spoke, one at a time, and I could tell they loved me by the way their words sounded and by the way they touched my arm or leg. I began to ask myself questions, but the doctor inside me would not answer. He had no diagnosis for failing skin and floating toes and fractured thoughts. My brain flowed toward a horizon that jumped back and forth from Iowa to Iraq. My thoughts all abandoned me. They were traitors. I was neither soldier nor doctor, alive nor dead. I was something, someone in between—an object drifting.

In a haze, I searched frantically for a medevac helicopter—for a weapon—for my medics. Where are my medics? Let's move! I wanted to send a distress signal. I tried to form a word, but my mouth locked in defiance. I tried again, once more, and then finally managed to force a word to the back of my teeth, where I pressed it firmly until it slid from the corner of my mouth. Collin bent over to hear me. I puffed my lips and made only a low-pitched hum. She stroked my right arm: nothing. I needed her skin, our skin. I needed to say a word, to gather my wits, and legs, and arms and lift myself to the edge of the bed. Instead, I floated and twisted. I drifted seamlessly from hospital to war, from patient to soldier. The bloody smells of the wounded alarmed me. The sterile smells of my room confused me. I lost partial control of my bladder, but I did not feel the warmth.

I maneuvered through the streets of Baghdad. I smelled the medicinal smells of hospitals. I felt the percussion of an RPG. My body shook as I pushed against the heavy door of a damaged Humvee. A soldier moaned garbled words in a combat hospital. Surgical lights filled my room. I opened one eye . . . closed it . . . opened it. The doctor I saw was strangely familiar. He told me the anesthesia would wear off soon, that the numbness would go away, that I needed to rest. Collin stroked my arm. I watched her smile as I drifted back to war.

A fire in my helicopter burned my skin. I tried to scream but could not scream. I felt the thud of metal, a missile hitting the aircraft: the doctor dropped my bedrail. Bullets pinged and pierced the aluminum skin. Several hit my legs: a nurse tapped my leg repeatedly. Shrapnel hit a soldier next to me. I moved to his side, but a safety harness pushed me back: Collin's hands trying to calm me. A helicopter warning signal blared: an intravenous monitor alarm sounded. The helicopter spun toward the ground. Soldiers screamed. One jumped from an open door. I struggled to free myself from my harness, but was slammed to my right, hard against the ground. I startled and opened my eyes. Collin stood near with my children. Justin said, "Dad." I stared at them and mumbled to Collin, "I'm hurt. My leg . . . numb. Something's wrong."

Diagnosis

TWO WEEKS AFTER my medevac flight from Landstuhl, a surgeon from the orthopedic department at the University of Iowa Hospital in Iowa City outlined my treatment plan. The Army had transferred me from Fort Bliss to the Rock Island Arsenal in Illinois, where a Wounded Warrior Project case management team contracted with university and private hospitals throughout the Midwest. In response to the overwhelming numbers of soldiers returning from Iraq and Afghanistan with injuries, the Army decided the transfers would expedite the medical care of soldiers.

A series of operations was scheduled on my left shoulder, left hand, right ankle, and right leg. Surgery would be followed by the appropriate months of physical therapy. I was also scheduled for maxillofacial surgery to repair some upper jaw damage from an infection. The surgeries began in March 2006. During the following year, I had eight operations; five involved my leg, shoulder, and hand and three involved my upper jaw and sinus. Doctors in each specialized field took turns. Following each surgery, physical therapists spent months working my joints to help me regain strength and range of motion. Each surgery went as planned. No surprises. But with each successive surgery, I had a progressively longer recovery. There was more pain than I expected and longer periods of post-op physical therapy.

The second week of May 2007, I woke up one morning with severe nausea and vertigo. I had to crawl to the bathroom, because I couldn't stand without losing my balance. I had no history of vertigo, so I went through a mental checklist of diagnoses: Ménière's disease, labyrinthitis, infection, brain tumor, brain stem stroke, intracranial bleeding. None of them made sense, but I felt I should see a doctor and at least get a shot or some medication. I asked Jordan, who had been home for a month preparing for her wedding in June, to drive me to the University of Iowa Hospital. I told the emergency doctor that I just needed a shot, but he insisted on a full workup, a brain CT, and a neurology consult. It was standard medical practice, but I wanted to avoid going down that path and discovering a serious diagnosis right before Jordan's wedding. If my symptoms didn't resolve, I would get the full workup after the wedding. When I tried to sit up for the exam, a flood of nausea hit me and the room spun around. My eyes jerked back and forth in rhythmic saccades that made everything appear jittery. I grabbed the sides of the bed to keep my balance.

The workup revealed an aneurysm at the base of my brain. The ER doctor gave me the diagnosis with a serious look that to me conveyed the sense that I was in trouble. One thing came to mind: bleeding. I had treated several patients in my career with ruptured brain aneurysms, and the resulting hemorrhages always pushed them toward death. The quick shot of medicine I wanted might alleviate my symptoms, but it would not cure an aneurysm. In disbelief, I simply responded, "You serious?"

The consulting neurologist reviewed the CT scan and concurred with the diagnosis, but he thought my symptoms unusual for an aneurysm. He did further testing to determine if I had central vertigo from brain pathology or positional vertigo related to an inner ear or vestibular nerve problem. He diagnosed an inner ear problem as the cause of the vertigo and concluded that the aneurysm was incidental. I had seen similar cases where, in the process of making a primary diagnosis, other secondary and incidental findings often revealed themselves in lab work or imaging studies. Sometimes the secondary findings became more significant for the patient than the primary diagnosis. After he gave me a shot and performed a maneuver that repositioned the small otoliths in the vestibular system of my inner ear, my symptoms resolved almost immediately. He ordered a brain MRI and a neurosurgical referral for the following week.

After several hours, Jordan came to get me from the waiting room. She wanted to know all the details.

"So what did they find?" she asked me.

I deliberately chose not to mention the aneurysm. "I had an inner ear problem and the neurologist gave me a shot and fixed some rocks in my head. Maybe a virus. We don't know for sure, but I'm better now and we can go home."

"I always knew you had rocks in your head, but all that for an ear infection?" We both laughed.

"It's slightly more complicated than that," I said. "The rocks are needed for balance. I can show you in an anatomy book at home if you want."

"That's okay, Papa," she said, rolling her eyes.

And with that, we left the ER and drove home. On the way, I decided not to say anything to Collin either. The word "aneurysm" was sure to set off alarm bells. I still had an MRI and neurosurgical referral and I wanted to make sure of the diagnosis. I told Jordan and Collin about my follow-up appointment but said the neurologist needed to evaluate the underlying cause of vertigo, which was in fact partially true, but also partially false, for which I felt a tinge of guilt.

The MRI and neurosurgical appointment confirmed the diagnosis. The neurosurgeon said the aneurysm's location at the base of my brain complicated the surgical approach. He recommended endovascular surgery and the placement of a small titanium coil by an interventional neuroradiologist. The procedure, he explained, was much like a cardiac catheterization for a coronary stent or a balloon angioplasty, except they would thread a vascular catheter up through my carotid artery and into my brain, where they would release a coil into the aneurysm, preventing it from expanding or rupturing. This was the safest surgical option.

A neuroradiologist visited with me after the neurosurgeon. He reviewed the MRI and walked me through the procedure again. "Should be less than two hours and you go home the same day," he said slightly rushed. "All you need to do is schedule it. Any questions?"

"You're sure I need this procedure?" I asked.

"The size of the aneurysm is at the minimum for treatment, but if we do nothing there is always the risk of expansion and rupture. You have a history of high blood pressure, which adds to the risk." He sounded the way I sounded when explaining a medical risk to patients—precise and with a bit of warning.

"I know about the risks, but it all comes as such a surprise. I have no symptoms."

"Small aneurysms rarely produce symptoms."

"I know. But I don't particularly want somebody digging around in my brain. You've done this before, I know, but I just want to make sure you know what you're doing." I thought he might become defensive at my comments, but he answered with a brief and professional explanation.

"No, it's a perfectly legitimate concern. Patients ask it all the time. We've done hundreds of coils and most have no complications," he assured me. "You know there are risks of bleeding and stroke and infection, but those are rare—not nonexistent, but rare."

"I know, but I just never expected to have brain surgery."

"Nobody ever does," he said dryly.

There was always a difference between providing clinical facts and clinical assurances, and the more risky the procedure, the harder that difference was to bridge. The doctor had given me reasonable assurances, but I still walked out of his office with the heavy truth of needing brain surgery. As I left, I felt a sense of near-betrayal by my profession, as if it were shunning me. I asked myself how it was possible that I needed brain surgery. I wondered how, as a doctor, I could have known all the things that conspired to hurt other people without understanding how the same things conspired to hurt me. I had given my life to medicine. How could it turn on me?

I decided to continue keeping the diagnosis secret from my family, at least until I made it past Jordan's wedding. I wondered what Jordan and my other kids would think—their dad keeping secrets about things they deserved to know. And I wondered what Collin might think—a husband who decided to keep her at a distance. I wanted to let them all know, but in my own time.

The week before Jordan's wedding stressed our family, as weddings tend to do. I tried to remain calm but couldn't help thinking about my aneurysm and pending surgery. When I ran around doing last-minute details for the wedding, I worried my aneurysm might explode. I imagined standing next to an IED in Iraq, afraid to move for fear of triggering it.

I needed to let somebody know, so I pulled the pastor aside before the rehearsal dinner. "If anything happens to me, it's because of a brain aneurysm. Call 911 and tell them to get me to neurosurgery," I said. I briefly told him about my diagnosis and pending surgery.

"I understand," he said. "How is Collin coping?"

"I haven't told her yet."

He gave me one of those pastor stares that blended concern and blame. "Are you sure you don't need to tell Collin? I had a sister die of a ruptured brain aneurysm."

"No, I just want to get through the wedding before I tell her. Just keep this between us."

I felt an urge to warn Collin so she wouldn't get blindsided by a medical emergency, but I didn't want to risk putting a spoiler on the wedding. It was Jordan's time and I wanted it to remain special and untarnished by a family medical drama.

On Sunday, the first week of June, I walked Jordan down the aisle. As we entered the church sanctuary, I turned to her and told her how much I loved her. It was one of those father-daughter moments when the world stops turning and the only thing that matters is the love between a father and his daughter. That precise moment held all the joy of fatherhood wrapped tight like a seed ready to take flight in a summer breeze. As I said "I love you," my words had a double meaning for me. One meaning conveyed that father-daughter bond that looms when daughters get married and leave home, the other held a sub rosa connotation of last rites: "I love you" meaning *I might also be leaving home, but not for beginnings, rather for endings, and I will never see you again. I am sorry that you will grieve, but I will grieve too. And even when I am dead, I will always love you.*

At the wedding reception, we danced and ate and laughed. I toasted the newlyweds and danced the traditional father-and-daughter dance. The dance got to me. If I wasn't going to die of a ruptured aneurysm, I might have died from a broken heart. Jordan was my first daughter. When she was a child she had undergone heart surgery to correct a congenital aortic defect. In her first junior high year she had scoliosis surgery. The surgeries and the rehab drew us close as a father and daughter, so when she announced she was getting married, I wanted to hold on just a little longer and a little tighter, which I did during the dance. And when the music was over, I kissed her on the forehead and let her go, and like my words "I love you," the kiss had a double meaning too.

The day after the wedding, I asked Collin to go for a walk. She figured something was up, because a casual stroll was out of character for me. As we walked around the block, I mentioned how my leg and shoulder had really been improving since my operations.

"So what's going on?" she asked. "I know you didn't bring me out here to talk about your operations."

"Well, I need to go over something with you and it's kinda tricky. It's nothing about the kids, or us or another tour. And it's not necessarily a bad thing."

Collin stopped walking and faced me. "You're scaring me."

"No. No. I don't want you to be scared or to worry."

"I'm already worried."

"I know, but don't be. Everything will work out. It's not that bad, really. I just need to have a small surgical procedure."

"A procedure? What kind of procedure?" Her question wasn't so much a question as it was an alarm.

"Well . . . I kinda need brain surgery."

Collin froze mid-stride. She turned to look at me and I couldn't tell if she hadn't heard me and didn't understand or if she had heard me and understood. She blurted a puzzled "What?" I had never seen her turn suddenly pale in our forty years of marriage—not through childbirth or the broken bones of our children or even after my post-deployment surgeries, when I looked like a zombie and my leg swelled to twice its normal size. Her face looked more the color of the side-walk than the color of skin. I understood how revealing such diagnoses always caused a sort of emotional shock wave, but I didn't expect Collins's visceral reaction, and as we talked I wished I could have broken the news differently. She had carried the weight of deployments and extended tours and the uncertainties of war, just as I had, and now she would have to bear the impact of this new diagnosis. It seemed so unfair.

"It's not a brain tumor or cancer or anything like that. I have an aneurysm at the base of my brain. It's small right now, but I need surgery to keep it from breaking and causing problems."

She pressed for more detail. "Is that what they found in the ER?"

"Yes, but I didn't want to say anything until after the wedding. I didn't want everybody worrying about it. It's not that big a deal."

"It sounds like a big deal to me. You should have told me." She wasn't angry, but she did look disappointed. Whenever I tried to minimize the impact of bad news, she tended to see through my words right to the heart of the issue.

"No . . . I didn't want to upset anybody, especially you. The important thing now is I need some further evaluations and then we need to schedule surgery. I just need you to be aware of what's going on."

"Ya think?" she replied. She took my hand as we continued around the block. I tried to answer her questions, but there was a flood of unknowns for her and for me. We both questioned what would happen *if*. And the answers were vague and complicated. We decided to take things one step at a time.

I had to report my diagnosis and get a deployability assessment from Colonel Danny Smith at the Wounded Warrior office at the Rock Island Arsenal. Danny was an affable and seasoned military physician and personal friend whom I had served with in the Iowa National Guard for nearly fifteen years. He had been overseeing my post-deployment care and recovery since my transfer from Fort Bliss. When we discussed my diagnosis, he ruled out any further deployments until surgery and recovery were complete. We considered a medical transfer to the Bethesda Naval Hospital in Maryland, but rather than deal with the logistics and the family upheaval, I opted to stay in Iowa for the surgery.

Brain imaging and visits with University of Iowa physicians occupied the entire following week. At the conclusion of all the testing and consultations, we scheduled surgery for the third week in July. I talked to Jordan and Justin on the phone and explained the details as best I could without trying to alarm them. Darren and Katelyn were still home from the wedding, so I discussed the surgery with them individually and tried to answer all their questions. Justin decided to come home for the day of surgery. Jordan had just relocated to Washington, D.C., so I insisted she didn't need to come back home. The whole business of telling my children about my brain surgery reminded me of the times I told patients they needed to call their families. That meant surgery was serious, as it always was, but calling a family together held its own kind of subliminal message. I tried, as my own doctors had tried for me, to assure my children that the procedure carried minimal risks and was one of those things in medicine that caused lots of unfounded fear and worry. I told them that the words "brain surgery," like "cancer," whipped up all kinds of crazy emotions, when in fact I had better surgical options than most patients needing brain surgery. We all believed that reasoning because it made intuitive sense and offered hope. Still, there was that lingering, gnawing understanding that brain surgery still harbored the potential for significant complications.

In the remaining days before surgery, Collin and I were rushed and weary. Over dinner at home we wondered together if we were ready. We decided we were not but that we had to keep moving forward anyway. We talked only tangentially about the procedure itself, without dwelling on it.

"This is one of those procedures that usually works just fine," I said. "But if there are any complications, at least we're prepared."

"I understand," she said calmly as she pushed her food aside. "I just never imagined."

"I never imagined it either," I said quietly

The doctors had explained all the risks of the surgery and mentioned death as a rare complication. That got our attention, and although we knew on paper that the risk fell below 1 percent, even a remote possibility of death by surgical complication was more foreboding than the risk of death by combat. I had signed on for combat. Collin understood that risk from her own father's military career and from mine. But neither of us signed on for neurosurgery and its possible untoward outcomes, no matter how rare. More significant than death, at least for me, was the potential for a brain hemorrhage or a stroke.

We had both stopped eating and just sat and talked at the kitchen table. At first we talked about some legal issues. "The wills are up-to-date, the insurance policies are paid, and I have a list of financial details in a file. The lawyer has a copy just in case."

"Thanks for getting all that stuff in order," she said.

After a while, we had nothing left to say about the paperwork and we just sat quietly. I finally blurted, "If I have a bleed or a stroke it will change everything, but doing nothing is not an option. If the aneurysm were to break, I could die."

"I understand," Collin said. "It's so scary though, especially for the kids. Everybody hears stories about brain surgery. If you need it, it's not good."

"I know. It's scary for me too. I'll try to answer their questions, but I don't want them to be all stressed-out, so we have to be calm about this."

"Calm. When have our lives ever been calm?" she asked.

I chuckled just a bit. "I always promised that you would never be bored if you married me."

Collin grinned at that. "Boredom might be good for a while."

THE MORNING OF the surgery, we all packed into two cars like a squad of soldiers on a mission. It was quiet in our car. No last-minute questions. No small talk. At the hospital we said our goodbyes and hugged each other in the pre-op waiting room. I told Collin and the kids how much I loved them and they said the same to me. A surgical tech came to get me for surgery. We all said another round of goodbyes and Collin blew me a kiss as I rolled out the door.

In the operating room, nurses slid me from the gurney to the operating table and hooked me up to monitors. The medical residents verified my name and repeated information about the procedure and the risks.

"We're going to place a coil in your aneurysm using a vascular catheter," said one of the residents.

"Yes, I know. I'm a doctor. Just don't break anything," I half joked. Nobody else laughed.

"Don't worry. We're very careful and we've done hundreds of these procedures. We should be done in an hour or so. You'll wake up in post-op recovery."

"Yes, I know the drill," I said, as if I really did. Truth was, I didn't know the drill. Everything done to me since the initial diagnosis was out of my area of expertise and I had to depend on the knowledge and experience of other physicians. That was both comforting and discomforting, a sort of emotional balancing act of trust versus control.

The anesthesiologist said we were ready to get started. "Okay, Dr. Kerstetter, I'm going to give you some sedation. You should feel a little tingling in your lips and begin to drift off to sleep."

The voices in the room quickly became fuzzy and distant. I noticed the promised tingling in my lips. A nurse started to prep my groin for the catheter puncture. The antiseptic solution felt cold on my skin. I heard the busy surgical talk of physicians and nurses. Large computerized monitors linked to a fluoroscope were crowded in among the dozens of intravenous bags of saline. I caught a single image of my brain. It all took me back to my time as a medical student when the operating rooms at Mayo were the greatest of all possible places in the world. The anesthesiologist leaned over his station at the head of the bed and asked me to take some deep breaths. I took two deep breaths as I watched a surgeon position the operating room lights. They were blue and white—like the light of a glacier. The lights stayed there, fixed, intense; then they faded.

Discovery

T HE RECOVERY ROOM was quiet. Collin had sent our children home sometime after I was wheeled in from surgery. They had all taken turns near my bedside before they left. As I lay in my bed, half sleeping, half waking, a doctor came into the room and asked me to move my legs. The right one didn't move. I looked at the doctor and Collin. I said my leg felt numb. "The anesthesia will wear off soon," the doctor said. He explained that surgery was complicated because my aneurysm turned out to be an infundibulum that wouldn't hold a coil. I stayed alert long enough to hear the explanation, then fell back to sleep.

After noon, a different doctor came to examine me briefly before my discharge home. He checked my leg where the catheter had entered and then listened to my heart and lungs. I said that my leg was numb and something was wrong. He examined me more thoroughly, then assured us I could go home after the discharge paperwork was done. Within an hour, Collin and a nurse helped me get dressed and into a wheelchair. Discharge papers in hand and a plastic urinal in a hospital bag, off we went. The halls seemed foreign, as if I had never seen them before.

When we got home, it was about three o'clock. The kids were out. Collin decided to park in the driveway to give her more room to maneuver in getting me out of the car.

"Stay put," she said.

"I feel sick," I responded "I'm going to vomit."

"Take some deep breaths."

"Hurry up," I pleaded. "Get me in the house."

Collin ran around the car to my door and held it open for me. We didn't have a wheelchair. We didn't expect to need one.

I swung my feet out, put my hands on Collin's shoulders, and pushed off the front seat. Up on my feet, I felt like I was riding ten-foot seas in a rowboat.

"Sit back down!" Collin shouted.

That wasn't difficult. My butt hit the car seat as my legs flailed between Collin's feet.

I mumbled. "You'll have to hold me up."

Collin weighed maybe 110 pounds in a winter snowsuit. I hit the scales at a solid 200.

"We can't do this," Collin said. "I'm calling Bev to help us."

Beverly was a retired nurse and a friend from church. She lived only a few miles from us and within five or so minutes was at our house. Bev and Collin tried to get me up and walking, but I wobbled too much to make it more than a few steps at a time. They finally decided to get a chair from Collin's computer room and use it to roll me into the house. Once inside, they got me into my recliner near the fireplace. I felt like I had run the Army Ten-Miler. I fell asleep with a large bucket at my side in case my nausea gave way.

The next morning my leg and my arm still felt numb, but I could move them a bit more. Collin helped me to the bathroom and I shuffled the twenty feet, feeling dizzy. I said something was off, that everything felt weird and hazy. She had to hold me up in the bathroom and help me with my pants and with washing my hands. I kept dropping my toothbrush with my right hand and we both thought that was unusual. I was tired, more tired than I expected, and we thought that might be a post-op effect. Collin got me back to the recliner and repositioned my leg. "Maybe we should call the doctor," she said.

"No, let's give it some time. Let's see how I am tomorrow," I replied. I slept for most of the day.

The second day home I was more alert, but I couldn't remember many of the pre-surgical or surgery details. I struggled to put sentences together. My words came out, but they were out of order and some made no sense. My right arm and leg remained numb. Small patches of skin on my arm tingled when I touched them. I had a vague premonition of something gone wrong, something more serious than numbness. And I felt a nudge of fear about surgery and my brain. When I tried to test my fine motor coordination, I couldn't tap my fingers and toes or pinch with the thumb of my right hand. When I stood near the recliner, I wobbled like a bobblehead doll mounted on a dashboard. I recognized the living room, the kitchen, and the bathroom, but my collection of Native American art seemed nothing more than a collection of meaningless color and lines. I flipped through a book. The words seemed distant and meaningless; sentences were invisible in the upper right corners of the pages. I skipped around the pages but that gave me a headache, so I quit. I decided the anesthesia was still in my system, that I would be fine in another day.

Darren was there to help and he and Collin took turns with meds and toileting and feeding me juice and crackers. I mostly slept, and when I needed anything I rang a tiny brass bell on the end table. By post-op day three, the pain in my groin incision had mostly subsided. I still wobbled when I stood, my attention drifted, and my memory was erratic and dull. I was aware of my off-centeredness but assigned it to the lingering effects of surgery. Collin was concerned and wanted to take me back to the hospital. I thought she was being a bit too cautious and told her we could wait until the follow-up appointment.

Months prior to my surgery, Collin had made plans to visit her cousins for their annual cousins' caucus. When I announced that I needed brain surgery, she called the airlines and wanted to cancel her nonrefundable tickets for medical reasons. They balked at a refund, but agreed to give her an open ticket to use later. After breakfast, I asked Collin if she could get me some things at the grocery store. While she was gone, I decided that she needed a break and should go on her trip. Darren said he could help me at home and drive me around if necessary. When she came home, I told her I was feeling so much better and she should go to her cousins' caucus.

"You have an appointment in a week," she said. "I need to be here to watch you."

She insisted on staying. I insisted she leave.

"You have the tickets," I pointed out firmly. "You've been counting on this for a year. There's nothing you need to do that Darren can't do. He has a phone and a car. If I need a doctor, they're only two miles away. I'm fine. Now, get packed and go."

Collin had always been one of those people who wanted all the loose ends tied before she went anywhere. But in her striving to make things smooth and uneventful for everybody else, she often shouldered the burden and stress of all the extraneous crap that surfaced when things didn't work as planned. I told her she needed to let go and trust us. Darren and I could manage. Reluctantly, she agreed but only after making detailed lists: medication, emergency phone numbers, schedules for feeding me, and instructions for feeding the cat.

"Mom, we'll be fine," Darren said. "Just go."

"I don't know about this." She hesitated. "I'm going to call Bev to let her know."

I was edging toward frustration. "Collin, we'll be okay," I said. "We have a phone. Darren knows what to do. Go. I love you. Go."

Still cautious, she left in the late afternoon.

On the fourth post-op day, I woke about 8:00 a.m. Darren was downstairs in his bedroom. I needed to go to the bathroom and wanted to try it without help, so I didn't ring my bell. As I stood up from my recliner, I planted my feet wider than shoulder width. I experimented with my stance by moving my feet closer and then wider apart. Feet close, a bobblehead ornament. Feet wide, a shuffling passenger on an ocean cruise. An ultra-wide stance worked best for balance. I shuffled toward the bathroom with a gait that may have suggested I was carrying a load in my underwear. In the bathroom, I balanced myself like a camera tripod with my legs spread wide and my left hand against the wall over the toilet.

On the way back to my recliner, I tried to walk without holding on to the wall. As I moved down the hall, arms out to the sides, I teetered as if I were walking a tightrope in a circus. *I can do this*, I said to myself. *One step at a time.* When I reached the sofa I didn't grab hold but let my leg press against it, which felt like a violation of some mythical rule of gait and balance. Confident that I could negotiate the remaining ten or twelve feet, I took a firm, wide step with my left leg. I made a good strong step forward away from the sofa. My head and upper body followed. My right leg stayed fixed. I started to fall and tried to compensate by twisting my trunk. The twist rotated my hips and my arms began to flail. I made one stumble step forward and launched myself into a fall. Before I hit the floor, I managed a crude effort at grabbing the back of the sofa with my right hand. My arm more or less dragged across the top of the sofa as I fell forward.

The torque and the pressure were enough to rip my shoulder. The thud on the floor and my yelp brought Darren bounding up the stairs.

"Dad!" he yelled. "What happened? What are you doing?"

"I tried to make it to the bathroom and back. I hurt my shoulder."

"You're supposed to ring the bell for help."

"I didn't want to bother you. I figured I could make it. Just help me back to my chair. I'm fine. Don't call your mom."

Darren helped me back to the recliner, where I rested and tried to make sense of what had happened. He brought me a pain pill and some water and put a pillow under my leg. My left hip and right shoulder throbbed. I suspected I had broken my right clavicle, but after several minutes I realized it was okay. My shoulder continued to ache and throb.

As I recovered, I knew something was terribly wrong. The natural movement of my right leg had failed; my hand lacked the strength and coordination to grab hold. I began to think and focus on causes of falls and reasons for failed balance. There was nothing about lingering balance issues or leg and arm numbness or a loss of concentration on the sheet of instructions about post-op care. I thought again about the fall. I tried to think clinically, diagnostically. I told myself I could figure it out. Nothing clicked.

Later in the day, after lunch, Darren helped me to the bathroom. As we walked toward the hallway, I paused to look at a painting hanging on the living room wall. It was an impressionist oil done by a Native American artist. It depicted a warrior on horseback thundering toward a campfire in the foreground. Standing close, I could see only scattered colors and the broken lines of a larger image. The intersections of reds and blues caught my attention, as did the energetic lines and splashes of paint. The brushstrokes portrayed an explosive energy and a defiance of normal lines. As I stared at the art, it dawned on me that my thinking matched the broken lines and scattered blotches of color. I had no linearity of thought, no immediate connection of lines or logic. My thoughts were like the wild brushstrokes of an impressionist artist. The painting struck me as odd and beautiful at the same time. Odd because it defied the usual realism of many Native artists. Beautiful because its impressionism released color and form like I had never seen before. As I looked at the warrior painting, something clicked. The scattering of lines, the brokenness of the whole, the patterns of oil and texture, and the wild, almost incoherent brushstrokes began to make visual sense. The thought "brushstroke" lingered. "Brush" and "stroke." Two words. Two meanings. The realization hit me. I caught the meaning of "stroke" in the context of art, and then I caught it in the context of medicine. Stroke. Everything fit. Surgery, post-op numbness and weakness, imbalance, my mind and its wanderings. How could I not have seen it?

"Darren," I said spontaneously while staring at the painting. "I think I've had a stroke."

He didn't know exactly what that meant, so I tried to explain.

"There might be some damage from the surgery," I said. "I need to go to the doctor."

THE EXAM ROOM smelled like a hospital. The chairs were worn, the floor tile was dated. The clock on the wall ticked and the second hand seemed stuck. I sat and waited with Beverly, who sat in a chair next to me. Darren had already arranged to meet with some friends that afternoon, so I told him to go ahead and I would call Beverly to take me. He balked at first, but I assured him it would be okay.

After thirty minutes or so, a young doctor entered the room. I vaguely remembered him from before the surgery. He was doing his fellowship training and worked with the staff neuroradiologist, who, he explained, had left town for a meeting. The doctor told me he was looking at my MRI—that he had some concerns. That word "concerns" bothered me. I used it in my own medical practice. I knew what it meant.

"Let's take a look on the monitor," he said, directing me to bring my chair closer. I struggled with the chair and Bev helped me. An MRI flashed on a computer screen. My name appeared on the upper right corner of the images. It was the first time I'd seen my brain since a month before surgery. The images looked like a cross-sectional atlas of human neuroanatomy; the details showed everything. The numbered frames revealed the intricate details of my grayscale anatomy. I recognized cortex and ventricles, cerebellum and midbrain. The brainstem, of course, looked like a stem. The medulla and pons bulged slightly from their stalk. I saw white matter, which on an MRI was not really white but a shade of gray. In a brain MRI, white could indicate an abnormal finding. I remembered that much from my training. I saw no white in my brain.

The doctor pressed a computer key and the screen advanced twelve frames at a time. Miniature brains appeared as fast as he pressed a button. "You're going too fast," I said. I couldn't get a feel for what I saw.

"We can slow down a bit." He clicked through all the images for an overview, still faster than I could comprehend; then he flipped back to the first frames. I saw no abnormal white. He paused on a frame in the middle of the first screen of my brains. He enlarged it and tapped it with his finger. "Here," he said definitively. "There's a spot here."

I saw the white where he pointed. I paused . . . tapped my right leg: nothing. I looked away from the images and then to Bev. She pursed her lips, said nothing, and gave me a slight tilt of her head. I looked back at the brains. The spot remained.

The doctor said, "Okay, then." His voice was flat.

He flipped through the images as if scanning the pages of a book. "Here's another," he said. "This one hit the pons, this one hit the caudate nucleus, this one's in the cortex, this one's occipital. There's a large defect in the brainstem." He told me they were real, not artifacts.

He used the words "embolic" and "infarction" to refer to the spots. I knew the senses of the words, but I did not know their exact meanings. They were words I had used in my medical practice. I saw the spots as he pointed to them. At first there was just one, but then another, and then more, scattered from cortex to brainstem. I counted: five, six, seven—more. I tried to say the medical words for "brain pathology." I could not. I called them "spots."

"I see them. That's not a good sign," I said, sounding as detached as I could.

"No," he replied, equally detached as I had sounded.

I looked at Beverly. "I've got spots on my brain." As I said the words, I felt my sphincter loosen.

The doctor adjusted the frames of the MRI. Again I saw my name on each screen. *Those brains have stolen my name.* The images enlarged; the white spots came into focus. I decided that the brains belonged to some other patient. "Are you sure this is my MRI?" I asked suspiciously.

The doctor persisted. He nodded his head and said, "Yes."

I thought he was confused. *He's an asshole.* He pointed to the shaggy white of pathology. He gave them special names. Cortical and occipital and brainstem infarcts. Again I asked if they were my scans, insisting they belonged to some other patient. He said they were unfortunately mine and that they were real. *Arrogant prick.* More than thirty images, sectioned into millimeter slices, projected the same white spots from different angles and different depths. *The images cannot be my brain. Doctors make mistakes.*

He asked if he could examine me. I wondered why. "For what?" I blurted.

"We need to correlate your exam with the MRI findings."

I didn't want him to touch me, but I said, "Sure, go ahead. But remember, I'm a doctor, so I'll be grading you." I chuckled just a bit. He didn't respond. Beverly helped me onto the exam table, and when I got situated, the doctor took my shoes and socks off and rolled up my pant legs. I couldn't feel my right leg and foot and I knew he would discover the same thing on his exam.

He pricked me with a pin, made me tap my fingers, and told me to flip my hands back and forth, faster and faster. He peppered me with questions that I could not answer. I knew I was in a hospital, but I didn't know the date or recall the words he asked me to remember—just three small words. I grunted to force them out of my brain. I guessed one word was "apple"; it was "ball." *An apple is a kind of ball.* Three plus five became thirteen. I counted backward by sevens. One hundred minus seven . . . The numbers dissolved before they hit my mouth. I wobbled when I stood. My body shook in a rhythmic ataxic stance when he made me bring my feet close together. I failed to walk a straight line on the floor—a drunk test. I felt drunk. I listed to the right. I began to fall. He and Beverly caught me. The doctor told me the MRI spots correlated with the exam, that the spots were real. *He's a bastard.*

He explained to me that a piece of atherosclerosis from my aorta might have broken off during the procedure and caused an embolic stroke or that it was possibly air bubbles that inadvertently entered the catheter system and blocked the flow of blood in several arteries feeding different areas of my brain. And he explained how, during surgery, the procedure revealed that my aneurysm was really an infundibulum, an aberrant widening that couldn't hold a coil. "Either way," he said rather bluntly, "you have a multifocal stroke."

"In other words, surgery didn't go so well," I responded, still distant and rather clinical. "Beverly," I said, "this can't be good."

The doctor interjected. "This was part of the risk we talked about before surgery. These complications can happen."

"I know, but this isn't supposed to happen. Are you absolutely sure the MRI is mine?"

"Yes. I'm sorry. It's your brain."

I sat silently for a moment. Nobody said anything. The room was too warm. I needed fresh air. I defied the truth of the images, the doctor, and the fact that complications were real. I asked to look at the MRI one more time.

For the sake of argument, I agreed. Yes, the brains were mine. They were a set of images that showed my brain had been damaged and that I was in deep trouble, or at least in need of a good neurologist. The doctor reviewed each image again. I studied the frames one by one as if studying for a board exam. I put my finger on the spots and nudged the computer screen to erase them. Nothing changed. We looked at each brain again; the white spots remained. I finally said the word "infarct," then "multiple," then "embolic." The doctor reaffirmed my diagnosis and told me once more about the normal risks of surgery. The words "normal" and "risk" seemed to float in the air like my right leg and foot, insensate and unreal. They made the room feel hot and dry like the desert in Iraq. I said nothing. I wondered how Collin and our kids might react, and I didn't want them to find out. The doctor finally said the stroke could interfere with my medicine practice for a while, but that he would refer me to neurology for further testing. I didn't know what that meant, "further testing." Hadn't I already been tested enough times?

I sat back in my chair and looked around the room. Silence . . . a crack in the universe, the pure space of nothing. Then a heartbeat, then a breath, then a single isolated thought—stroke. I saw the spots of pathology and I finally understood their meaning and the meaning of the doctor when he spoke of my career. The spots were real; the pixels did not lie. I saw my life diminish as I vanished into the darkness of nothing.

Stroke School

BEVERLY DROVE ME home from the hospital and helped me back into the house. I sat in the recliner—thinking, not thinking. I didn't phone Collin to tell her what happened. Three hours later, I got up to go to the bathroom. I held on to the sofa and used the hallway walls to balance. I stared at myself in the bathroom mirror. I asked the mirror what I was going to do. No answer. I fumbled with my pants, pissed, looked in the mirror again. I saw a stranger. Back in my recliner, I rested and reread my post-op instructions. The part about sudden headaches was circled in red. I had not had a headache. I wanted a headache, something to feel inside my head. Instead, I felt nothing except perhaps the weight of a diagnosis.

Darren came home late, and when he asked me how the appointment went, I told him I was right about the stroke.

"What does that mean?" he asked.

"I'm not sure yet," I answered. "I have to see a neurologist this week. It probably means my walking will be off for a while."

"Did you call Mom?"

"No, I'll call her tomorrow."

I didn't call her. She called me—in a panic. Somebody from church found out about my stroke and the pastor put me on an e-mail prayer chain to the general congregation: "Pray for Jon Kerstetter. He has had a stroke." At her cousins' caucus in California, Collin checked her e-mail about noon and got the news. She called home immediately. I answered.

"What's going on? I just got an e-mail saying you had a stroke."

When Collin was anxious she became more direct and shortened her sentences.

"I didn't send any e-mails."

"I don't understand. Are you okay, then?"

I hesitated. There was no way to hide what had happened. "Well, not exactly. I had to go to the doctor and he said I had a stroke during the operation. It was either a blood clot from my aorta or air bubbles."

"Why aren't you in the hospital?" Her short reply wasn't a question; it was a scolding wrapped in disbelief.

As with telling her about my brain surgery, I wanted to minimize the impact of what I was saying, but she was already seeing through me. "I'm not bleeding and there is nothing that can be done now. I have to see a neurologist and Internal Medicine in the next few days."

"I'm coming home today."

"No, there is nothing you can do. The doctors repeated an MRI and there's no emergency. It's not like I need another operation. I can wait until you come home to see Neurology. It's only a few days extra."

"I don't care. I'm coming home now," she insisted.

"Don't be upset. There's nothing you can do."

"I'm not upset. Why didn't you call me when you went to the hospital?"

"I don't know. I didn't want to upset you."

"I'm not upset."

For a flicker of a second, I saw the irony in our back and forth. Having a stroke deserved some upset, maybe even demanded it. Yet we both tried to check our emotions.

I had several follow-up appointments with my internist and a neurologist. My internist, Dr. Leslie, saw me first after my stroke diagnosis. She performed a complete neurological and mental status exam. I flunked both. Dr. Leslie was tall, fit, and persistently kind. She had worked in an Internal Medicine practice in Dubuque during the same time I worked at the Finley Hospital there. She was one of the rare internists who didn't complain and moan when called to come to the ER for consults or patient admissions. Instead, she displayed an uplifting manner with her patients as well as her professional colleagues.

She tapped my knees with her percussion hammer and tested the sensation on my skin with a cotton swab and a pin.

"Close your eyes and tell me if you feel anything," she said, her voice conveying a doctor's clinical objectivity.

"I feel soft on the left. I feel sharp on the left. I feel something on my right shoulder. It's not the same as my left," I said. I didn't feel the cotton or the pin on my right arm and leg.

"Squeeze my finger," she instructed. I did. And I could tell my right hand was weak.

She walked me down the clinic hallway with a nurse at my side. My ataxic gait had not changed from my initial stroke diagnosis just a few days prior. "I walk like I'm drunk," I said.

Back in the exam room, Dr. Leslie continued with a cognitive exam. "Let's have you count backward from one hundred by sevens. I'm going to give you three words to remember for later. Do you know who the president is? Can you tell me where you are, and the date?"

I knew who I was, at least my name, and I knew I was in Iowa City, that she was my doctor and a colleague that I had worked with at the Finley Hospital in Dubuque, Iowa. I had chosen her as my internist because she had trained at the Mayo Clinic and had a reputation of excellence and thoroughness, and her patients loved her. Beyond all her medical acumen, she was a doctor who made patients feel confident that, under her care, they received the best practices in medicine. I felt the same confidence, but I also felt loss as she examined me. With each tap of the hammer, each touch of a pin and movement of a muscle or joint, I added up the deficits and felt the impact of the words the interventional radiologist had said as we looked at my MRI: "This may affect your practice of medicine." When he said that, I decided he was at best mistaken, at worst a liar. Nothing short of death could ever keep me from being a doctor. Not war or disease or accidents or life—nothing. Period. So, to hear a young doctor still in training tell me that an untoward surgical outcome could potentially damage my abilities as a doctor was simply unacceptable. But as Dr. Leslie completed her exam and discussed the findings with me, I had to consider her diagnosis to be grounded in truth, because I knew she would not tell me otherwise. When she said the word "stroke," I knew the diagnosis was real.

"Well, Dr. Kerstetter," she said calmly, "your exam is consistent with your diagnosis. I've already seen your MRI and talked with Neurology. You're going to need stroke rehab and I'm working on setting that up for you."

"How long before I can go back to work? I was planning on another deployment soon."

"We need to talk about that. Your stroke is going to prevent you from working until you recover. Your gait, your motor weakness, and your cognitive deficits—all added up means healing will take some time."

I had seen Dr. Leslie in clinical practice. She had the ability to talk with patients and their families in a way that encouraged calm understanding instead of panic or fear, even in the most critical of situations. That was how she was talking to me.

"I know, but how long is that?"

"I don't know yet. What I do know is that you've had a multifocal stroke and some of your injuries will require a long course of therapy. Some of the deficits could be permanent, but it's too early to tell. For now, I can only recommend that you remain on medical leave. You have to let yourself become a patient and let me be your doctor."

"I understand," I said. As I replied, I knew I didn't understand. Hearing Dr. Leslie say words like "permanent" and "long course" hit me hard. I knew that strokes were serious, but I wanted one that came with more options, ones that I could control.

"Good. Now I need to talk to Collin and you together," she announced.

Collin joined us, and we sat side by side in the exam room on office chairs. She patted my leg a few times before Dr. Leslie started talking. Her touch conveyed to me that she knew, just as Dr. Leslie knew, that this was going to be one of those doctor-family meetings where we talked about a prognosis because we simply had to face it and that it would lay bare the things we feared the most. I felt the heaviness of becoming a long-term stroke patient whose career was at risk. It was a force like the weight of war. I wanted to resist it, get a do-over, repeat the surgery, consider one more opinion, but the doctor in me knew that the doctor before me was right and there was no need for anything further.

"Will his symptoms get better?" Collin asked after Dr. Leslie had explained my stroke. Her question seemed to cling to the walls of the exam room. It was the core of all the questions she asked and I was afraid to ask. And she asked it with all the sincerity and concern that belied any assumptions that my recovery would be quick and easy.

"It's too early to tell. We'll likely see some improvement, but it's hard to predict how much function will be recovered and the time frame for recovery. We should know more as therapy proceeds."

"Is he at greater risk for another stroke?" Again, Collin was asking the same questions I wanted to ask but didn't.

"It depends on the underlying cause. If we find plaques in his aorta or carotid arteries or generalized arterial disease, then yes. High blood pressure adds to the risk. We need to complete our stroke workup before we know more."

There it was. I was a stroke patient. No equivocation. No bargaining. No way out. No time frame for recovery. Collin gave my arm a little squeeze and I choked up a bit and swallowed hard. I blinked back a few tears, because I was a soldier and a doctor and no goddamned stroke was going to do me in.

Dr. Leslie had already discussed my case with a neurologist and had arranged for stroke rehabilitation at the University Hospital in the departments of physical therapy and neuropsychology. A physical therapist would work on my gait and physical deficits. A neuropsychologist would work on my cognitive deficits. She also prescribed a cane to help with my balance. That one small item, a cane, angered me, and I revolted in her office.

"You can prescribe anything you want, and I honestly appreciate your help, but I'm not using a cane. No way. No how. I'm just not going to use it," I protested.

"Dr. Kerstetter, you know as well as I do the risk of falls after a stroke. Why are you resisting this? You've already fallen at home. Your balance and gait need attention."

"Well, I can walk just the way I walked in this office."

"You mean off balance and ataxic," she replied with a clinical barb. I snarled. "I don't want a cane, period."

"Why? Because you're concerned with how people will see you, or because you don't believe you need it?"

"I just don't want to feel like a stroke patient," I said. I was stubborn, resistant, and in want of an exit. I wanted to go for a walk and smoke a cigar.

"But you *are* a stroke patient. You have cerebellar and brainstem infarcts, along with the others. You've seen the MRI."

"But I don't want to have this stroke."

"That's not a choice you or I have, is it?"

THE FOLLOWING WEEK, cardiologists at the University Hospital performed trans-esophageal echocardiography (TEE) to look at my heart and aortic arch for evidence of atheromatous plaques that may have dislodged during surgery and caused my stroke. The results were normal, which meant my particular kind of stroke didn't increase my risk of another stroke. That was something positive and I clung to it as if it were news of cancer in remission. After more follow-up appointments with Dr. Leslie for monitoring my blood pressure and adjusting my meds to keep it within a normal range, she asked me about my plans for the Army and for emergency medicine.

"I suppose as soon as this is all over, I'll return to duty and continue with ER medicine or teach in the flight surgeon academy at Fort Rucker," I said.

"Did you discuss this with your Army staff?"

"Colonel Smith is informed. He said I had to stay on medical hold until rehab was finished."

"And that means no deployments, right?"

"Right . . . for now."

Dr. Leslie looked at me and leaned forward in her chair. She waited until she had my attention. "Dr. Kerstetter," she said with emphasis, "I want you to understand that your rehab is going to take longer than you expect and you need to be prepared for that. Your stroke is complicated because it affected so many different areas of your brain."

"Yes, I know." I couldn't think of anything else to say. No clinical insight. No comeback to question the validity of her counseling. Just a shallow consent, "I know," like an impudent teenager being told about exercising proper safety while driving. *Yes, I know, I know. I know how to drive. I'll be safe.* Dr. Leslie was right. My stroke was complicated. I was a doctor. I understood. I would do my time in therapy, recover, heal, six months max. That was the course set before me.

My FIRST PHYSICAL therapy appointment at the University Hospital was three weeks after surgery. The therapy rooms looked like large, open-spaced fitness centers sans bodybuilding weights and treadmills. Patients and therapists worked their sessions on mats and tables and exercise machines. My physical therapist, Peggy, who had been a physical therapist longer than I had been a doctor, introduced herself to Collin and me and told us that we would start with a baseline assessment. If quick, pressured action had characterized my practice style in the ER, then Peggy's style was exactly the opposite. She exuded a calm and unhurried manner, a different kind of clinical control than I was used to.

"There is a battery of short physical tests we need to do," Peggy said to us. "It helps us evaluate and plan your motor recovery." Her demeanor reminded me of Dr. Rhodes, my professor of pediatrics at Mayo. They both spoke with an unhurried wisdom that made me feel confident that I would learn something great if I would be patient and listen.

"I didn't know there were tests for that," I said. "I just thought we did a bunch of balance exercises." I wasn't trying to belittle therapy; I truly didn't know what would happen.

"Well, exercises are an important part of the plan, but we also need to assess your starting point and set goals based on the specific motor injuries you have. Make sense?"

It did make sense. And she explained things in a way that acknowledged my experience as a physician while at the same time bringing me up to speed with the nature of stroke rehabilitation. She talked as if therapy applied to both of us, to Collin as well as me, even though I was the one with the stroke.

"You both go through therapy," Peggy explained. "What we do here affects you both and you will both have to learn new things and work together. Collin, I'll give you instructions on how to continue therapy at home. Jon, you will have to remember that Collin is as much a part of your therapy as any physical therapist, and if you work together, you'll have a better outcome."

Peggy led me through the assessment and scored it using some clinical rubric I was unfamiliar with. The whole idea, as I understood it, was to quantify each motor deficit and then design a custom physical therapy program based on the assessment. Gait and balance were my greatest physical deficits. Peggy explained how the stroke damaged the sensory and motor cortex controlling my right leg and arm, foot, and hand, and areas of the cerebellum responsible for coordination and balance. I also had issues with left-right discrimination and fine motor skills, particularly with my right hand and fingers.

Before the end of the one-hour session, we started my first exercise, a walk between parallel bars meant to test my compensated gait. As I walked between the bars, gait belt attached and Peggy near my side, I assumed my ultra-wide stance and began to walk. I shuffled, listing toward my right with my eyes tracking the position of my feet. The experience reminded me of a medical school clinical rotation in physical medicine. I observed patients learning to walk after brain injuries, and though it was interesting to watch, I always felt uncomfortable because they struggled so hard for so little gain. When I found myself between the bars, I felt that threatening sense of struggle. Would I stare at my feet forever?

"Look up and straight ahead," Peggy coached. "Hold the bars and steady yourself. Raise your chin. Look out across the room."

"If I look up, I'll wobble and fall. I have to look at my feet to know where they are."

Peggy didn't back down. She controlled the pace of the session—calmly, yet purposefully. "I understand, but let's focus on a more natural gait and posture. Concentrate on your posture and let's make some small corrections in your stance. Try again."

I started over. The length of the bars was no more than ten feet but it felt like ten yards, not because of pain, but because I couldn't balance. *Focus*, I told myself as I set up my stance at the end of the bars. I started again without holding on and tried to bring my feet closer together. Before Peggy could stop me, I took two bold steps. Bang! I crashed against the right-side bar. Peggy grabbed the gait belt and kept me from falling. Collin watched from a chair across the room. She watched intently but didn't say anything. I could tell she was scared. I was scared too, but I didn't want to show it.

"Use the bars to hold on," Peggy insisted. "Lift your head. If you feel out of balance, stop and gain control. Pay attention so you don't get hurt."

"I *am* paying attention." When I said it, I knew we had different meanings. And with those floundering steps between the bars, I saw myself reduced to an infant learning to walk, so dependent on the steady encouragement of parents. I didn't want to be that dependent kind of person, but I could hardly claim to be independent.

"Start again. This time use the bars. Get your feet settled, find your balance, then take a step."

I stood with my hands gripping the bars, looked across the therapy room with my chin up, and took a step with my left foot. My right foot was slow to follow, but it did follow. I cheated and looked down to see where I had planted my feet. My left foot was just a toe ahead of the right, nothing close to a normal walking step. Peggy asked me to look up and said that was a good step.

"Much better," she said." Let's do another length and finish."

"That's all?" I asked.

"We had a good start. Let's finish strong and we'll go over your home exercises. I'll see you back in two days."

Before she let us go, Peggy explained the testing and her findings. The tests related to central nervous system control over muscle groups and motor functions. Walking, she reminded us, took significant skill and control, and brain damage that interfered with that learned skill would manifest itself in the tests. Mine was not an unusual case—complicated, but not unusual in that motor, sensory, and cerebellar damage came from an embolic source of injury. She cautioned us that progress would take time.

"This is one of those fields in medicine where progress is often measured in inches and months—not in all cases, but in many," she said. "I suspect we'll be working together for several months or longer. You will need to give yourself time and permission to heal."

Permission to heal. I had never heard that before. Time I understood. Permission I did not. I hadn't given myself permission to have a stroke. Why would I need to give myself permission to heal? I said I understood and nodded my head, yes.

I SCHEDULED SESSIONS three times a week—Monday, Wednesday, and Friday—for the first few months, then two days a week, Monday and Thursday. On the calendar, I labeled the appointments "Stroke School." The first weeks were hell. They were not as physically painful as I had predicted they would be, but they were painful emotionally and mentally. Every exercise reinforced that I had neurological deficits. Every session reminded me that I belonged to a special group of patients—stroke patients. And the reminder carried a clinical significance that was impossible to shake; that some deficits might remain forever.

In addition to the gait training in the parallel bars, I walked on a blue taped line stuck on the floor, tandem walking. A physical therapy student helped. Peggy and the student gripped my gait belt as I brought my feet closer together and took a step on the tape. I never managed more than a single step before I fell off the line. The instant I brought my feet together, ataxia took control and the exercise degenerated into preventing a fall. If I was able to take a step, it was either off the line or crooked. I looked like I was taking a roadside sobriety test from a highway patrol officer. I was grateful that we spent only five minutes or so with that particular exercise.

I practiced walking through a slalom of tiny orange cones. The soft weave challenged my attention and balance. We alternated the slalom course with walking down a hallway with pictures hung every ten feet or so. When I got in rhythm and my gait actually moved me forward without weaving to either side, Peggy would ask me to look at a picture as I walked. My head always aimed straight ahead and tilted down so I could watch my foot placement. When I turned to look, my feet froze and my trunk wobbled in ataxic gyrations. I couldn't do both. It was all or none, one or the other, walk or chew gum. We did that art walk every session for three months, and whenever I looked at a picture, my legs stopped working. Just for a change, Peggy would ask me a question as I walked. Same result.

"So, tell me your name and address."

"Jon Kerstetter. Two-three-eight-eight . . ."

And before the words left my mouth, as they were forming in my brain, my legs halted their staccato march down the hall and I would weave back and forth, stuck to the floor like a field mouse caught in a glue trap. Peggy got me to push through with my gait, but when I was able to do so, my words came out garbled or stuttered or I missed parts of my address. I spoke one word, took one step, stopped, spoke another word, then took one more step. All or none, sometimes both, but chopped into fragments of words and steps. Peggy said the choppiness was from brain neurons wiring a new connection for unattended gait, like when an infant learns to walk. I didn't know about that, but what I did know was how much concentration it took to walk down a hallway without falling over, especially when it involved dividing my attention over two tasks at once. I got angry with myself and said "Shit" or "Dammit" when I couldn't walk and talk. Peggy reminded me that I was making progress and needed to breathe when I walked and look up and not overthink it. "You're being too hard on yourself," she said. "Remember to give yourself permission to heal."

Despite the sort of droning pace of physical therapy, Peggy made it engaging and even fun at times. When I walked the slalom cones, she asked me to pretend I was a race car driver or a skier. Sometimes she walked me into the large therapy room, where many therapists worked on patients in an open space. I saw other patients with injuries and strokes. Some, I could see, had deficits far greater than I had, and it made me grateful that my stroke was not worse.

When Peggy wasn't looking, I watched the clock in the therapy room. It always seemed stuck. I suspected that she had rigged it for longer sessions, but they always timed out after fifty minutes, after my mind was spent like a bullet fired on the range. At the end of each session, she offered me water and talked about my healing and my progress. I wasn't always sure I believed her, but I kept going back for more. "See you in a few days," she said as she reminded me to breathe. "Take a deep breath."

The same week I began physical therapy, I started cognitive therapy with a neuropsychology team just down the hall from Peggy's office. Collin dropped me off and promised to pick me up afterward. The staff explained in the first session how they measured cognitive deficits and then worked to rebuild compensatory strategies and possibly new neural connections for patients with brain damage. It sounded like the same treatment philosophy as for physical therapy.

In the first session, I completed a series of diagnostic tests and an interview with the neuropsychologist and therapist. The cognitive testing took hours. A neuropsych technician and a graduate student worked on my case. One tested me while the other scored the tests and made clinical notes. The technician asked me to remember and repeat words from a list that she read. "Ball, train, toy, apple, couch, book, banana . . ." She read until she finished a list of thirty or so words. As I concentrated on remembering, I repeated the words in my brain, the first word, then the second, and then the third. By the time she read the third or fourth word, I forgot the first word. When she read the fifth and sixth words, I had forgotten all the previous words. When asked to repeat them all back at the end, I struggled to remember any of the words and recalled only three or four. We repeated the process several times, same list, same sequence. Same recall phenomenon. The tech kept reading and I kept forgetting. After three trials I said, "I can't remember shit." The tech told me to do the best I could and not to worry about it. It was a diagnostic test and there were no right answers. But, for me, there *were* right answers, the answers that recalled all the words I was supposed to remember.

I added numbers incorrectly, spelled words incorrectly, read passages from one-page short stories incorrectly. The tech timed my reading. I answered questions about the meaning and content of the stories. *Dammit! I know how to read. Why are they testing me?* I drew a clock and she asked me to draw noon and six and three and nine. I did it correctly. *Ha! I showed her. I wasn't so stupid.* When she asked me to draw nine-thirty, I got the minute hand mixed up, and did it again on six-thirty. I couldn't put blocks in sequence—building blocks, the kind that children play with. *Just put the damn blocks in order.* When the grad student wrote things down, I knew it meant I was stupid and he was making note of it. We took a break halfway through and I wanted to go home, because I didn't see the point of taking a test that I couldn't have prepared for. "No right answers," they insisted. *Yeah right*, I told myself. *If there weren't right answers, why are we doing the test?*

At the conclusion, the staff neuropsychologist visited with me and asked questions about my work, home, and family life. What kind of medicine did I practice? What was my job in the military? Did I drink or use drugs? How did I cope with illness and stress? Did I know I had had a stroke? Did I know what that meant for my long-term prognosis? Had I ever been depressed or sought mental health treatment? *Hell yes, I knew what a stroke is, and hell no, I'm not crazy.* After the barrage of questions the neuropsychologist introduced me to my cognitive therapist. Her name was Cher, like the singer, and she was half my age. She had a tattoo on her ankle and she spoke confidently and professionally. And despite my professional doubts about therapists in general and about cognitive therapy and neuropsychology in particular, she made me feel at ease. Maybe she read my hesitation as I looked around her room; maybe she was sensitive to our age and professional differences. However she knew I was skeptical, she addressed it without a blink.

"Dr. Kerstetter, my name is Cher and I'll be working with you." She offered a handshake as she took control. "Have a seat and let's go over a few things and then I'll see you next week with your results. I understand you've had a stroke and that you're a physician."

"Yes, I had an aneurysm and surgery didn't go as planned." I glanced around her office. Books and professional journals about neurology and neuropsychology filled the bookshelves, and she had several models of color-coded plastic brains.

"I see your wife isn't here today, and that's not unusual for the testing day. Will she be joining us next week?" Cher took notes as she talked, but she also made eye contact that kept me on track.

"She's planning on it, but she had a prior commitment today."

"Good. I just want to emphasize how important it is to have her attend that session."

"Sure. How many sessions will I have," I said impatiently.

"Depends." With a single word, Cher defined the essence of therapy. It did depend—and there was no amount of my impatience that would make it go faster.

"Oh. I thought it might be a set number, like ten or so. I don't know anything about this kind of therapy, so I don't know what to expect."

"Everybody has different needs, so it's hard tell exactly how we'll proceed and how long your therapy will last. Any questions you have of me?"

"Well, I don't know exactly what you're going to do. I know I did poorly on the tests. Are you going to retest me?"

She gave a courteous smile. "It's not a matter of doing poorly or not. They're diagnostic tests. They give us information to guide our therapy. Yes, we retest to monitor your progress. I can tell you're concerned about the results, but please don't be. They are a starting place and, yes, they make everybody self-conscious about their intelligence."

I didn't want to ask direct questions about a damaged intellect, because doing so would have revealed my fear that the tests had marked me as unintelligent. It wasn't that I didn't trust Cher, but I didn't trust

the testing, the process, and the significance of doing poorly on diagnostic tests. Maybe that actually translated into a lack of trust in her.

Instead of dwelling on the issue of damaged intellect, Cher turned
the conversation to my roles in the Army and in emergency medicine
and asked me to explain each of them. She sat forward and listened attentively as she took notes.

When I left her office, I considered her professional enough but still
much too young for a therapist. And I wondered if a therapist named
Cher with an ankle tattoo and a room full of books and models of the
human brain could help me recover. I decided she probably could not,
but that I would give it a go anyway. I'd try the whole neuropsych-
testing, cognitive-restructuring, mind-twisting, and suspicion-raising
thing called stroke rehab, and in the end, if it didn't work, well at least
I tried.

THE STAFF NEUROPSYCHOLOGIST met with me for the first half of
the next weekly session. He reviewed my test results and walked me
through a list of cognitive injuries and outlined a therapy plan for
each one. Several deficits shared a common theme, the loss of memory. Short-term memory had been markedly affected, as had long-
term memory. Defects in executive functioning were pronounced and
kept me from structuring and organizing information for complex
problem solving. Fine motor skills, elicited by the metal peg exercise,
showed strain, especially on the right side. There was more. Reading
speed and comprehension measured in the third percentile—third,
not thirtieth. My attention and focus resembled that seen in a patient
with attention deficit disorder. And there were concerns about a con-
founding issue of PTSD from my recent combat tours, which to my
thinking was not an issue. So, by the end of the first thirty minutes of
that second cognitive therapy session, I had been given a crap load of
things to consider about my brain and my stroke, if considering was
even something I could have done or wanted to do, given my cognitive status. As the neuropsychologist highlighted each specific deficit,
together they seemed to grow like an accretion of malignant cells in

my brain, all wanting to invade as many normal cells as they could and render me useless and untreatable.

In the second half of the session, Cher asked me about my reaction to the test results as she took notes. "Tell me about your test results," she said.

I couldn't answer her question spontaneously because I didn't yet know what my reaction should be. Should I have been pissed or depressed or sad? Should I have been thankful that I was still alive and that my stroke hadn't killed me outright or dropped me into a coma? Maybe I should have been grateful that I wasn't strapped in a chair and shitting my pants or drooling on my shirt. I didn't know what to think because I wasn't thinking. I was revisiting my life, the one I knew as a doctor and a soldier and the one where things generally went the way I wanted them to go. And I was questioning whether my brain damage was more like the truth of a broken arm or more like the truth of an amputation.

I finally answered: "It sounds like I have no brain."

"Oh, you have a brain," she said thoughtfully and gently, "and it's full of valuable information and experiences."

Her words seemed to counterbalance the emotional pain I was feeling. Cher put her pen on her desk and made eye contact. "Dr. Kerstetter, it's important for you to understand that a stroke does not make you less intelligent. It makes memory formation and recall difficult, but we'll work together to help you compensate. A stroke can't make you less than the person you are." Her message to me was as powerful as it was comforting. I needed her insights to unravel my fears. I was scared for my future, for my brain and my life, and I needed to hear and understand exactly the message she had for me, because without it, even hope was broken.

In the next weekly visit, Cher started me on list making and journaling. It was a technique to pull me into the therapeutic process and to get my mind reengaged on the skill of focusing on details. I was lousy at it. Sporadic. Incoherent. Sloppy and incomplete. But I did it. I wrote pages of notes and fragments of thoughts. I made rudimentary lists. They were supposed to help me with executive functioning and ordering of tasks, something of a paper brain. If I didn't make a daily list of things to do, I often did nothing except go to doctor or therapy appointments. I was to review the lists with Collin each night or morning. I usually forgot and Collin had to rescue me. I tried an electronic PDA with a calendar and a to-do list and a reminder app. I got it all mixed up with a paper list and a desk calendar where I wrote appointments. I said "Shit" and "Damn" and tore up my lists when they didn't match and I couldn't figure out which one was accurate. Cher would go over my list making in the session. About ten weeks into therapy, I grew overly upset in a session when she mentioned lists.

"Were you able to track your appointments and tasks this week?" she asked.

"No," I answered abruptly. "I don't need a list." I wasn't trying to be mean-spirited or caustic, but it had become apparent to me that my mind was wild and hurt and on the loose. I couldn't make a list, much less keep track of one.

Cher paused and looked at me. "Tell me what's going on," she said.

"This isn't working," I blurted. "I would have been better off dying in Iraq. At least it would have had a purpose. Now I can't even manage a list, let alone a patient." I stood from my chair. I wanted to run or hide, but all I could do was weave in my ataxic stance. Cher asked me gently to sit back down. I felt trapped and wanted to free myself from therapy because I was a soldier and a doctor and if anybody could fight their way out of a stroke, it should have been me.

"Let's just sit for a moment," Cher said calmly. "Take some slow deep breaths." After I settled down, she continued. "And how many weeks have you been making lists now?"

I didn't answer. I looked at the plastic brains on the bookshelves.

"I think you've been doing it for less time than you would give a patient in your care," she said.

"I don't want to be a patient and I don't want my kids to see me like this. I feel dead!" And when I said it, I put my head in my hands and stared down at her desk and said nothing for the longest time, and I bit the tip of my tongue to keep from showing emotion.

She let me sit in silence for a while, then finally said, "But, Dr. Kerstetter, you're *not* dead. You are still a doctor and you are still a soldier, and you're experienced and intelligent. A stroke cannot make you less than who you are. Do you understand that?"

When I heard her words, I wanted to weep and wail and let my tears finally run free and fill up her therapy room and wash away my anguish and fear and loss. And all my suspicions about Cher's lack of military knowledge and her tattoo and her age, her profession and the fact that she was not a doctor, all disappeared. She told me I was grieving for the parts of my body and brain that were injured, and that I likely feared I might never recover and would never be a doctor or a soldier again. She was right. Exactly right. And in that session I finally understood clearly that I had clung to those identities, soldier and doctor, because I felt they made me who I was and a stroke had broken me. But there I was, still alive—injured, to be sure, yet still quite capable of thinking and fighting and moving forward.

Before we concluded, Cher said she was fortunate to work with me and asked me to explain some things about military medicine and how doctors treated patients in a war zone. I asked her for a marker and said it would be easier to draw her a diagram on her whiteboard. As I drew a line sketch of a military battalion and the multiple echelons of care, I was surprised that I could remember details about the military. After five minutes I had drawn a schematic of an Army medical unit in war and had explained the medical evacuation system, how we transported patients from the battlefield to military hospitals in the States. She thanked me and said what a great job I had done. The next week when I returned, the drawings were still in place. She asked me to expand on the explanations: "Tell me the difference between a battalion and a platoon, between the responsibilities of a captain, a major, and a colonel. Where is the forward edge of the battle? What is asymmetric warfare? What does a flight surgeon do exactly?" I answered her questions, and it took the entire session; and when I was done, I felt like a flight surgeon again, but I was a bit puzzled about my answers.

"How could I recall those military details and no other details about medicine or what my wife told me to do this morning?" I asked.

"All strokes are different," she said. "You have mixed deficits. Your medical knowledge is most likely still intact, but the neural pathways have been disrupted and are not easily accessible. Right now, you have short- and long-term memory deficits and neither are complete, but you also have attention deficits, which makes things trickier to manage."

She pulled up my MRI on her screen and we counted the infarcts and the different levels of brain involvement: cortical, white matter, gray matter, motor, sensory, mid-brain, cerebellar, and brainstem. "If you had a patient with that MRI, would you tell them to expect a simple, uncomplicated recovery?" she asked.

"Not really," I said. "I see your point." And I did see, or at least I gained some initial insight. I began to understand that my stroke had hurt me more than I deemed possible and that ongoing therapy was essential to my recovery.

"Dr. Kerstetter, you'll get through this," Cher said confidently. "You have a great capacity for learning. Look at what you've done in your life. Yes, you have some significant neurological deficits—nobody here is going to tell you otherwise—but you also have a therapist and a team of doctors who are willing to help you. And we need you on that team."

That session was a crossing point, a breakthrough. The hard shell of my professional personality cracked just enough to allow some room for a therapist to draw out my military and medical experience as a tool in our therapeutic strategy. And although I didn't immediately transform into a model patient and didn't automatically rid myself of denying the reality of my stroke and its sequelae, I did make a mental crossing that allowed me to trust a therapist, and that, I would eventually learn, helped me move from one stage of healing to another, from denial toward acceptance.

Reading

THE NEXT WEEK after our breakthrough session, Cher started me on a rehabilitative reading plan. My first task was to read a novel with a simple plot—follow-up appointment in one week. I was supposed to read it with Collin and discuss the book as we went through it. Cher intentionally left the choice of the book to me. At home, I decided to do things on my own. There was just something too remedial about the assignment, and I balked at having to read with Collin. She had spent time in our neighborhood grade school as a reading mentor. I didn't need mentoring or a reading coach, so I chose a book about theoretical physics and string theory. As a college student, I was fascinated by the subatomic universe and the cosmos, so why not start in earnest to understand it? But after "reading" numerous chapters about folding gravity and time warps and vibrating subatomic strings, I couldn't explain a single concept to Collin or Cher. I probably could not have understood string theory prior to my stroke. I didn't understand my reasoning for selecting a physics book, but it may have reflected a belief that I was above reading therapy. The appropriateness of my selection, Cher pointed out, was one of the goals of the task.

I didn't immediately give up on string theory, thinking perhaps my brain just needed a little warm-up time. I kept on pushing through it even though nearly every word was incomprehensible. In a follow-up appointment, Cher was less than impressed, maybe even stern. I did think, however, she was amazed at my tenacity, however misplaced it was. She gave me high marks for denial and zero marks for coming to grips with the truth. Again she pulled up my pre- and post-stroke

MRIs on her computer screen and asked me if I could interpret the images. I could, with some difficulty. I noted the numerous small lesions of dead brain on the cerebral cortex and in the midbrain and on the brainstem. I muddled through what the lesions meant in terms of brain function and how a person with that sort of brain would experience cognitive difficulties. She asked me to help her construct a therapeutic plan for cognitive rehab.

"That's not my field," I said. "But I'm familiar with emergency neurology and the basic neurosciences."

"Good. So let's try this: I'll give some general ideas and you can tell me if you think the plan is reasonable or not."

She asked me if reading would be a good task for cognitive rehabilitation.

"Yes, that's a good idea," I answered.

"Speed of task processing. Slow or fast?"

"Well, you need to go slow at first."

"Any particular reason?" she asked.

I thought I could sense her direction. "You have to avoid confusion. If the patient gets confused by the therapy, then it's not therapeutic."

"Good. Good observation."

My mind wandered off a bit. *Ha, I knew I could do this. I'm so damned smart. I should be a therapist.*

"Graded difficulty?"

"Huh?"

"Difficulty," she said. "Should there be a gradual or graded difficulty in the exercises?"

"Oh, I was back on slow versus fast."

"Okay, let's focus here. You with me?"

I think I blushed a bit. "Yep."

"Would you introduce new reading material based on difficulty level, with basic reading first?"

"Yes. You have to bring the patient along slowly and then advance the difficulty as progress is made."

"And where would string theory fit into the plan, if at all?"

"Ah . . . at the very end?"

"And where do you have it?"

I hesitated. *Therapists are a sneaky crowd. You have to watch them carefully.*

"Okay, I got it," I said. I wanted to move on, change directions.

Cher continued. "And can you tell me the name of the patient on the computer screen?"

Silence. Silence for a long while. I looked at the plastic brains on her shelves. I wanted to hide from that name on the screen. Instead, I swallowed hard and faced her.

"I need you to read the name on the MRI for me," she said quietly.

"It's me. Jon Kerstetter. They left off 'MD.'"

"Dr. Kerstetter, you're right. You're still a doctor, but you have a brain injury just like some of the soldiers you treated. Only this time *you're* the patient and you have to run with that. That's what we have to work with, and it's going to take all your cooperation to get this patient better."

"I still don't think it's me. I mean, I know it's me on the screen and I know it's me when I try to walk and read. But I keep thinking tomorrow I'll wake up and find that everybody was mistaken or that I'm caught in some crazy dream."

"Would you like to talk with the surgeon or the neurologist to verify the findings?"

"No. I know where this is coming from. I'm the one who treats other soldiers. I'm a doctor. I'm supposed to give medical care, not get it. Army doctors don't get hurt. They can't get hurt. Everything is backward. I'm not supposed to be the patient."

"But you *are* the patient. That's *your* brain we see. What do you want to do?"

I paused and looked at the MRI on her computer screen. The images were real; she was real; therapy was real. I tapped my leg and felt nothing.

"Can I start over?"

— — —

FOR MY NEXT book I choose Ayn Rand, *Atlas Shrugged*. Same problem as string theory but without the math. We had the same discussion in therapy again, only Cher pulled a plastic life-size model of the human brain down from her bookcase and asked me to name the various color-coded parts. The model split down the middle in a sagittal plane that showed the left and right hemispheres. I struggled but was able to name about a third of them. I felt so smug and so smart. Then she pulled up my MRI on her computer and asked me to find my injuries and point them out on the plastic brain. I used a pointer to show her the spots on the model that corresponded to the spots on the MRI. *I'm so damned smart. I could be a neuroscientist.* My mind wandered to stroke patients I had treated in the emergency room.

"Focus," she said. She told me to pretend she was a patient with that kind of brain injury and then asked me to explain the things she might experience and what prognosis she might expect. I did so, but with a bit more struggling. Again I knew what she was up to.

Sure enough, she asked me to explain what to expect in terms of the time it would take for healing and recovery. I told her how slowly brain function tended to recover, and that she might see little progress at first, but that it was important to keep trying and to not give up and to trust her therapist. I choked and stammered a bit because I knew it was a role-playing exercise and I was really not talking to her but to myself. But I wanted to be honest with her, as if she were my patient, and so I told her the facts as gently as I could.

"Cher," I said, my voice sincere and starting to break. "There's no question about the significance of your stroke. That, you can't change. But what you can change is how you do your therapy. That will impact your recovery more than anything else."

She sat attentively as if she were a real patient and she nodded her head in agreement. "You're absolutely right," she said. I continued by telling her the importance of working together with her therapist; then we concluded the role-play.

She was genuinely moved. "I could sense by the way you talked to me that you are an excellent and caring physician. If you were really my doctor, I would have been confident with your approach. It's obvious that you care for your patients," she said.

I had to breathe slowly as I considered what she said. I did care and I wanted nothing more than to continue caring.

"I have a question for you," she asked me gently. "Can you give yourself the same care and concern as you gave your own patients?" When she asked, her eyes welled up just a bit, and I sensed that she touched the heart of my struggle. I needed to care for myself the same way I had cared for my patients. It was that "permission to heal" that Peggy had mentioned. And when I realized that she had exposed my weakness, I wanted to yield to the power of therapy. I wanted her to see inside my brain, into the parts that held my fear and pain and confusion, into the spots that were broken and into the areas left undamaged. I wanted her to see all the things I had done in war and to understand all the crossings I had made in becoming the person I was. I wanted her to know how much I needed my soldier and doctor identities, because I was dying inside without them.

Spontaneously I said, "My brain hurts." But I really meant to say, "My soul hurts," that my innermost being was lost not knowing who I was, what I was, or if I would continue as a doctor and a soldier or as a patient forever. I said nothing more. Cher said she understood. I believed her.

She assigned me a book of short stories for my next appointment. As I listened to her instructions and looked at the plastic brains, then back at her, I understood that I was a patient whose life was redefined as much by stroke as it was by war. I saw myself as a boy and a doctor, a soldier and a survivor, and finally as a patient with a stroke. And in that compound glimpse of myself, I sensed the polar ambiguities that had come to define my life, and I knew I faced both limitation and possibility.

READING CONTINUED TO challenge me over the many months that followed. It was a struggle of distractions, the deletion of words, the substitution of words, the incomprehension of meanings, and the inability to discern plot and story development. I could generally understand only three- to four-page stories; anything longer gave me difficulty. I wrote notes about the characters and the meaning of individual paragraphs. Literary imagery and metaphors often took me off into different directions that the story never intended, some of the directions triggered by words that brought back memories of war in Iraq. I didn't know then that my reading would recover so slowly, that it would take more than two years to read the entire 1,600-page anthology of short fiction compiled by Ann Charters, *The Story and Its Writer*. I read classic stories by Chekhov, Hawthorne, Poe, and Conrad, and more recent stories by Sandra Cisneros and Sherman Alexie. I read them every day. I underlined sentences I didn't understand, which in the beginning were most. I read some sentences and paragraphs four or five times, some even more. And when they made no sense, I closed the book and went for a walk with my cane. Sometimes I imagined my boyhood and the mountains where I hiked. Life was simpler then, or so it seemed. In high school I read books like *The Catcher in the Rye, Franny and Zooey, The Pearl, Nineteen Eighty-four,* and *Animal Farm*. I used to thrive on literature that challenged my intellect and the norms of society and culture. Reading was so enticing, enriching, and natural, a skill as essential as walking. When I compared the kind of reader I had been in medical school with the kind I had become after a stroke, I felt like Charlie in *Flowers for Algernon*: a man rendered childlike by a developmental brain disorder, then treated by scientists whose experiments held out a chance at recovery, only to eventually fail. In the end, despite a period of hope and improvement, Charlie regressed to his childlike world.

I never thought my life would regress. I saw myself as a person who would always move forward to challenge new boundaries. I was educated, smart, and self-confident. I was a thinker and reader and explorer. I believed in the substance of human will and the science of the universe. Electrons always spun in molecules, planets stayed in their orbits, medicine cured disease—and none of it wavered, not even one ripple. But then there was a complete reordering of my ordered universe and, instantly, simple words that had served me so well in transforming my life evaded any effort at comprehension. My brain could only quiver at words and their meanings, and the damaging effects of a stroke loomed larger than any cosmic storm.

I continued making efforts to read. I made slow, visible progress despite my stumbling comprehension. Many of the stories in the Charters anthology were simply too complex, but I muddled through. The good stories, the ones I understood and could retain and retell, I read several times, only to forget them within a few days. A new story displaced one read just days before. If I didn't read a story in one sitting, I had to start over because I had no context for a mid-story paragraph. But the literary energy and the human connection and the ingenious insight of the stories were enough to keep me going. And on those days when comprehension evaded me, I went to the city library and walked among the stacks. I picked out books, fanned the pages, and smelled the ink and the paper. I lingered on pictures and reminisced about my first school-age library trip. When I finished with the fiction or nonfiction section, I perused the children's shelves and checked out *Charlotte's Web* and *The Prince and the Pauper* and other similar titles. Sometimes I read them there in the library at a secluded table, embarrassed that I might be seen mouthing words and reading at a child's level. Other times I took them home and read them secretly while Collin was at work. I laughed in the places where I was supposed to laugh and was serious or sad when appropriate. The stories moved right along in a linear plot. They pulled me into their niches of time and consequence, just as they had when I read them as a child. That was fine with me and far more insightful than string theory. And I knew if I could read a children's book, well, at least that was a start.

Winter Dream

I N   T H E   M I X of specialists taking care of me, Psychiatry got involved in my case because there was a concern about depression. I was told over forty percent of stroke patients developed depression. I didn't feel depressed in the clinical sense—loss, yes; clinical depression, no. In my first appointment with Psychiatry, the resident psychiatrist asked me the usual questions about suicide and mood and feelings and libido. My answers must have been too terse, because he asked if I was upset that I had had a stroke.

I responded abruptly. "Wouldn't you be upset if you had a stroke?"

"Yes, I would," he said. "That's why you're here, to make sure your mood and reactions don't interfere with your ability for recovery. We are part of your therapy team."

"Okay, but I'm not depressed. And my libido is fine."

I didn't want to talk about my mood or my feelings. I knew how I felt; I knew the pain of a stroke, every emotional and physical thread. Stirring it up only risked more pain. As an alternative, the psychiatrist offered a low-dose antidepressant, citing an academic study of stroke patients on low-dose therapy as recovering better than patients receiving a placebo. I consented to the treatment because the benefits seemed real enough, but I still resisted the monthly follow-up appointments and the persistent efforts to peel back the layers of feelings about my stroke.

In November, Colonel Smith and the medical command at Rock Island Arsenal requested an assessment regarding my prognosis and likely timeframe for return to duty. My therapists, Dr. Leslie, and the neuropsychologist were asked to respond with a written summary.

They visited with me about their assessments and it became clear that they considered me non-deployable for military service. The neuro-psychologist summed up their position.

"Dr. Kerstetter, what is your level of confidence that you could return to duty as a military doctor right now?" he asked. He was probing, infiltrating.

"Well, none. I know I'm not ready yet," I said.

"And we don't think you are ready either. It's too early in your recovery. Colonel Smith has a sense about that, but we need to document your prognosis for the Army."

"Yes, I know," I responded coldly.

"Your clinical findings are already documented in the chart, but in summary I am going to recommend that you not practice medicine or be deployed until you have recovered enough cognitive and physical ability. Do you understand the reasoning?"

I responded with a stare and a pointed question. "You're concerned about *me* practicing medicine?"

"Yes, but do you know why?" That was a clinical trick to make patients own a decision—throw it back on them, get them to voice the hard logic of a difficult outcome. "Well, I suppose you think I can't remember how. I know I'm not ready to return to medical practice or active duty. I know that. Colonel Smith knows that and if you document that in the chart, the license board will know it. They could suspend my license."

"I'm not saying you cannot return to active duty eventually, but not right now and not in the immediate future—not until you have some significant recovery of function."

I wanted to curse but decided against it. "I get it. I need more progress."

"More function," he responded.

I wasn't sure I knew the difference. His semantics were bullshit to me. I knew exactly what I needed. Time. I finally said I agreed and left it at that. And I judged him as a bastard, because he gave the Army the idea I wasn't fit for duty, and he told me I wasn't fit to practice medicine, and goddamn him and the therapists and the psychiatrist who said I might be depressed. What the hell did they know? Wouldn't they be depressed if they were me? Hell yes, I knew my brain was injured, but how about some time? Give me time to heal and I would do the work. All I needed was time.

THROUGHOUT DECEMBER I wrestled with the notion of non-deployability and with a possible hold on my medical career. My right shoulder degenerated and it gave me persistent pain. The fall I had taken the first week of my stroke had torn my right shoulder rotator cuff, and my orthopedic surgeon advised surgery. We scheduled it for the first week of January 2008. It would be my tenth surgery in twenty-four months since returning from Iraq.

Our children came home for Christmas and we had a wonderful family celebration. They all put their money together and bought me a motorized recliner with the standard wooden lever on the side replaced by buttons to press for raising my legs up or down. They were all supportive and concerned about my surgery. I didn't want us to dwell on my health, but rather on our family Christmas.

The January surgery did go well, except for a temporary setback in my balance, which, if I had the sense to think it through, should have been expected. I stayed an extra day in the hospital and was discharged in the afternoon of day three. The orthopedic surgeon was satisfied with the surgical repair and arranged for physical therapy to start in the following six weeks. I had the usual incisional pain and post-op pain that kept me down for a week or so. I slept in my new recliner and Collin watched after me and gave me meds on schedule. I wore a shoulder immobilizer that secured my arm to my chest to aid in healing.

On post-op day four, my second day home from surgery, I felt good, with only moderate pain. Collin helped me to the bathroom and had to pull down my pants and hold me up while I pissed. I told her I could handle it, but she insisted I might fall. I was weaving from my pain meds and stroke and that concerned me a bit. I slept off and on throughout the day. Collin woke me about 8:00 to get me ready for bed. After helping me in the bathroom she got me settled back in my recliner and covered me with a blanket. She started the gas fireplace and gave me a pain pill and my little brass bell with stern instructions to ring it if I needed help. She left the hallway light on and promised to wake me at midnight for another dose of medication. A kiss, a gentle hug, the tight snug of my blanket, and I lay back to sleep.

I DREAMT ABOUT the helicopter crash of my second tour in Iraq.

An Apache and a Black Hawk collide in the desert in northern Iraq. The survivors huddle in a desert ravine, dark of night, fifty miles from their base. All are injured. Four soldiers from the Black Hawk maintain a defensive position. They have limited ammunition. The commander orders a security and medic team to respond. The teams move immediately to the crash site to recover the injured soldiers. I command the medical team.

The response team is a flight of three aircraft, two Black Hawks and one Apache gunship. The soldiers load into the helicopters and begin the flight to the crash site. The flight proceeds in a flurry of movement. The medics buckle in. Engines start. We fly off into the night. The pilot makes a radio announcement: "We are five minutes out. There is intermittent small-arms fire at the site. Expect a hot LZ." He starts another string of updates, then abruptly chops his radio transmission. The aircraft jinks hard left. Several of us slam our arms and heads against the sides of the aircraft. I anticipate a warning light or a fire. Nothing happens. I expect to lose altitude, but our Black Hawk continues to fly. I catch a glimpse of red tracers on my side of the aircraft. Fear mounts.

Time to LZ: 30 seconds. Focus. Clear the landing zone. Initiate medical intervention. Recover the dead. The aircraft attitude pitches upward to slow the helicopter. The pilot hovers just above the ground, then finally touches down. We run straight out of the doors to our 9:00 and 3:00 positions.

As we move out, my feet sense a new kind of threat—rocks. Rocks scattered in icy mud. Rocks that break soldiers' legs and ankles. They lie in wait for the exact moment when they can break some unsuspecting bones. They can wait for years. Rocks wait for soldiers in just that way; then they strike and they never give much warning. My mind snaps back to the mission.

The medic team is two hundred yards from the crash site. I move slower than I want. I curse the rocks and the mud. I feel a sense of panic and a need to pick up the pace. Don't panic. Stay calm. Lead the mission. The team humps the first fifty yards without incident. Sweat now runs down my forehead and neck. I am hot. The cold desert air hits my skin and chills me. My legs feel heavy and tire too quickly. I keep pushing forward until I step on a rock and twist to my right. I slow the pace of the team and signal them to advance with caution. I look back toward our insertion point and forward toward the objective.

A sudden burning sensation floods over my chest and right shoulder. I feel my heart pounding and pulse quickening. Sweat beads on my forehead and then drips in my eyes. I signal a halt and crouch low to the ground. There's a painful swelling over the front of my deltoid. It will not budge. I tell myself to disregard it and keep pushing forward.

I struggle to move the team toward the downed aircraft. My mind races forward one hundred yards. I keep the team on target with the shooters on the flanks. I smell aviation fuel and the chemical smoke of an aircraft fire. I see the burning Apache.

Sweat flows from my neck and forehead. Suddenly my footing is off-center. My balance tilts and I can't adjust. I fall forward, striking my shoulder on a rock. My right shoulder erupts with burning, ripping pain. I imagine the pain that a tracer round causes when it hits human flesh. The pain disappears. I feel feverishly hot. Pain stabs my shoulder again. I tell myself I'm hit, but I hear no crack of enemy fire. I hear nothing at all. My arm is still moving. The pain fades but then flares up quickly and tears at my shoulder. I hesitate. I am lost in confusion. I recover from the fall and holster my pistol after wiping mud from the grip. I recheck the medics. They follow haphazardly. I yell, "Don't bunch up. Keep moving." One of the medics fades in and out of view, trudging forward, then dissolving backward. The other medics are advancing at a crawl. I feel my skin tighten. My heart beats so loudly I focus on its rhythm.

I advance so quickly that I outpace my team. I halt and wait. The medics are moving too slowly. My right shoulder spasms in pain. I cannot move. I signal the medics to advance to my position. They finally reach me in what seems like hours instead of seconds.

"What the hell is going on?" No answer. "Somebody answer me." I clip my speech. "Let's do this mission. Move."

The shooters are on the flanks, two on the left and two on the right, medics in the middle. I take point. Docs never take point. I take point. We advance once again. My mind runs a checklist. I advance another twenty-five yards. The team is on target. Walk in the park. Stop!

Seventy-five yards at my ten o'clock, I see movement. I signal my team to halt and take cover. Eight Iraqi insurgents come into view and are moving directly toward the downed aircrew. They have a grenade launcher. The Apache flying cover is not engaging. It doesn't matter. I am in position. I need to engage the enemy before they get to the aircraft. They are moving fast, almost at a run. They have not seen me. I have tactical advantage. I signal for my shooters to fire on my command.

"Open fire!" My team does not respond. I repeat the order, this time yelling loud enough to be heard in Baghdad. "Open fire! Open fire!" The shooters fire and hit two of the insurgents. Their leader hits the ground and positions his men to return fire. A quick barrage of gunfire splits the air. I now face six insurgents. I have four shooters. I signal our medics to move to the aircraft crew. They shift to the right, then run to the Black Hawk as the shooters lay down suppressing fire. I must control the fight. I want to call in air support but cannot work the radio with my hands. Something is jammed. I cannot wait. I decide to move forward and focus my firepower. I hear myself yell, "Kill!"

I don't have enough men to try flanking or enough time to try anything fancy. I advance straight up the middle. I tell myself I don't belong here as I push forward in a full upright stance and run toward the enemy. My feet adjust to the rocks and I feel like I'm actually running above the ground instead of on it. I become instantly aware of everything in my past and everything in my present. My brain creates a collage of movement and sound. I hear rapid startled movements, the burst-mode firing of assault rifles and the metallic click of bullet casings ejected from their firing chambers. I hear the sound of my heart in my neck and feel the cold winter air against my sweat. Broken images appear. Some vanish quickly; others attach themselves to the corners of my retina. The images coalesce: burning aircraft, wild desert ter-

rain, winter mud, and endless sand. Parts of soldiers materialize, then dissolve. I catch full glimpses of body bags. The rapid flow of blood murmurs as it rushes through my carotid arteries. My screams and commands roar above the sounds of firing weapons. I hear the indecipherable yelling of my enemy as they position themselves for cover.

I move with the full force and intent of killing my enemy, who has the full intent of killing me. I reach for my holster, attached to my tactical vest. My right hand squeezes the pistol grip. I yank to move it into firing position. Pain instantly wrenches my shoulder and shoots down my arm. I shout and groan. My pistol is snagged. I cannot pull it free. I cannot move my arm. I know I will die in a matter of seconds. I am an easy target. I shall die today. Today is my day.

The Iraqi leader charges straight ahead, directly at me. He matches me stride for stride. He raises his weapon and begins firing rapid chaotic bursts. I see the muzzle flashes. I'm sure I am hit, but I feel nothing. I feel suspended in time—trapped in a slow-motion movie that I am watching from overhead and left of center. I hear the now-muffled sounds of gunfire. A single round of ammunition explodes from the barrel of my enemy's assault rifle and cuts through the air. The round scathes through the fabric of my uniform just below my left hip.

Reflexively, I grab at my holster again. I loosen the retention strap with a flick of my thumb and strain to jerk my pistol free. Nothing! Nothing except a wrenching pain in my shoulder. The pistol does not release. I yell at my men to fire at will. The yell becomes a scream, and I can hear it reverberating in the cold air. "Fire! Fire!" I am close enough to see the right index finger of my enemy as he pulls the trigger of his weapon, close enough to hear the metallic zing of spent casings as they spin through the air.

I know one thing: I shall die in this moment of battle, in this finite moment of war. I know it because I cannot fight as I was trained. I know it because I stand exposed to an enemy whose orders are to kill. I know it because I let my tactical advantages become tactical errors. I should have waited for air support, dug in, flanked, or moved directly to the injured aircrew. I know I shall die because I have become confused and have lost my focus. I can hear myself screaming a prayer: "God! Help me!"

I fade in and out of something that is real and something that is an illusion. I scream in pain. The terror in my screams jolts me. I thrash and struggle.

In a final terrified attempt to return fire, I yell some guttural animal sound and rip my pistol from its holster. I pull it up and across my body, centered into firing position. My index finger strikes the trigger and begins pulling in rapid succession. I see the wild spray of bullets as my enemy fires his weapon. We lock on the target of each other. I feel every pain I have ever felt in combat, but I feel them all at once, compressed into a single pulse of time, compressed into a rush of adrenaline and fear, like the sensation people feel in that suspended second just before they are hit in a high-speed collision. I feel the burning of a bullet as it splits my skin. I'm hit! I'm finally hit! The force knocks me to the ground. The fever I have felt sporadically now floods my body and I drip with the warm flow of blood. I am floating in air, flying in slow motion. I feel the shearing of my arteries and the tearing of muscle. I hear the splintering sound of shattering bone. Time moves backward like a cheap home movie that rewinds itself over and over, showing a clip until it's worn thin and bare. I see that my rapid-fire bullets found their mark in the center of my enemy's chest. The movie runs forward again and I know I am still alive, but my shoulder has been hit. From my position on the ground, I survey the scene. The medics are alive and huddled together. Three of the enemy insurgents lay dead, covered with sand. I cannot see the others. I hear the faint sound of a helicopter mixed with the sound of an approaching scream. My wife fades in and out of the battle scene. She screams my name. She wanders aimlessly at first and then finally stands on the far edge of my visual field, as if to watch from the sidelines.

I yell frantically, "Get down! Get down!" I must be dead after all. Yes, I decide I'm dead. My wife is coming to my funeral. She's early. God, she's here in Iraq. She's not supposed to see me like this. I yell for her to get away. I hear myself yelling. How can I hear myself yell if I'm dead? I'm not dead.

My shoulder rips in pain and I struggle to stand. I fall. I yell at my wife to get down.

"Look out! Get down!"

She yells in return, "What's wrong. What's the matter?"

"I'm hit! Get down! Get down!"

"You're not hit! You're okay!"

My left hand reaches to my right shoulder. I feel pain and swelling. "No—I'm hit. I'm hit!"

"No! Wake up! Wake up! You're in Iowa. You're home. Wake up!"

COLLIN'S VOICE FINALLY penetrates the dream. The soldiers around me fade. The enemy vanishes. The desert dissolves. The helicopter disappears. My wife struggles to hold my flailing arm. I can feel her touch. "You're okay," she says. "Don't move your arm."

Our living room comes into focus. I feel the surgical dressing on my right shoulder bulging over my deltoid. The post-op shoulder immobilizer that held my arm to my chest dangles loosely at my side. My right arm is free. I feel stabbing and tearing pain in my post-op shoulder. Sweat soaks my shirt. I see our fireplace kicking out its gas-log flames. My recliner rests only ten feet away. An extra blanket is wrapped around my legs in a tangle. Collin coaxes me back to reality. I finally hear her voice clearly. I see her face. I am home, in Iowa. I emerge from the stranglehold of a nightmare.

FOR SEVERAL HOURS I had thrashed and struggled in my recliner. My nightmare entangled two realities into a third where I faded in and out of the real and the imagined. The "real" from my post-op pain translated itself into the "imagined" struggles of combat. On a winter night in Iowa, I experienced a time warp of sorts—a post-traumatic stress nightmare where the force of one kind of memory collided with the force of another, where time and experience collapsed into a singularity, a black hole where my mind could not define cognitive boundaries.

In a post-surgical dream, I found that I had become a time traveler. I traveled in a parenthetical world of war, a world bound by the forces of PTSD.

St. Luke's

Ａ FTER SURGERY AND during physical therapy, I had difficulty with ongoing pain. Sometimes it hit me like a sudden rip of thunder. No warning—just a frightening boom and a shaking of the earth. Other times, it started like a dandelion seed parachuting down on a puff of wind, its weight no more than the heft of a childhood memory. It felt like the tiny barbs of a rose leaf drawn across my skin. When pain came hard and fast, a scream bubbled from my throat. I tried to choke it off, but usually I let it fly like the screeching caw of a crow. If it started like a seed, it was tolerable at first, maybe 2 or 3 on a pain scale of 10. Either way, thunder or dandelion, the pain festered and grew so in the end it felt like I was being tortured or burned or pulled through a keyhole. My pills did not work. I bit the back of my hand or cupped my ears. I was cursed by the witchcraft of pain.

During recovery, I wore a shoulder immobilizer for six weeks, and my arm and shoulder muscles atrophied so much I could feel the tubercles on the bones. The pain didn't resolve with surgery; it got worse. Added to that, my stroke affected the strength and sensation of my right arm and leg. The combination created an extra therapeutic challenge. Pain reinforced weakness, weakness reinforced pain. Peggy and the orthopedic surgeon told me it would dissipate over time.

The first weeks of post-op shoulder therapy were the worst. Pain shot from my shoulder to my back, and even into my legs. Its onset was mostly the thunder variety. Peggy worked slowly at first, and then gradually added arm stretches with a rope pulley and another stretching routine where she held my arm and gradually, but firmly, raised it to my side and overhead as far as it would go, which in the first sessions was about twenty degrees. When she stretched it to a limit where scar tissue and pain kept it from going farther, she held it there to the count of ten while I breathed slowly to control the pain; then she would move it a fraction of an inch past that resistance point and I usually screamed and panicked.

"Okay, okay. That's far enough!" I screamed. It sounded like a cross between a plea and a warning. We did full sessions, and afterward I would feel drained and nauseous.

On alternate days I went to cognitive therapy. Cher continued with reading and some work on brain exercises. It had been six months since my stroke, the time frame I had initially thought it would take to get back to normal. I felt impatient and wanted to push my cognitive recovery, but I didn't know how. She cautioned me that overreaching might be counterproductive.

"Recovery takes time," she tried to convince me. "If you try to push too hard, it only makes you stressed and frustrated. You'll get a slower recovery."

"I just didn't think it would take this long to see results," I complained.

"But you *have* seen results. You can manage a list and you are beginning to restructure your reading skills." She sounded encouraging, but I was thinking more about what I had lost instead of gained.

"I should be able to do more than make a list or read a children's book. I used to recall emergency protocols and complex dosing equations in seconds. Now I can't remember shit."

"Are you the same person you were six months ago?"

"No, but I want to be the person I used to be. I'm tired of having a stroke."

"So you *do* recognize the difference."

Cher always had a way of digging into my psyche with facts. They were like being hit with a thump on the chest. I had tended to view cognitive therapy as a hybrid of voodoo and neuroscience and psychology, yet Cher practiced a nuanced approach that encouraged critical self-analysis. And that hard reflection led me to the truth that my brain had changed—was changing—and that I was a significant stakeholder in the radical thing called therapy.

"Yes, I understand the difference," I said, resigned to the notion of having had a stroke, but still wanting to slough it off as if it never happened. "I get it. It's real."

"Yes, it is," Cher responded. "Think of it as a battle injury. It has real consequences."

We left it at that, at the reality of having survived a stroke and the reality that cognitive rehabilitation demanded far more than just showing up for a therapy session. I knew all that, but I wanted more. I wanted to push limits, like I had as a soldier and a doctor, but the limits seemed hard and fixed. I didn't know how to unstroke a stroke. I felt stupid: stupid, unintelligent, uneducated. I wrote four block letters in my journal—STPD. It was a mnemonic for "stupid," Stop—Think—Plan—Do. I never used it because I couldn't remember it.

Adding to my emotional and cognitive frustration, persistent pain from my shoulder surgery blocked my full efforts with Peggy and Cher. They adjusted their sessions accordingly but wanted to keep going so I didn't lose ground. We continued as best I could, working around the pain.

Collin continued to drive me to appointments between the exercise classes she was teaching, and when I wasn't in therapy I wanted her to drive me to a coffee shop because I was so tired of sitting at home alone. In the month of January I went to forty-five medical and therapy appointments. During one particular week I had eighteen appointments. Collin wanted to scream, did scream.

At the end of the first month back in therapy, it was clear that my progress had come to a standstill. Cher had me retested and some of the tests showed a regression instead of an improvement. I suspected the neuropsychologist thought I wasn't trying hard enough. I was frustrated with therapy and could tell that my therapists were frustrated too. Cher explained that they weren't frustrated with me but with the distractions interfering with my therapy, namely my recent surgery, the persistent pain, and possibly PTSD. She was concerned about my continued resistance to PTSD therapy.

"Did you understand that your test results were positive for PTSD?" she asked.

"They would be positive for anybody just returning from war," I countered. The discussion would go back and forth and I would never agree or never consent to any presumed need for therapy.

As GOOD AS my outpatient therapy was at the University Hospital, Collin and I both felt it lacked the continuity and intensity of an in-patient stroke rehab program. We needed more progress because, frankly, we were both on the near side of desperate. Our lives had begun to revolve around my stroke and its persistent reminders of all that we had lost together. That was our primary focus and neither of us would let the other live like that.

We had asked Dr. Leslie about inpatient rehab and she suggested St. Luke's Hospital in Cedar Rapids, Iowa, as a possible alternative. St. Luke's promoted an intense hospital-based stroke and brain injury rehabilitation program and had a reputation for clinical excellence. Dr. Leslie consulted with Neurology and with my military case managers at Rock Island and recommended an inpatient approach. Within a week, the Army made arrangements for an admission to St. Luke's.

On the day I was supposed to be admitted, a late March blizzard hit Iowa. The Highway Patrol cautioned that some roads would be closed if conditions worsened throughout the day. One of those roads was Highway 218 to Cedar Rapids. Collin was afraid if we drove to St. Luke's, she might get stranded or have an accident. Rather than run the risk of delaying my admission, we called a friend and he agreed to drive us. It took more than an hour to drive the thirty miles and we arrived at about 11:00 a.m. The blizzard reminded me of the blizzard that hit Minnesota the morning of my medical school interview at Mayo. As I had with that storm, I refused to let a blizzard keep me from a hospital.

St. Luke's was a five-hundred-bed hospital, a combination of an older redbrick façade and modern steel accents. When Collin and I arrived, we rode up the elevator to the sixth floor. The physical therapy reception area had an open feel to it and there were several patients coming and going in wheelchairs. I saw pictures of Midwestern scenes on the walls, and overall it didn't seem so much like a hospital. After my room assignment, I met with the doctor who led my therapy team. He specialized in physical medicine and rehabilitation and focused on brain injury and stroke rehabilitation. His bookshelves held plastic brains similar to the ones in Cher's office. Over the course of thirty minutes he laid out a complete therapy plan and answered all our questions. Therapists who worked exclusively in stroke and brain injury rehab would work with me in different therapeutic blocks. I would participate in rehab sessions at least six to eight hours a day. Therapy was diverse: physical, speech and language, occupational, and even recreational therapy as well as psychology. If I needed medication for pain or a trigger point injection, the doctors there would provide whatever I needed. In essence, it was one-stop shopping for stroke rehab. It held the promise of preserving my body and career—medical and military.

When the doctor finished the intake interview, Collin took me to my room and we said our goodbyes. I was expected to remain at St. Luke's for four weeks.

"I think this is the right thing to do," she said with conviction.

"I hope so. Something has to change."

I was hopeful, yet also at the limit of hope. Collin and I needed the St. Luke's program to work because it seemed everything else was working too slowly or not working at all. And it wasn't that Cher and Peggy didn't help me. They did. But there were limits as to how much family stress we could bear. At one point, Collin and I wondered if a nursing home might be more appropriate for a while. And in my own mind, I struggled with the ever-present and growing threat of losing my career in medicine.

"Tell the kids I'll be all right," I said. "Call me when you get home, but I might be in therapy, so keep calling."

"I will. I Love you." She did love me. I could tell. But I could also tell she was worn from therapy, just as I was.

"I love you too. Be careful going home."

Our brief goodbyes reminded me of our goodbyes at Fort McCoy.

We embraced and then Collin left and I was alone in my room, in a hospital dedicated to stroke and head injury rehabilitation. My stroke had claimed parts of my body and brain and was threatening to take my career. I was trying to fight back with a grand scheme of inpatient therapy at St. Luke's. And that was as daunting as the desert in Iraq, something larger and more frightening than I had imagined. It was a beast that could swallow me whole or take me piece by piece. Collin and I had put maximum leverage on four weeks of hospital-based therapy, a gamble with stakes so high I wondered if we had chosen wisely. I worried that I might fail or that the therapists would find me untreatable. I was cautiously optimistic because of the positive recommendations Collin and I had received, but just below the surface of that optimism lay the "what-if" questions about my future.

What if I spent the rest of my life zigzagging on the sidewalk, watching my feet in anticipation of falling to the ground? Would my stroke confine me to children's books forever? Would I think no more complex thoughts than perhaps *What's for dinner?* Would I become a burden and a chronic nuisance to my wife? At the core of those questions was the one that mattered the most: Would inpatient therapy allow me to continue as a physician?

JUST AFTER LUNCH a therapy assistant knocked on my door, which I left half-open. "I'm here to get you for therapy," she said. She was matter-of-fact yet pleasant. No cajoling, no excess small talk.

This is the beginning, I think.

I respond to her with a single word: "Okay." She helps me to the wheelchair and off we go, rolling down a well-lit hallway toward the therapy bay. As we roll, the hallway grows and elongates, like a scene from *Alice in Wonderland*. I am off to my first therapy session and in my head I am the perfect storm of anxiety and anticipation, bewilderment and excitement. I hope that hospital therapy will provide exactly what I need, yet fear it will provide nothing at all. I notice the doors of patients' rooms as we pass them. Most are painted tan; some have bright colors. My wheelchair has a wheel that squeaks and I joke that I need oil and laugh a bit. She chuckles in return. As we come into the open therapy room, I am surprised that it is filled with so many patients and therapists. Fifty, I think, but the number is certainly fewer. Large brown therapy tables and blue mats cover half the room. The other half is covered with parallel bars and exercise equipment and a mock kitchen. She parks me just inside the room next to another patient and tells me that my therapist, Cindy, will be with me shortly.

The patient waiting by me is drooling. Her skin is pale. Her fists are tight and her arms contracted. She has an obvious head injury—a car accident, I assume. I study the room. It's a lair, maybe a beehive. A patient near the opposite wall is screaming at her therapist. She refuses to get out of her wheelchair. The therapist is working at getting her to stand. The patient lets out a string of curses and the therapist says, "Stop! That won't be tolerated." Then the therapist rolls her over by me and my drooling companion and tells the screamer that she can cool down. The screamer yells, "You're a whore!" The therapist says nothing and walks away.

Cindy comes to get me just as the screamer calms down. She introduces herself and tells me she is going to be my therapy team leader. She rolls me halfway through the room and helps me to a table where we sit and she goes over my schedule of exercises for the day. We will start with gait and balance and then do some shoulder work and finish with speech and language therapy.

"I'm ready to go," I say, anxious to get started, yet also intimidated by all I see, by the lair and its imaginary wolves. Cindy instructs her therapy assistant to grab a gait belt. I tell her I don't need one. She says I do if I want to do therapy. I can tell she takes no prisoners. Gait belt on my waist, they help me to my feet.

"Okay, let's just take a short walk down the hall," Cindy says. "Tighten your stance, look up. Breathe. You're tensing up. We need you to relax."

I bring my feet together and ataxic gyrations take control of my body. I am a wobbling toy top at the end of its spin. The therapist and assistant each take hold of my belt. I take one step. *Shit*. I make a wild gyration that twists me 45 degrees off-center. "That's okay," Cindy offers. "Let's try again." I make a concerted effort to watch my feet and think of every step. Cindy puts two fingers under my chin and pushes it up. "Look up," she says. "Your feet know where to go."

"I need to watch my feet," I counter.

"You need to trust your feet," she counters back.

I think she is using a cute little mantra she learned in physical therapy school. *Trust my feet. Whoever heard of that?* We start again and I manage to walk maybe twenty feet with the therapists holding on. I weave and stutter-step as Cindy encourages me to keep my head up and breathe. I turn to look across the room and crash, but my gait belt saves me. "Concentrate," Cindy says.

I *am* concentrating—on all the activity going on around me. On the screaming patient and her therapist, on the drooling head injury patient, on the others working their limbs and their hands. The lair, the hive, the therapists. I've never seen anything like it. More screamers emerge whom I hadn't noticed at first. They're more reserved, polite, but still in agony over something in their therapy. Other patients, like me, walk to the rhythm of their therapist. Some do quite well; others, not so much. One patient with ataxia cannot walk a single step. Another is hooked up to a computerized treadmill. He has one prosthetic leg. I think he might be a soldier too, but I don't ask. The therapists look like they don't take crap; they keep pushing. They might pause but they don't stop. And as I take my first walk in my first hour of therapy at St Luke's, I wonder about the kind of patient I will become. Will I crash to the floor, scream at my therapist, weep in shame? Will I fail therapy? Will it fail me? I sense that I want to run or hide, but I cannot; the therapist knows my room number, my case file—my name.

Cindy walks me slalom-style through a set of orange cones on the floor, just as Peggy had done in outpatient therapy. We walk slowly, then fast, in a circle and then on a line; on carpet and on linoleum, and up and down a set of practice stairs. I walk with and without my cane. I step over a fake curb, a line, a crack, over or around tiny obstacles on the floor: a shoe, a piece of paper, a spill of water. I wobble and weave up and down a ramp like a boxer on the ropes. I walk until I think walking is overrated. After thirty minutes Cindy says it's time for some balance routines.

"I thought we were doing balance," I say, slightly puzzled.

"That was gait training. Balance is different."

We do five minutes on a large blue exercise ball. I fall to the sides and Cindy catches me. We repeat. I fall again. It's like being drunk without the booze. I say "Shit" more than is necessary. It doesn't help.

From the ball, I graduate to the balance beam—a gymnast's balance beam, only fixed to the floor with a double set of mats on either side. No way can I walk on a balance beam. No way.

"Am I supposed to walk on that?" I squeal, my voice up nearly an octave.

"We use it for balance. Don't worry, we're here to hold you up. We're going to start with one step. Your left foot first, then your right."

She has me stand on the right side of the beam with my feet together as close as I can get them. She and her assistant hold me with the gait belt. My left foot goes first. It's my good foot. They tighten their grip on my gait belt and lift. And as quick as I am on, I am off.

"That's good," Cindy says. "Try it again. This time, remember to breathe."

I start again by standing and breathing. When I am ready, I am supposed to lift my right foot onto the beam. I will never be ready. Never. I pause longer than is apparently allowed. Cindy and her assistant start putting pressure on my belt. That's the sign. Pressure. It's time to move.

"I'm not ready," I protest.

"Raise your right leg to the beam and let it rest there," Cindy insists.

She's not stern, just clinically pushy. I raise my right foot onto the beam and let it rest. All my weight is on my left leg. Cindy and the assistant guide me with pressure on the belt. I am on the beam and Cindy holds me steady and starts to count. She gets to three and a half before I fall and they catch me. After one more trial she has me practice the balance beam routine on a line on the floor. It's not any easier for my balance but not nearly as threatening as the beam.

Cindy finishes my gait and balance session and walks me back to my wheelchair. My next session starts in about ten minutes. I drink water and watch the other patients. The screamer has gone back to her room. I'm glad. She made me nervous. I *am* nervous. I think my gait and balance training have gone poorly. I want a redo, but I can't have one. I feel like a temporary interruption in the massive machinery of therapy, and when I am finished with the days and the weeks before me, I shall walk out the door of this hospital and onto the thin mantle of a tenuous life.

Somebody calls my name. I answer, "Yup," and raise my left arm. Another therapy assistant comes to my side and says we're off to an occupational therapist, Charlotte, for some hand and shoulder work. I simply nod. At a table next to the wall where the screaming patient started out, I sit on a chair and the therapist sits next to me on her chair. She is older than the other therapists, older than me. Her hair shows hints of gray, but she is trim and fit. She tells me she has been at St. Luke's for fifteen years. As she begins the session, we talk about my motor deficits from the stroke and my recent shoulder surgery. I am comforted to learn she has had years of experience in recovering fine motor skills and shoulder mobility "Well," Charlotte says, "you have several issues that we can work on at the same time. Do you have much shoulder pain?"

"Yes, every time I move it," I answer. "I have a catch that always hits a nerve when I do my arm circles or lift it to the side."

"We'll work on that," she replies. She sounds clinical and objective as she gives a little smile. "Okay, let's have you stand and do some small circles with your arm. Just pretend you're stirring a pot, only let your arm dangle in front of you. Balance yourself with your feet."

I start the motion. My arm swings loose like a pendulum. I am making eggs instead of circles and Charlotte tells me to let my arm swing round to my front. If I do that, I know electricity will surge down my arm. She gently pushes on my upper back so I'm more parallel to the floor and my arm is swinging directly under my shoulder joint. It is more aggressive than I wanted, more dangerous for eliciting pain. "Small, round circles," she encourages.

My arm rotates slowly. Round and round. The tiniest of circles, no larger than the diameter of a softball. There is no pain, but there is no real effort at pushing the edges. I'm doing well, I think.

"Good," Charlotte says. "Now make a larger circle. Use your body to swing your arm. Make sure to breathe."

"I thought I *was* breathing."

"You tend to hold your breath."

I take two big breaths and swing my body. As I begin, I lose my balance just enough to throw me off. My arm swings wide in an arc that almost reaches the table and the pain shoots down from my armpit to my fingers and into my back. It's a combination of electricity and tearing and burning. I hear my joint snap and rip. It makes that sucking, tearing-cartilage sound a drumstick makes when pulled from a roasted chicken. I scream and yelp both, simultaneously, then I hyperventilate as a tsunami flattens everything in its path. I grab my right arm with my left and hold it steady so it doesn't dislocate, even though it won't. I taste the salt of bile at the base of my tongue. I retch the dry retch of pain. Charlotte grabs hold and sits me in my chair. "Breathe slow, controlled breaths," she says as she massages my arm.

I have no control over how I breathe, no real control over the heat that rises within me. I cannot fight the pain that bores unrestrained into my arm and through my joints. I am gored by a bull in Pamplona, hit by a bullet in Iraq. I am down and trampled and bleeding. I think the pain will mark the end of the session.

Charlotte tells the assistant to get me a cool cloth so we can recover and start again. *Again.* I hear the word, but I think she is mad, a mad scientist or just mad in general. I cannot start *again*. I am spent. Samson has lost his strength at the hands of Delilah. The wet cloth on my forehead provides a tiny distraction, but when Charlotte stands me up again, the pain is too much to bear. "Let's just stand and breathe and let your arm rest at your side. You need to relax your whole body. Your tension adds to your pain."

I protest loudly. "It hurts, dammit!" The three words come out angrier than I want them to. And I don't know if anger is what I feel. Maybe it's the surge of natural hormones in response to pain. Maybe it *is* anger; if it is, I think I might be angry with myself for having a stroke and that's confusing and pain is confusing.

"I know it hurts," Charlotte responds. She sounds factual, neither challenging me nor comforting me, just informing me that she knows the facts about pain and therapy. "I want you to bend at the waist and let your arm move forward naturally. Don't force it; no circles. Just let gravity take it where it naturally wants to go. Let's do that for a count of ten."

"I can't," I plead. I think that *ten* is the same as infinity. I hate gravity. I hate my arm. I hate my therapist.

"Bend forward slowly. You're in control. Remember to breathe."

Charlotte puts slight pressure on my neck to inch me forward. I do not respond. She puts her other hand in front of me to indicate how far I need to bend—four inches, maybe six. If I can move that minuscule distance, I have a chance at healing. I take a breath and hold it, getting myself ready to bend. "You're holding your breath again," she reminds me.

"I think I need to stop," I beg. "My shoulder hurts too much."

"Let's do five more minutes. An inch at a time. You're doing fine," she insists.

I am *not* doing fine. That's doctor talk or therapy talk for "This is going to hurt like hell, but we're going to ignore you and push through it anyway." That five minutes will become the Hundred Years War. I rest; then I bend, one inch, no more. The pain edges forward with me, ready to pounce and twist me into submission. Charlotte tells me how well I am doing and to bend just a little more. "A few more inches," she says. I listen to her voice, her assurance. I feel her hand on my neck, the supposed hand of experience, and for one unredeemable second I decide to trust her. I am still a soldier. I suck it up and push back the pain. I bend the full remaining distance to her hand. The bull thrashes its head, the inquisitor turns the wheel on a rack, and I see the gray darkness of unconsciousness mixed with pinpoint sparks of light. "Jesus!" I scream. "Stop!"

I know that other patients are watching me the same way I watched the screaming woman in my first hour. And I am ashamed and embarrassed. I see that I am broken and gored and racked and weak. I have failed the test. I cannot master pain. My life is diminished.

By week two I had assigned my therapists secret names: Attila the Hun, Charlotte the Barbarian, Julia the Inquisitor. I even fantasized that one of them was a dominatrix, whip in hand, black fishnet stockings revealing muscular thighs, her spiked heels digging into my chest as she pinned me against the therapy mat. "You're not screaming," she snarled in an Eastern European accent. Then she wrenched my arm or leg and I screamed, not because I wanted her but because she hurt me. I let her continue, because in some bizarre way pain became the equivalent of healing. I would yield—one millimeter per session, one twitch of a toe, a single step.

The same exercises and routines continued daily over the following three weeks. Some days crushed me; others made me feel like an artist with a new palette of oils. My therapists advanced my therapy in increments that challenged my mind and body and resolve. I solved puzzles and word games and wrote basic sentences. The speech therapist made me read out loud from a book, like a child in kindergarten; it *was* kindergarten in some ways. I put blocks on top of blocks and matched colored tiles to colored tiles. I added numbers and subtracted numbers, and memorized lists of objects and didn't repeat them back in order. I read stories and told the therapist what they meant and then I repeated the process. Different day—Different story. I learned to walk and talk at the same time, and did them both reasonably well. To retrain my hand-eye and limb coordination, I played one-on-one "volleyball" with a brightly colored inflatable beach ball. My feet stuck to one spot on the floor while my arms swung at the ball. Down I would go, therapy assistant attached at the gait belt.

In the afternoons the therapists took me outside to teach me how to cross a street. I flunked. I would just strike out off the curb, forgetting to look both ways. I said "Damn" or "Shit." They said, "Think."

"Think before you walk," they harped. "Learn to recognize danger and risk."

"I *am* thinking," I said.

I told them I knew all about danger and risk and that I had fought a war. They countered by telling me the only battle I had to fight was concentrating on walking and being safe.

In my final week of inpatient therapy, the therapists all talked with me about my progress in various areas of therapy. It was clear that I had indeed made progress, especially with gait training and some aspects of cognition, mostly with the ability to focus on my immediate surroundings and to assess environmental risks. I was much better at things like crossing the road and planning my day and participating in complex tasks, but the deficits from my stroke would need continued outpatient therapy. Each therapist laid out a plan for continuing therapy. Balance and gait training remained high on the list, as did cognitive therapy for my brain.

Before my discharge, I had to pass a written and simulator driver test. That was tough. The reaction time of my right side had been significantly impaired. My cognitive processing speed and reading speed were also markedly affected. I got two practice sessions with the simulator and with a sample written test. I would get only one chance at the real test. I barely passed with minimum scores, but I did pass. I would be legal to drive—impaired, yet legal.

Beyond the big test of driving, I took practical tests of my ability to function independently at home with activities of daily living (ADLs). The mock kitchen I saw the first day came into play. I had to cook a grilled cheese sandwich while an occupational therapist watched and scored my performance. I burned the sandwich and the pan because I was not paying attention. She would recommend in my final summary that I not be allowed to cook alone in the kitchen and that when I did cook, Collin had to monitor me.

The last of the ADL tests was in the area of bathroom and dressing skills. Tying my shoes was challenging to the point of frustrating because my fingers would simply not do the complex trickery of knot tying. The solution: stretch shoe laces or slip-on shoes. Making the bed was a breeze. Putting on my shirt required extra gymnastics; my right arm was still painful and without a functional range of motion. I had to sit on the edge of the bed to put on my jeans; otherwise I fell over when putting my foot into a pant leg. Toileting was a pain. Showering was dangerous. I recognized that and so had Collin. I had seen plenty of senior patients in the ER who had fallen in the shower and broken a hip. The shower in my hospital bedroom had more bars than a county jail. When showering, I held on with one hand while leaning against the sides for balance. I didn't dare close my eyes to the beads of water when I faced the shower, because I would immediately become ataxic and fall. To wash my chest and face, I learned to sit on the shower chair, face the faucet, then soap and rinse. On my final test, a therapist named Rachael came to my room and watched me put on my white athletic socks and take them off. She hovered as I put my feet into my pant legs while sitting on the edge of the bed. I dressed myself with aplomb and flair just to show off.

"What do you do for the shower?" she asked, looking straight at me, clipboard in hand.

"I hold the bars and sit on the shower chair and have my wife standing nearby. I take my time and don't rush. There is a big risk of falling," I pointed out. I sounded as if I were giving answers for a medical board exam. I hit each of the safety points right on target.

"Okay, so let's see you do it," she said with her almost-pushy therapist voice.

"But I already took my shower this morning," I said.

"And I need to see you take one before you leave. It's a matter of safety."

"You mean now?"

"Yes. I need you to show me how you manage in the shower."

I had experienced far worse things than showering in front of a therapist, gender embarrassment aside; but to me, it was demeaning and yet another reminder of how much a stroke had changed my life, how it had destroyed my self-esteem and self-control until I was reduced to a soldier with elastic shoelaces needing to demonstrate that I had enough smarts and balance to stand in a shower without falling on

my ass. Dignity in hand, or perhaps in the toilet, I undressed in front
of the therapist and then stepped into the shower. I sat on the gray
plastic chair and soaped myself as my therapist made notes about the
whole ordeal.

Passing these tests meant I could function at home within certain
parameters of safety and wisdom. There would be the usual assistive
devices: jar openers, cane, shower chairs, and a temporary driver's license, renewable only at the discretion of my doctors. I would have
to adopt a new paradigm of functionality and daily living, one that
would always reflect the pure and unassailable fact that I was a stroke
patient and would remain one forever. And that fixed, clinical reality
was a hammer that struck against the image of how I imagined my life
proceeding.

I didn't make the functional gains I had expected of inpatient therapy. I was not cured. I had made clinical progress and it was visible
and meaningful, but it also established that my recovery still remained
a work in progress. Hospital-based therapy had propelled improvements in my physical deficits; equally important, however, it forced
me to confront those deficits and the real limitations they imposed.
That was especially true of my cognitive and memory deficits. During
my speech and cognitive therapy sessions, I had come to a realization
that my patterns of thinking weren't just impaired, they were broken,
and no amount of inpatient therapy crammed into four short weeks
was going to repair the damage.

That was my greatest lesson and my greatest disappointment, the
double-edged sword of inpatient therapy; it made me clinically and
emotionally aware of exactly who I had become. And that was the person who in a few short days would go home from St. Luke's not as
the imagined patient with his doctor skills fully intact and his mind
sharpened, but as the real person whose fears had become concrete.
I would not emerge from therapy with all the recovery that I had
dreamed possible, yet I was not a therapeutic failure. I was simply and
profoundly a stroke survivor.

Elephant Man

I N JUNE, SEVEN WEEKS after I left St. Luke's, the Army medical corps invited me to Fort Knox for a medical review board. Up to that point I had been classified as non-deployable and given a chance at recovery with outpatient and inpatient rehabilitation. The clinical summaries from my doctors and neuropsychologists at the University Hospital in Iowa City and St. Luke's all gave no firm date or prognosis for my likely return to military duty or emergency medicine: they simply stated that I did not, at the time of my evaluations, have the capacity to practice medicine or deploy as a soldier. Colonel Smith, at Rock Island, had discussed his summary with me before he sent it on to Fort Knox. As a friend and colleague, he struggled with his recommendation for non-deployment status. His final decision reflected Army medical standards and regulations. I agreed with it. I would have made the same decision.

At Fort Knox, in the shadow of the gold repository, my medical review board proceeded with a series of physical examinations and a review of my therapeutic progress. A young nurse who had done a tour in Iraq in one of the Army hospitals, helped me get to the exam rooms and made sure we checked off each box on a two-page checklist. She had just been promoted to captain and told me she wanted to make a career of the Army. As she walked me to the different stations for X-rays and lab and an EKG, she asked me about my tours. We had served in Iraq during the same months. Her combat experience gave her insight and empathy that encouraged me to feel at ease.

She reminded me of the nurses on the Globemaster medevac flight, the way they would comfort their patients to help them endure the stress of a medevac. At one point she took my arm and helped me balance, and when she touched me I sensed that she was also comforting me. The exams, the X-rays, and the standard medical questions to that point had all been so formal and procedural; not that the doctors or medical personnel were aloof or uncaring—they were exactly the opposite—but there was a certain fatalistic undercurrent in proceeding through a board review. By the end of the day, a medical officer would sign a form stating that I was no longer deployable and that I met the criteria for a medical discharge. Nothing personal, nothing random, nothing unexpected. The mechanics of the process gave me a hollow twinge of hopelessness. When the nurse held my arm, her touch was a lifeline.

The review board physicians met with me individually throughout the morning. They extended their gratitude for my tours of duty and my service and addressed each of their concerns with me. In the afternoon, the board conferred together; then the ranking officer met with me to review their findings. Physically, I failed Army standards. I could not run or sprint or manage a weapon to protect myself or a patient. My right arm and leg were weak. My right arm muscles had become so atrophied that one of the doctors told me I should not expect to use that arm again. Cognitively, the Army retested me to make sure they had an accurate and up-to-date assessment of any residual cognitive deficits. They found several: reading, memory, focus, executive functioning, threat assessment, and the management of critical information. The psychologist summarized their findings. He told me I did not have the cognitive capacity to accurately assess and use complex clinical data and on that basis, I was a risk to myself and to patients. I could no longer be deployed or function as a military physician.

In the last ten minutes with the psychologist, he reiterated the board's appreciation for my service and then indicated that I would be discharged from the Army with a medical retirement. He walked me out of his office to a waiting room where I was to wait for an administrative officer to help me with all the necessary details for a medical discharge. I thanked him for his time. He gracefully said, "No, thank *you*." And with that final courteous gesture, my career as a military medical officer and flight surgeon in the United States Army ended.

I sat in the waiting room, eyes roving about. I felt like I had felt so many times in doctors' offices after my stroke. The substance of all that had happened that day carried a substantial weight and I was weary. I could never go back to the Army, never go back to medicine, and never back to the person I had become over the arc of so many years. The Army would move on without me. The nurse who helped me in the morning was now helping another soldier; the doctors who had reviewed my case had closed my file and moved on to the next case. And I thought that if there ever was a time when I had felt abandoned—like I was the only person alive in the universe—it was there in that lobby, waiting for my final discharge paperwork.

By July 2008 it had been a year since my stroke. In the beginning, I had decided that stroke therapy would not extend much beyond eight to ten weeks, an idea for which I had no clinical foundation. A year later I wondered if therapy might never end. It was different from what I had expected or hoped for. I puzzled over the pace of recovery, angry at times, perplexed at others. I took walks and sat at coffee shops, thinking of all that had transpired in the past year. I wasn't looking to fix blame. I just thought therapy would have gone faster and I would have returned to medicine and the Army. That was a topic that Cher and I discussed: the nature of recovery, its speed, and the ongoing need for further therapy.

In August and September, Cher and Peggy began preparing me for an outpatient transition to the VA hospital. As soon as my Army discharge became effective, I would no longer be on active duty, and therefore no longer eligible for continued therapy under the management of the Army Wounded Warrior team at Rock Island and their contract at the University Hospital. I really didn't want to transfer my care to the VA, but my outpatient therapy at the University Hospital had run its course, and the next natural step involved the Veterans

Administration Hospital in Iowa City. Cher encouraged me to keep an open mind and to use my military leadership to an advantage.

"Use your Army skills," she said. "View the change as any change in the battlefield. You told me how your training taught you to adapt and overcome. It's time to use that training."

She was right. Stroke therapy was all about adapting to change, and after a year of such adapting, my progress had become more dependent on my participation and less dependent on any particular therapist or program. Cher offered to make the needed calls and introductions to the staff at the VA. I agreed and the plan was set into motion.

In our few remaining sessions before my transfer, Cher let me talk about anything I wanted. I led the discussion and essentially the therapy. It was a twist. I felt like I was a doctor again, like I was counseling some patient facing a life-altering diagnosis. I started by asking her a question.

"Did you ever see that movie *The Elephant Man*?" I asked her.

"The one with Anthony Hopkins as a doctor, in black-and-white?"

"Yes, that's the one. It was modeled after a real patient named John Merrick at the London Hospital in the late 1800s. A doctor named Treves rescued the elephant man from a London freak show. Merrick wore that cloth hood on his head to hide his deformities, and he dragged his leg and slurred his speech."

"Where are you going with this," Cher asked, a bit intrigued.

"I remember two scenes. The elephant man tripped over a little girl and knocked her down. A crowd of people thought he tried to hurt her, so they chased him to a dead-end street and were going to beat him. They tore his hood off and Merrick shouted: 'I . . . am not . . . an . . . animal.' The crowd finally left him alone."

"Do you relate to him?" Cher asked me.

"Yes, I do. Not to his awful condition and his disfigurement, but to his awareness that he wasn't an animal to be beaten into submission. Not that therapy does that, but sometimes I feel like an animal beaten by a stroke, and then I have to remind myself that I am not. Then I center myself and keep going in therapy."

"Excellent observation." Cher had a pleased look and slight smile, as if to convey she was proud of me. "It's a sign of your ability to think in the abstract. What's the other scene?"

"Toward the end of the movie, Merrick is having tea in Dr. Treves's home and he asks a question: 'Can you cure me?' Treves answers, 'No, John, I can't cure you.' And Merrick replies, 'I thought not.'"

I told Cher how the scene lingered there with the emotional weight of a man coming to a final understanding of his own mortality and destiny.

"That scene is me," I said to Cher. "It is where I am at right now in my life and my therapy. So I'm asking you the same question. Can you cure me?"

I had seen Cher in therapy for the better part of a year. She had forged a clinical bond that allowed me to reveal the hardest insights and deepest fears about myself and my stroke, and especially about my future. It was probably a bond that few therapists ever make with their patients. I was grateful for how much she had pushed me into discovering who I had become and, in many ways, into discovering the resilience that defined my life. I had seen her become emotional a few times during our sessions, to the point where her tears would well up and she would grab a tissue and sometimes offer one to me. The story of *The Elephant Man* moved us both. She, like Dr. Treves, paused in silence before she answered me.

"No, Jon, I can't cure you. I never could." And at that, a few tears fell and she held a tissue to her eyes.

"I thought not," I replied quietly, my own tears welling up as we sat in silence.

I saw Cher once more in therapy. I had made her a present at home, a collage from a drawing of a medevac chopper and one of my battle patches and the insignia from the Army Medical Corps. I gave it to her at the start of the session. She jokingly said, "So therapy has been like a battle?"

"Kinda," I replied. "No, actually, I wanted you to have the patch because it signifies the unit I went to war with. And I want you to know that you are the kind of therapist I would trust in combat. So it's kind of your combat patch, if you will."

She thanked me and we discussed what it meant to wear a combat patch. It was more than the unit emblem sewn onto a uniform, and even more than the sign of serving in combat. It was a symbol of identity so closely held among soldiers that it bound them together in the mutual pride and gratitude of having served and survived together. And she said she was humbled by it and would keep it on her desk.

We talked a bit more about my gains in therapy and then we switched to talking about the idea of a clinical plateau. Some of my doctors had suggested that I had reached a one-year plateau in recovery and might not experience further gains—not that therapeutic gains would be impossible, but that efforts at some point could become counterproductive. I had partially bought into that line of thinking, yet had experienced several plateaus in my therapy and was able to work past them to gain more function. The Army doctors on the review board told me that the deficits remaining at the one-year point were likely to remain and that the therapeutic goal would shift from gaining more function to adapting to residual deficits. Dr. Leslie, Peggy, and Cher had all discussed the issue with me, but we all agreed that the clinical notion of a therapeutic plateau was not a law of therapy but something observed in many patients. I usually countered that I wasn't "many patients" and then we discussed the role that resilience and personal will played in recovery. Everybody involved in my care, including me, had seen patients who defied clinical expectations, ones who pushed beyond the practical limits of therapy. I believed I might be one of those patients, but I didn't have the expertise in stroke therapy to validate that belief. I wanted to believe that I could surpass and keep surpassing plateaus, but I wasn't sure if they were hard rules of therapy or merely clinical constructs. I would have to find the answer in the coming months and years.

We finished the session by reviewing my transition to the VA.

"I'm excited for you," Cher said. "You'll do fine with the therapists there."

"I don't know that I'm excited, but I am open and I know I can adapt."

"And that's a positive sign of healing. That's the soldier in you."

I nodded and smiled just a bit. "I think you're right," I said. "I figured something out last week. I know I'll never practice medicine again. I've known it for quite some time."

I told her what I had known to be true and discovered and rediscovered so many times in therapy. I had felt the weight of it ever since my brain surgery and had pushed back and refused to accept it. But in that one definitive statement, I told the truth and let it flow unrestrained and saying it made it somehow less oppressive, as if I could see it as a doctor with some clinical distance.

"That's been very difficult for you. Do you know why?"

"I wasn't prepared for the loss. I was afraid of facing it. I felt like I didn't have anything else."

"*Do* you have anything else?"

"I don't know yet, but I know it's not medicine or the Army. I've decided that even if you were to sign something permitting me to return, it would be unethical. I can't put myself in a position to harm patients. That's a line that I cannot cross."

We talked about my decision and the ethics of it, the weight and finality of it. Cher told me that it was the kind of decision that many patients never made, but that my willingness to accept my limitations would ultimately help me live with them and move forward. She reviewed some of the high points of therapy and my progress.

"When you consider all the things you've done in your career and all the places you've been, you have had a truly remarkable life. That's not something a stroke can take from you."

"When you say it like that, I can almost feel what you're saying."

"Almost?"

"I have a sense of it—that it's true. I've done a lot with my career, but it's hard looking back and seeing it come to an end the way it did. But I don't want to dwell in that mind-set. I want to keep moving."

"And that's more a sign of healing than any test we could give you. It tells me you're going to do more than be a stroke survivor."

Therapy: VA Style

THE VA IN Iowa City was an older brick hospital built in the 1950s across the street from the University Hospital. Its hallways on some patient floors had dated vinyl flooring and the rooms seemed cramped. Part of my reluctance to go to the VA was its reputation. I had heard from other soldiers that care was slow and some of the doctors seemed uncaring. Residents in training from the University rotated in the VA under the supervision of staff doctors. Some of the residents were excellent; others lacked knowledge and sensitivity. The VA had so many patients requiring mental health services, including neuropsychology, that those services were relocated to a separate clinic facility in Coralville, about three miles away.

In August, the first provider I met at the VA in Coralville was Harvard-trained neuropsychologist Mike Hall, PhD. His office shelves held a collection of academic texts in neuroscience and behavioral science. The mandatory neuropsychologist's plastic brain models sat on the top shelf. As he spoke and interacted with me in that first meeting, I decided he was a type A personality, atypical for a provider in mental and behavioral sciences and very different from what I had expected. He spoke to me like we were two clinicians conferring on a case, not that I was a colleague, but more that he recognized my capacity to understand clinical language. He was still the neuropsychologist and I was still the patient—that was clear—but it was also clear that my background as a physician made our provider-patient relationship different.

After we talked and familiarized ourselves with each other, Dr. Hall ordered a battery of neuro-cognitive tests that would pinpoint specific deficits. Some of them were the same tests I had taken at the University Hospital. He also referred me to a VA psychologist for a PTSD evaluation. He scheduled the tests and evaluations for the following week. The tests reaffirmed multiple stroke deficits and proved positive for PTSD.

The PTSD diagnosis, while not a total surprise, did make me curious, because I felt my war dreams and startle responses had settled down since I had returned home from Iraq. The VA psychologist, Heather, also a PhD, who was relatively new in the mental health department, discussed the scope and ongoing nature of traumatizing war experiences. She projected an interest in soldiers and in PTSD and she was sincere and kind, but when she spoke about war and trauma, it seemed to me she did so from the vantage point of a textbook or a VA seminar on treating soldiers.

"Let's discuss the criteria for PTSD," she began. "There is a traumatic event, recurrent memories, nightmares, avoidance, and a list of changes in mood or thinking." I imagined her giving a lecture.

I didn't need a lecture or a primer. I knew the criteria on the list. I had *lived* the criteria on the list, real-time, in combat. Fair or not, I dismissed her talk as lacking the real bite of combat experience and trauma. She had never been to war; I had. She had never been a trauma doctor. I had seen the emotional and physical trauma of combat.

Despite my initial misgivings, Heather impressed me as a therapist who genuinely cared for veterans and their causes. Still, I judged the tests for PTSD little more than voodoo because of their reliance on patient self-reporting. I also criticized the diagnostic criteria as being much too broad to yield any reasonable specificity for the diagnosis. There were no concrete lab tests or CT or MRI criteria. If the psychologist said you had it, you had it, period. To me, the diagnosis lacked clinical objectivity. I didn't deny that it was real and that soldiers experienced it, but I battled against it with a military frame of mind, the toughness/weakness paradigm: soldiers are tough; PTSD is a sign of mental weakness. Consequently, I distrusted the diagnosis because I did not fully understand how behavioral and emotional actions, so functional in combat, could become so dysfunctional at home. I hated the term "PTSD" because of its overwrought emphasis on the word "disorder" and its implied status of emotional incompetence.

Heather continued to work with me even though I was reluctant to open up. She doggedly pointed out that I showed the signs and symptoms and pestered me about different aspects of reliving and avoidance, hypervigilance and irritability, violent dreams and nightmares.

"Tell me about one of your dreams or recurrent thoughts," she said in one of the early sessions.

She was a spy. I could not let her see my secrets. "I don't really want to go into it," I replied coldly.

"Why not?"

"Too violent, maybe."

She pushed and prodded. "Maybe? Can you be more specific or descriptive?"

"Well, it might be more like, I don't know, something out of Dante's *Inferno*, something hellish or evil."

"Can you describe what you saw that makes you feel that way?"

Psychologists were always probing how I felt about things and sometimes I wanted to scream, "Shitty! I feel shitty or inhuman, dammit!" But I never did, because I knew that was what they wanted to hear, and saying it would only prove their point, that I felt something deep and dirty and horrible that I never wanted to surface. So instead I just said I felt sad. And I did, but that was the small of it.

I feigned confusion. "Describe what I saw?"

"Yes. Describe the surroundings or the person or the incident that makes you think of hellish things," she said.

I wanted to just get through the session without delving into my wartime psyche or the patients I remembered, but part of me wanted to shock her, maybe as a way of saying I knew more than she did about trauma. I picked a case I remembered often.

"Okay. I saw this soldier—well, not actually the soldier. I just saw his empty Kevlar helmet, and it had a hole in it from a rocket-powered grenade. That was all I had left to look at—the helmet. The rest of him went inside a body bag. So his Kevlar was burned and frayed where the grenade hit it, and the char of the helmet stunk and the inside of it was greasy and it still had a chin strap attached. Is that what you mean?"

"Yes, that's what I mean. Was that the worst thing you saw?"

"No, but it is one that keeps coming back in dreams."

"Could you draw me a picture of the helmet?"

I thought she was nuts. I had plenty of pictures in my mind; why draw one?

"No, I don't think I can. I can't draw very well."

"I'm going to give you some paper and a pencil. Just make an outline," she said.

And so the session went. Images and memories. Horrific memories and a crude drawing of a soldier's helmet with a hole in it. I gave it to her and she kept it in my file, but I didn't want it there, touching my other pages. I wanted to get rid of it. Out of my recall and dreams, out of my brain.

A FEW DAYS LATER, I met Gina, a VA speech and language therapist who worked with veterans needing a wide variety of therapy for issues related to speech or language or cognition or all three. Her department saw older and younger veterans alike; ones with throat cancer, some with head injuries, others with PTSD, and veterans like me with cognitive stroke deficits. Gina, like Dr. Hall, treated me not as a colleague but with the appropriate recognition for my medical knowledge so I felt like I was part of my own therapy team—which, if I had thought about it, I was. Her personality didn't fit my stereotypic image of a therapist. I imagined her as sort of maudlin or mega-serious or always poised to dig into the secret feelings about my stroke or make me take brain tests to show how much I had lost. She was anything but what I had imagined. She took a practical and more lighthearted approach to therapy, one that allowed me to fumble an exercise and not take it so hard. I felt at ease with her because she was obviously smart and experienced in her field, but also because she had mastered the art of working therapy so it wasn't so weighty and intangible.

"Okay, Dr. Kerstetter, our first task is working with some numbers. Do what you can, and we'll repeat the exercise and chart your progress."

"I'm bad at numbers."

"That's okay. You'll get better over time."

Better over time. Those words helped me believe I could go beyond the therapeutic plateau that cornered me up against a wall like the crazed mob that cornered the Elephant Man. It gave me hope that if I cried out loud enough, my limits might dissolve and I could push further.

With Gina, there was never the question of my being able to complete a specific task, only the idea that I would try and that I would show incremental progress. Every exercise and every session focused on the very practical goal of improving functionality. The exercises meant nothing if at the end of therapy they did not help me become more functional in some aspect of cognition or life skills. In the beginning therapy sessions, we focused on exercises that used number and letter sequences. I put them in proper order or tried to recall numbers and letters from different lists. I grouped color-coded words together. I forgot my instructions in the middle of an exercise and Gina would simply stop me and review the instructions.

"That's okay," she would say in her soft clinical voice. Forgetting was forgivable. Imperfection pulled me one step closer to perfection. The universe did not come crashing in on my brain if I bungled, simply because there was no such thing as bungling. An exercise was an exercise; it helped improve my brain. I repeated the exercises in our sessions and eventually we saw improvements in accuracy and speed. One week led to the next, one new dendrite touched another, one at a time, and my memory and sequencing and focus began to improve.

Gina was patient. I was impatient. I compared my speed and complexity in recovery to the kinds of tasks I used to do in emergency medicine.

"That's not a fair comparison," Gina would say. "Don't beat yourself up by measuring your progress against how you used to do things."

"But I feel stupid and slow."

"Your intelligence has not changed, only the speed and access to information."

And when she assured me that I was still a doctor with stores of knowledge and experience, I wanted to work harder and recover more function.

I ALTERNATED PSYCHOLOGY and cognitive therapy, so I rarely had them the same day. I needed the time in between to recover and think, especially as it related to the more emotionally traumatic sessions of PTSD therapy. I still struggled with the diagnosis and with the whole approach of confrontational therapy. After sessions, I always felt drained and wanted to distance myself from the sessions. About a month or so into therapy, Heather asked me specific questions about my dreams.

"Do you ever wake with night terrors or thrash around in bed?" She was prying again. I felt the hard edges of her question.

"Rarely," I answered. "I had more of that when I first returned from Iraq."

"And what about the dream wakes you? It is always the same one?"

"It's usually the same one. An enemy is attacking me and we fight, hand-to-hand. I kick or punch with my fists and that's what wakes me up. Sometimes I roll around and get caught in the sheets. That always gets me riled up, because it feels like someone is grabbing me and sometimes I yell out and scare my wife."

"Have you ever hurt yourself or your wife in a dream?" she asked bluntly.

I didn't want to go down that path. I wanted to shade my answer without having to violate the truth substantially. I felt I had earned the right to keep some things to myself.

"Not really. I did kick the wall by the side of the bed a few times, but other than a bruise, I was all right."

"How often does that happen?"

"Rarely anymore. It's mostly gone."

She raised her eyebrows and tilted her head just a tad. "Completely gone?"

"Not a hundred percent, but I'm fine. My dreams are mostly okay."

Heather wanted to keep digging, but I wanted to move on. Dreams were dreams. Nothing could be done to erase the ones that had already occurred, and nothing could prevent a nightmare from slipping through a mental crack now and then. I tried to change the subject, but she was a spy. Prying. Probing. Questioning. Her pestering questions threatened to grab hold of my secrets and make them public. Those secrets were mine; I could not let them out.

"How does your wife react when you have your worst dreams?"

"Well, sometimes she has to wake me up, but that was more when I first came home. Like I said, my dreams are okay now."

"Does she still have to wake you?"

"Rarely. Only once in a great while, and then I go back to sleep."

"Do you talk to her about the dreams?"

"Yes, just to give her an idea, so she's not scared."

The dream talk went on for more than I wanted it to, and when we got to the end of the session, Heather said she felt like there was more. There was, but I wasn't going to say anything, and she was making me mad with all her psychobabble questions. Exposing my dreams and nightmares contained its own kind of creeping vulnerability, so I decided to hold the worst of my nightmares to myself.

IN MY MORNING ROUTINES, I continued aquatherapy with an arthritis swim group. Ray, one of the leaders, was a Vietnam veteran and a former Army Ranger. We joked around in the pool and sometimes went out for coffee afterward. At coffee one day, he asked me how my VA therapy was going. I told him about my psychologist and the skullduggery of talking about dreams and war and PTSD. Ray was a shoot-from-the-hip sort of veteran and he would blurt out things that made complete sense but were often embarrassing or politically incorrect.

"Sounds like the VA thinks you're crazy, like me," he said, loud enough so the tables next to us could hear. That's just what I had wanted, my therapy as coffee talk for the other tables. He went on to tell me of his own VA psych experience and how he told the psychologist about his fits of nightmares when he first got back from Vietnam.

"Hell, yes," he said. "I almost strangled my wife several times. I thought she was sneaking under the wire to kill me, so I choked her before she got the chance. I don't know how she survived that first year back."

We both made light of it, as if to make it less serious, but he made his dreams sound so real. The enemy sneaking in to get him. His thrashing in bed, the night sweats, the absolute terror, and his yelling and fighting in bed. He said he was glad he locked up his guns or he might have shot his wife that first year back. I didn't know what to think. He wasn't trying to trivialize the experience or trying to play psychologist. He was more or less neutral or clinical, as if the incidents were unfortunate but natural consequences of war and nothing to be ashamed of. He said the North Vietnamese soldiers were always sneaking under the wire and infiltrating the camps, and that his greatest fear was getting knifed as he slept. He asked me if I ever had dreams like those. I said I did, then changed the subject.

In Iraq, enemy insurgents didn't crawl under a wire into our camps. Instead, they laid out roadside IEDs and beheaded people in front of video cams. They tortured and dragged captured soldiers through the streets, then burned their bodies and left the corpses hanging from bridges or tied them to a post for everybody to see. My greatest fear was being captured and beheaded. My nightmares centered on my arms being pulled out of their sockets and being marched in front of a camera with a black hood on my head, screaming as an insurgent took a knife to my neck. And when I dreamed them, I could feel the pain in my shoulders. The endings always escalated into a hand-to-hand fight where I thrashed in bed and got tangled in the sheets, and when the blankets rubbed against my neck, I attacked in a rage. I clenched my fists and punched at will. I kicked and clawed and screamed until

I got my hands on my enemy's neck and pressed on his trachea, which I knew was vulnerable. On the other side of my nightmare, Collin screamed and cried as she took the brunt of my war-fed panic. I kicked and kneed and punched her with a closed fist, and I didn't stop until she woke me up. Once, according to her, I got her in a chokehold and she panicked. When I finally woke to her screams, I felt fear and sorrow and shame. And I wanted to hide myself or run away so I couldn't hurt her.

In the next session with Heather, I decided to tell her about my pool buddy Ray and his traumatic nightmares. After a bit of her prodding, I leaked some parts about my dreams and how they became so vivid they distorted reality and how my wife became my enemy and I attacked her to survive. The secret was bare and open and the telling of it made me ashamed, but it also confirmed what we had both known and I was now facing.

"Would you refer a soldier for PTSD counseling if they gave you that same clinical history?" Heather asked.

I hesitated before I responded. "Yes, I would."

As I heard the logic of her question and my own short reply, I knew she was talking about me. And like the experience of finally admitting to my stroke and its consequences, admitting to PTSD and its sequelae gave me a sense of freedom and power to confront the whole truth of my injuries.

Heather wanted to introduce me to therapeutic writing, not just journaling but writing a short piece about an incident that was recurrent in my thoughts or dreams. In the previous session I had thought I might be done with the whole describe-your-worst-scenarios approach. That part of therapy elicited gut-wrenching emotions and horrific memories. The "fun meter," as I used to joke, stayed on zero for those sessions. I needed a break.

"Can we do that next week?" I asked.

Despite her lack of military experience, Heather displayed a mission-minded persistence that reminded me of a range sergeant: *we were going to stick to the task until it was completed.*

"Yes, we can, but I want to get you started on some short reading from trauma patients so you get the sense of how this might be helpful."

"Okay, but I'm tired of bringing up these memories. No offense, but I feel like shit after some of our sessions."

I thought she would be offended, but she wasn't. She remained professional and unfazed, like she had heard it before.

"That's natural. You're processing the most difficult of human emotions and it's not easy. If you can, tell me just in a few words what you might write about."

"If I had to pick one out of many, I would write about a postmortem identification of a soldier who was a colleague and friend. I had to identify him after a helicopter crash. I remember it all the time."

"That's all we need for now. Just an idea, no more. And if you feel like writing about it, just write details as they come to mind. Don't try to make sense of them; just write down anything that comes to mind, like a free-writing exercise."

I took the writing samples and over the next few days ignored them. Then, two days before my next session, I read them. Mostly they felt strained, as if the writers were trying to make a point but were at odds with writing short essays. There were four short articles. One described how a soldier had shot a dog in Iraq and how that affected the writer because the dog probably belonged to some Iraqi kid. The dog story made the most sense to me—not because I liked dogs, but because the writer connected how an incident of combat that had no bearing on war had a bearing on humanity.

When Heather encouraged me to write about the helicopter crash, it was October 2008. Four years had passed since I performed the postmortem identification on Lieutenant Michaels and his copilot. I expected the time was enough to distance me from the traumatic context. It was not. Writing about the incident triggered vivid and horrific memories, including the smells and even the prickly skin sensations I had experienced. The writing exercises dragged on for a month and, in my own clinical judgment, did not help.

Initially, I wrote at a table in a coffee shop. One paragraph or even one sentence took hours to write, each word stirring the deep emotions of that singular incident of war. Unavoidably, the hardest details brought me to weep, not for myself but for the soldiers I had cared for. I felt lost. Often, my struggle became so intense I left the restaurant and drove home where I sat alone in the basement trying to gain some distance from the memories. Sitting in the basement only made writing more difficult, as if the isolation concentrated my focus too much. For weeks, I repeated the same writing process.

Heather thought if I could frame the crash in a different context, one that did not inevitably collapse into an emotional impasse, I might make some progress. I didn't know how to do that so I tried approaching the writing as a clinician doing a medical investigation. Rather than forcing myself to expose hidden feelings and emotions attached to the crash, I simply described what I saw, writing only the objective findings of fact relevant to the postmortem identification. It was the same technique I had used in Iraq: focus on the objective nature of the findings; keep an emotional distance if you can. With that perspective, I found a paradoxical sense of freedom—in a sense, permission to explore the periphery of trauma. As I explored the edges, I was able to separate the facts of the incident from the emotion of the incident, creating a dual perspective where I finally understood that writing about a traumatic event was not equivalent to the event itself. That truth may have been self-evident to therapists, but to me, at my stage of healing, the distinction between what was real in combat and what was remembered at home became obscured by the diffusion of one reality into the other. Keeping them separate was not easy.

That initial small understanding about the dual nature of trauma, real versus remembered, allowed me just enough space to compartmentalize my traumatic memories into specific blocks of time where they had limited emotional momentum. During that time I wrote objective notes to myself. The process was often difficult. On many days I could not write. On some days I wrote one line in five or ten minutes, then I stopped and sat and relived the details, often writing nothing for hours. I used to get angry and cuss at myself for not being able to write and think objectively. On occasion I would break out in spontaneous tears when writing at a coffee shop, and I would pretend I had something in my eyes and rub them red, then leave in a hurry.

One morning, more than four years after my stroke, I could not bring myself to write. Like a soldier, I gave myself an order: "Cut the crap and start writing!"

I wrote one line, then one more, and that forced beginning opened a torrent of free writing that continued almost four hours. It included descriptions, emotions, and rants. It was messy, horrific, and shitty. It was raw. It was primal. Most of all, it was real. I wrote about the postmortem exam in all its horrifying detail. I described the mutilated pieces, the ravaged bones, and the smoked smell of charred muscle. I noted every torn and missing organ. I revealed my weakness, my sorrow, my fear—all the things that I could never write in a standard Army report or tell another soldier or my wife. I showed how I was confused and at the same time embarrassed, because as a physician I could not identify what I had seen in a body bag. I wrote how I struggled to say the word "decapitation." I let myself describe how worn and tired I had become, and how as a soldier-doctor I hated war yet loved war. Then I outlined how those incongruities tore at my spirit. At the end of my writing session, I wrote about the sound of the body bag zipper, how it distorted reality within the context of war. "In its simplest form," I wrote, "a zipper is but a pull-tab, a slider, and two rows of teeth. Yet in the context of war, it symbolizes the constant and horrible reality of death." In that context, the image and sound of a zipper helped me understand the struggle of having to bear the necessary imperative of combat—to kill and destroy. That was my greatest struggle as a soldier and doctor, blending the ethics of one into the ethics of the other. And that was a strained and binary ethic, one that touched the borders of love and hate, evil and good; it pitted the military dogma of killing the enemy against the religious dogma of loving the enemy. It juxtaposed death and dismemberment with rescue and healing and asked how they fit together. It questioned what it meant to be a soldier and a citizen, a father and a husband, a doctor and a patient. Mostly, it pressed against the compressed and easy answers that soldiers often give: "It was my duty or my job." Being a doctor and a soldier was always more than a job or a duty; it was life and death played out within the walls of a hospital tent and within the depths of human hearts.

After my writing about the crash and the sound of a zipper, I showed it to Heather in a therapy session. I mostly read it to her and we paused to reflect on certain key points. She was quiet and respectful, as if perhaps she were attending a funeral or a wake. Sitting forward on her chair, she gently asked me to slow down in a few places where it was painful for me to read and where I could see her tears mounting, and in those places we both wept for all the things we had lost in war. And I didn't care anymore that she wasn't a soldier or hadn't gone to war. We had both felt the force of its aftermath. I went back for a few more sessions with her, and then over a month or so I let them fade until I went no more. I wasn't displeased with her or with therapy, but she had taken me far enough in healing. The work I still had left to do I felt I could do by continuing to think and write and ask for help if I needed it.

I WORKED WITH Gina in cognitive therapy weekly and we made gains that finally showed on my chart. Measured gains. Real gains. I was faster in some forms of puzzles and exercises. I understood more words and more complexities. She custom-designed exercises using clinical vignettes and medical vocabulary. I advanced to "master list maker" and focused on sequencing and prioritizing multiple daily activities. I remembered to take my medication on schedule at least 70 percent of the time and learned to plan ahead for things that could interfere with my schedule and activities. We talked about my future. What did I want to do? What skills were transferable? Could I teach anatomy at the medical school? Teach something—anything? I was a model patient and Gina was a model speech and language therapist. Anything was possible.

At times, when needed, she brought me back to reality. She reminded me to maintain focus and intentionality when controlling my activities and my environment. I still needed therapy, but overall I had made so much progress that I felt like a list-making, stroke-recovering, cane-toting genius who had finally broken the therapy mold and uniquely declared, "I get it. I finally get it."

What I felt I was beginning to "get" was an understanding of all the changes, physical, mental, and vocational, that stroke brought into my life. But more, I was gaining an understanding that recovery involved more than a series of rehab sessions, it involved, no demanded, a change of mind and will.

WITH THAT UNDERSTANDING in mind, Gina and I worked toward a new therapeutic paradigm. We targeted cognitive strategies that challenged the notion of relatively fixed clinical plateaus that patients reached over time but rarely went beyond. The idea was nebulous at first, a flight of imagination, a look beyond the horizon, but it was there. We were talking about it, thinking about it, planning it. I still needed the routines of brain exercises and all the sequencing and calculations and readings that I had been doing. But if I chose, therapy would diverge from basic functional exercises toward higher-order brain functioning and problem solving that required more than brain exercises. The essence of this metacognitive approach meant that I would have to think about thinking and structure my own questions when trying to solve a real-life problem. I couldn't simply ask for another round of therapy. The approach held the promise of increased independence and functionality, especially with complex and multidimensional tasks. Writing was a prime example. At the time, I had difficulty structuring a sentence. How would I solve the puzzle of writing a short essay or managing the structure of a book? I didn't know, but if we were successful in our new therapy, I could figure it out or find resources to help me.

The List

Iowa City, Iowa; Summer 2009

TOOTHPASTE, TOILET PAPER, hamburger, ketchup, buns. Five items made a Saturday morning grocery list. Collin rehearsed the items with me, face-to-face, asking me to repeat the list. It was the only way she knew if I understood her. When she asked if I understood, I always nodded my head. On the way out the door, I double-checked my wallet for money, stuffed the list in my left pocket, and headed to the grocery store. Got it. Simple. Drive directly to the store, buy the items on the list, return home. Thirty minutes max. En route, I stopped at a coffee shop to relax a bit. I bumped into a friend and we bantered about the everyday stuff that coffee shops elicit: our families, current events, politics, and the recent trend in the price of gas. Two hours passed. As I finished my coffee time, I remembered that I needed to make a grocery store run.

At the store, I wandered the aisles and gazed at the shelves. I traveled every aisle, up and down, sometimes twice. I was looking for something, but I didn't know exactly what. The meat and seafood section was especially appealing. I watched live Maine lobsters and silver-scaled tilapia swim in Plexiglas cold-water tanks. Their movements fascinated me. I finally decided on one pound of king crab legs and two half-pound T-bone steaks. The demo lady at the end of the aisle near the seafood displayed a special cranberry horseradish sauce that she promised went well with steaks. I gobbled a sample on a cracker. "Wow, that's really good," I said. She smiled. I couldn't imagine we didn't have this at home. I added two jars to the cart.

In the bakery, the yeasty smell of fresh bread overwhelmed me. I gently laid two French loaves in the child seat of the cart, up high and out of danger from being crushed. I added four éclairs just for effect. As I thought about dessert, I sensed the need to get some other items, but I couldn't remember what they were. Whatever information was conveyed in the "nonexistent" grocery discussion with Collin had vanished, so of course I wasn't concerned that I didn't remember it. I only knew I was in a grocery store. I knew how I got there and that I needed to buy food. The list in my pocket did not even register in my mind. I had no agenda, no plan, no list—just this compulsion: buy food.

Following that general notion, I roamed the store. Pickles. I needed pickles. Barbecue sauce would be good. And cake mix. I added three milk chocolate, three French vanilla, and three lemon—all on sale. I savored the thought of Collin being so happy with me because I looked for discounts. Bright orange placards announced a temporary price reduction on cake frosting. I added six cans of various flavors, then rushed over to the dairy department and threw in three blocks of cream cheese because I always used cream cheese in my frosting recipe. Near the cream cheese aisle was the yogurt aisle. I couldn't recall seeing so many interesting combinations of fruit and yogurt. Ten cups for eight dollars. A steal. I arranged them artfully next to the French bread. The bread reminded me that a nice cabernet would go well with the T-bones. Off to the wine section I rolled my cart.

I spent a full half hour gawking at the artistry of the wine labels. I finally decided on an Argentinean blend with a nice colorful label. The wine reminded me that aged cheese would be good. I headed to the cheese display. Same treatment as with the wine. I spent thirty-some minutes eyeing the cheeses. In the cart went Camembert, a wedge of Canadian Black Diamond cheddar, and a new cranberry goat cheese spread. Cheese needed crackers. I added two boxes of gourmet crackers.

I continued my shopping spree until my cart was about half-full. I sensed that I didn't need all that I had decided to get, but I really didn't know what, if anything, I was supposed to get. So I added just a few more small items: jelly beans, tangerines (my wife liked them because they peel so easily), a few candy bars, and a quart of Ben & Jerry's ice cream.

At the checkout counter, the cashier asked if I had found everything okay. "Yep," I said. "Gonna have surf and turf tonight."

"How fun," she said. "It looks like you're planning a party."

"Just the two of us," I responded. She smiled. The tally went well over $100. I swiped my credit card and the bagger loaded the cart. Off to the parking lot I went with seven plastic bags for dinner.

I got home about noon. Collin was making lunch. I was so excited as I brought the groceries in and plunked them on the kitchen counter.

"I got you some jelly beans," I announced with a smile.

"Oh, no . . ." she began. "What's all this? What happened to the list?"

"What list?" I asked.

She moaned and shook her head, then reminded me of our grocery conversation earlier that day, of the list she made, of the folded slip of paper in my pocket. I told her that I didn't remember any list. She asked if I checked my pockets.

"Five things, that's all you had to get."

She was a bit upset with me. I pulled the list from my pocket.

"Oops," I said. I felt badly, but had no remorse. I was not sorry for things I could not yet control.

FOLLOWING MY INSTRUCTIONS from cognitive therapy, I made lists for everything: medication, medical appointments, errands, writing, reading, free time, and family time. I made lists for cooking and cleaning, for yard work and housework. Banking and taxes were on a list. Handling money was tricky without a list. Sometimes I lost checks for deposit because they were not on a list. I decorated the house with Post-it notes. Take meds. Feed cat. Gas car. Stay home. VA appointment. Read book. I left the cat out on the screened porch one day in the middle of winter. I didn't write a note to let him back in or set a timer to remind me. I left for a coffee shop and stayed for three hours. Collin returned home for lunch and found the cat—still alive. I caught hell from my wife . . . and the cat. If something needed to be done and was not on a list, it usually didn't get done at all.

Spontaneous events in my life created a greater emotional impact and tended to override my planned events. Colors of seafood, movements of fish, and the art of wine labels could evoke a stimulating diversion from the dull and inanimate world of lists. Interactions and objects that stimulated my senses usually altered my direction of thought and broke my focus. I literally became "listless" when under the influence of sensory details—something of a sensory attack.

Gina and Dr. Hall had told me that the executive functioning part of my brain was still recovering. Consequently, higher-order thinking, such as sequencing and prioritizing, problem solving and multitasking, did not operate as they should have. With the added deficits in attention processing and disruptions of short-term memory, the milieu in which I tried to order my thoughts became a torrent of distractibility and hesitation. The making of lists helped me accomplish basic everyday tasks. They helped me focus and maintain intentionality in everything I did.

At the top of one of my earliest lists, Cher had written in bold letters, **Kiss Wife**. No list—no action. In the first year of my stroke, I often felt like I was living in a never-ending labyrinth of confusing choices that overwhelmed my ability to discern the important from the unimportant. A crisis of apparent urgency or the impact of sensory details could derail an ordered thought or a detailed plan within seconds. I felt trapped in a cartoon strip where five or six frames told a story, but I could never make the connections between frames, and I could never completely understand the point or get the joke.

Cher had also told me I thought in scatter plots because of the type of stroke I had. She was right. I was always connecting the dots in my brain, but in the process I made chaos out of order. When I discovered something I needed to do, I stopped mid-stride from what I was doing and changed directions immediately. When I changed directions, I often forgot what I had been doing originally. I went blank—tabula rasa. I tapped my head to jar information loose that hid among the synapses of my brain. Information was in there—I just had to find it. It was like a cognitive treasure hunt. I found a clue, changed directions to find the next clue, and then jumped to the next one and then the next. I usually forgot the original clue, then had to start over from the beginning—changing directions one more time.

To help me compensate, my therapists used list making to keep on track, primarily with first-order thinking and daily tasks. I perfected the strategy as months of therapy accumulated. I got so good at it I tried to make lists in my head, from memory, spontaneously. Then, after a round of missed appointments or multiple runs to the grocery store for the same forgotten item, I would repent and go back to my list-making basics. Collin would remind me that I needed the lists to stay on task.

"What's on your list for today," she would prod.

If I hadn't made one, I would say, "I don't know."

"Well, I hope you get it all done, then," she replied, with just enough jab to make me feel guilty.

"I'm trying to work without a list," I would say.

"And how's that working?"

There was no way out and no way to win. I simply had to use a list, on paper or in my cell phone. No list—no action.

I HATED LISTS. They reminded me of bad friends who never called unless they needed help moving furniture. Lists reminded me of litmus paper that turned red for positive or blue for negative. My lists were litmus paper; and they always turned red for brain damage. They nagged that my abilities as a doctor and a soldier had been effaced by a stroke and that I was incapable of thinking with just the pure cognitive and imaginative power of my brain. Lists filled me with the desire for things not on the list.

More than anything else, lists reminded me that I needed a list. The reminder used to piss me off. When that happened I usually wrote my lists hard and fast. I tensed my shoulders and jaw. My breathing turned shallow and choppy. Sometimes I scribbled unintelligible words, a cipher for the things I was unable to do on my own. I often relegated lists to my pocket or left them on the kitchen counter, isolated, unattended, and impotent, unable to insult my intelligence and the skills I used to possess. If I was really in a rebellious mood, I crumpled a list and tossed it in the trash. Occasionally, I tore a list into pieces and threw it in the street—a sort of therapeutic littering.

I knew that I had to move forward if I was to accomplish anything, so I relented and made another list, and then yet another. I filled them with simple things that had to be done just to survive the day. I filled them with the complex things I considered important to me, and then I worked them hard, the simple and the complex—like a doctor and soldier at war. I kept moving. At times the movement was forward, then backward, then forward again. It was never linear. But I learned to adapt to the movement no matter how helter-skelter, no matter how insignificant the days may have seemed.

On good days I didn't need a list at all. Without prompting, I thought and acted in that wild, intoxicating bliss of spontaneity. I phoned my kids and told them how good it felt to be getting smarter, faster, stronger, to be learning new things. I talked with my wife, asked her questions about a scene in a movie; I reminisced about something we did when we were first married. I kissed her just because I could. She kissed me back, smiled, and caressed my arm. She reminded me that love didn't need a list. And in the strength of those moments, I crossed from a world of checked-box therapy into a world where spontaneous ideas flowed outside the lines like the crayon art of school-age children. That movement invigorated me, saved me, and reminded me who I really was.

Thinking Level 5.3

A S A NATURAL CONSEQUENCE of improvement in therapy, I wanted to recapture the ability to think like I used to when I practiced medicine. That desire created a major sticking point in therapy. I persistently looked back to the kind of thinking I had done as a physician. It was facile, quick, and confident. I prided myself in being able to forge order out of chaos. I acted with decisiveness and boldness in emergency and combat medicine. After my stroke, that all changed. I never regained the level of cognitive skill I had possessed in medicine, but I wanted to recover at least some ability to think with higher-order logic. Thinking only at the basic, daily activities level bored me and frustrated me. I used to get angry with myself for failing to understand conversations with more than one person at a time. If I read *Scientific American* or *Smithsonian* magazine, I just looked at the pictures and captions because the text was too detailed. I got caught in loops of sentences because I had trouble extracting meaning from analogies or metaphors. I tapped my forehead to help me think, as if the tapping could loosen a dangling word or free a thought.

My thinking resembled a nonlinear, random pattern of information. When I tried to understand the deeper meanings embedded within a story or a conversation or a complex problem, my thoughts became even more scattered and unpredictable. I could only see and think about things one frame at a time, but the frames didn't necessarily connect. My thoughts became fragmented, taking me in directions that had no apparent coherence or connection with reality.

In conversation and speech, I mispronounced words. *Medical appointment* could come out as "medcala appoint." *Brain* morphed into "bainir." My brain and tongue felt like they weren't connected at times. If I initiated a conversation, I could sound fairly smart; but if somebody asked me questions about medicine, or about a conversation I had the day before, or even an hour before, I faltered. I couldn't recall enough information to form an abstract thought and I couldn't process information quickly enough to make an intelligent-sounding response. Army doctors at Fort Knox, in their final assessment of my stroke status, said I didn't have the cognitive ability to process critical information. They were right. I had difficulty thinking. With respect to memory, on some days I couldn't recall Gina's name or Dr. Hall's name, so I asked the receptionist so I wouldn't be embarrassed. I feared losing memories of Collin and my children. Secretly, I contemplated getting their names tattooed on the sides of my fingers.

In the process of moving from basic to higher-order cognitive functioning, Gina and Dr. Hall modified my therapeutic sessions to include routines that emphasized complex and abstract thinking, executive functioning, and metacognitive processing. Much of cognitive therapy mystified me and I didn't fully understand the logic of brain exercises and repetitive tasks. It wasn't always clear how puzzles and sequencing exercises would eventually translate into complex thinking. Some of my sessions focused more on encouraging me to stay on track to hit a very fuzzy target—to be able to think about thinking, metacognitive processing. I felt like a stranger to myself and to Collin, though less to my kids, who didn't see the day-to-day impact of rebuilding cognitive skills. Gina or Dr. Hall had no specific or exclusive brain exercises that led to specific gains in metacognitive function. To me, the therapy tended toward the nebulous side of medicine. I didn't see any real progress from my perspective, yet Gina and Dr. Hall saw incremental improvements in my thinking and charted tiny movements in progress, so I kept going back to "brain school," as I used to call it, week after week, month after month.

My new therapy plan began in January 2009 and would continue as long as needed. The first steps used a series of prerecorded listening exercises in a program called attention process training. The goal was to increase my skills at focusing and processing more complex verbal instructions. Gina monitored my progress as I listened and wrote my answers. In any given session, she usually had to stop the tape one or two times because I got confused by the instructions or forgot them while I responded. The instructions included compound commands that raised the level of complexity tenfold, or at least that's how it seemed. The male voice on the tape droned on without inflection—a therapy robot: "Select from the card deck the red, even numbers only, then add them." Those simple instructions I followed, but the compound instructions lost me. "Select from the card deck the red, odd numbers, but only if the number is red and the word for the number is green. Do not select the red odd numbers if the number and word for the number are both red." I got confused trying to remember the permutations of colors and numbers or colors and words. The exercise required not only a great deal of attention but also relatively quick memory formation and recall. The slightest distraction in the exam room—the squeaking of a chair, the tick of a clock, a wave of Gina's hair—and I would lose my concentration and muff the exercise. In one session, a fly buzzing around the room landed on my head and changed my focus for the entire session.

When I first started the program, I wanted to kick myself when I left Gina's office. I knew she was giving me exercises meant to push my cognitive recovery, but they always made me feel stupid and inadequate. Gina noticed that and spent time reminding me that our goal was slow, incremental progress, not an overnight recovery. We pushed for weeks at a time, and then she changed the exercises to give me a "brain break."

We worked on attention process training and reading concurrently. I read so slowly that I got distracted by extraneous thoughts and memories. Certain words—for example, *run, fight, weapon,* and *desert*—triggered thoughts of war and Iraq. Less obvious triggers included words like *oil, watch,* and *water. Oil* reminded me of the burning oil fields in southern Iraq; *watch* triggered the images of my aviator friend killed in action; and *water* brought back memories of two-liter water bottles delivered on pallets by C-130s. The wanderings led me from the context of the story I was reading in 2008 to the context of the war I had fought from 2003 to 2006. I had no clue how to control trigger words other than to just keep reading and hoping that, over time, the power of triggers might dissipate.

In addition to trigger words, environmental distractions often derailed my reading. If I read at a coffee shop, typical noises in the restaurant caught my attention or startled me. Conversations from friends pulled me in and I would lay my book aside and join them.

In therapy, our metacognitive approach to solving reading issues involved discovering the root causes and proposing solutions. Gina didn't tell me what the corrective actions or strategies should be, but instead asked me to think about them until the next session.

"As you think about your reading," she said, "try to think about different things you could do to control the environment of your reading."

That extra logical task required me to perform a deeper analysis; it meant I had to think about thinking, to think about the variable components of a problem and its solutions. It was something akin to contingency planning in the military; it required multifocal thinking.

IN ADDITION TO distractions, we identified two specific reading problems, word substitution and sentence comprehension. When I read, I frequently substituted one word for another or one letter for another. Sometimes I dropped complete words or partial words from a sentence so it might read something like "Jack a Jill up hill to pail water." The word-chopping thing happened every time I read. At times it was so severe that I got lost in meaninglessness and would stop reading. At first I used to blame the authors, thinking they just wrote terrible sentences. I grew frustrated and wanted to pull my hair, but instead I held open books up to my forehead, trying to force my brain to understand sentences, as if osmosis might transfer the meanings directly from the pages. When that didn't work, I tapped a book against the sides of my head. That didn't work either.

Books became my enemies. I would start one book, put it away, and then start another. I used to have five or more books open and scattered around the house at any given time, each with a bookmark marking the places where I was lost. Sometimes I left them unread for weeks at a time, then tried to pick up where I had left off. I always had to start over from the beginning. I made notes in my journal about being stuck in sentences and lost in fragments, about being tired and wanting my brain back the way it was. Gina and Dr. Hall discussed that with me and said that the fact that I was even able to start making notes showed I was using higher-order thinking. I didn't know about that, but what I did know was that reading became tedious and painful. In my mind there was no solution. Gina asked me to continue reading and taking notes, not just about meanings and characters, but about process and structure.

On February 14, 2009, I finished reading *The Story and Its Writer*, the short story anthology I had started with Cher in August 2007. I wrote the date inside the front cover and celebrated by skimming the pages and rereading a six-paragraph short story by Sandra Cisneros, "My Name." When I read it originally, I responded to it by writing in my therapy journal about my own name, with respect to my title, "MD," and how its meaning had changed since my stroke. From a literary point of view, my writing was abysmal. Cher told me I had used another person's literary voice as my own and it didn't work to reveal my own personal insights about identity and loss. I was cheating, in a sense. I needed to use my own voice. It was my first try at writing something in depth.

When I reread "My Name" on the day I finished the anthology, I read it at least five times. I studied it. It portrayed what I had been grappling with in therapy; like Cisneros, I wanted a new name that would reflect the real me. Her writing came from the heart of a multicultural perspective and it made me think in a different way about issues other than recovery. As I read and studied her six short paragraphs, I wished I could write like her. In the space of a single page, she opened a cultural door that invited readers to explore the cultural and social meanings embedded in a name—her name. I wondered how I could ever do the same. I decided I could not. If I did write, I would have to discover my own voice, as Cher had said. At the time, more than two years later,

I had difficulty retaining my own identity as a stroke survivor let alone a distinctive voice. Gina and I talked about the reading in a session. She said I was gaining insight in my readings. I wasn't sure. She told me to keep reading, keep thinking, keep working the plan.

For Christmas in 2008, Darren had given me the first *Hunger Games* book by Suzanne Collins.

"Dad, I think you'll like this book," he said when he gave it to me.

He knew I was having difficulty reading and he thought the book would be easy enough to understand.

I thanked him and added it to my pile of books. In April, after Easter, I decided to read it. I knew it was a young adult dystopian novel and that was not really my genre, but I had enjoyed science fiction in high school and had a personal reading rule: if somebody gave me a book, I read it. I looked up *The Hunger Games* on several websites. It was referred to as a grade level 5.3 book. Grade level 5.3. The number stuck. I thought I was certainly capable. I started the book in my recliner next to the fireplace on a Saturday evening after dinner. I was still reading at 10:00 p.m.

It took a week to read the entire book. I put it down between readings, picked it up where I had left off. I didn't have to retrace any chapters because I could remember the plot and the characters. The story swept me in by its easy readability and its clean, tight prose. And the plot kept me thinking: *What's next? What's next?* I was so excited. I had read a book in a week and retained enough to repeat the story to Collin and then to Gina in therapy. Grade level 5.3. That was my level of comprehension. My reading speed was slower than my comprehension but I didn't care. I could think! I could read! Gina said my progress was remarkable.

The following week I discussed the epic event with Dr. Hall and he suggested it showed my improvement and that perhaps it was time to consider other vocational options for my future. I was retired from the military and from medicine, so I didn't fully understand what he meant by "other options."

"You mean like getting a job?" I asked.

"Not exactly. Something more like going back to school."

Wride (Write)

M EETING WITH DR. HALL was always interesting. He had an edgy yet professional demeanor and he would always laugh with me when I poked fun at my progress or at psychology. We often laughed at the twists and oddities of cognitive recovery. During most sessions we talked about therapy issues and he usually filled me in on the latest developments in mental health for soldiers. Those sessions tended to lean toward the serious end of a continuum. At the other end was a light-hearted treatment of all things clinical as if we were more like friends than patient and doctor, though I knew that was a relationship that held firm and couldn't be changed. One of the interns who sat in on our sessions asked me a zany question in her first interview with me.

"So, how's your disability?" she asked.

"Well, kind of disabling," I shot back. And I laughed until I was breathless.

Dr. Hall loved that anecdote, because it showed how both he and I could muster a sense of humor and laugh at our own circumstances. I joked about VA administrators and cognitive tests and exercises. "How can you tell how many administrators are on duty in the hospital?" I asked him. Answer: "You roll a donut down the hall." Laughter therapy.

At other times, when I told him I had felt less than properly treated in a situation involving a VA staff member, he would go to bat for me and get on the phone to resolve any care issues. He was tenacious on behalf of patients.

He addressed me as "Dr. Kerstetter" and frequently reminded me that my professional education and experiences gave me an advantage in therapy. On days when he reviewed my cognitive tests, he always put the results in the context of recovery. He would take a particularly poor testing result like reading speed and ask me to focus on a strategy for improvement rather than a test number. "Don't focus on the numbers," he would say rather forcefully. "Focus on recovery." And as I listened to him, his counsel made perfect clinical sense. Move patients forward rather than let them linger on what they had lost. That was his talent. And he made sure I felt clinically relevant in that movement forward.

I felt like he understood the gravity of treating a patient who equated losing a career with losing a leg. To him, I was more than a patient who had lost clusters of brain cells. That loss had caused a rift in my identity as a physician and a soldier, but he didn't spend much time in session pondering the weight of it. Instead, he created a therapeutic climate that stressed healing and the need to keep pushing forward to explore new boundaries. He and Gina were alike in that regard. Their encouraging interventional styles, coupled with my proclivities for challenging boundaries, formed a perfect therapeutic triangulation—self-motivation, cognitive training, and directed encouragement. That didn't necessarily translate into quick results, but there was something happening in my recovery that was certainly rare and special. When Dr. Hall spoke about the extent of my recovery, he always noted how high-functioning I had become and how some patients with less demonstrable brain injury did not recover to the same degree. In part, I thought of my recovery as motivated by the fear of becoming nothing, a person who would live only in the shell of a former life, devoid of the joys of professional identity. Yes, I had my family, my wife, my children and grandchildren. I had love and meaning as a father and husband. I had far more recovery than many stroke survivors. Added together, it all meant that I enjoyed a full measure of personal and family significance, but that wasn't enough. Love for my family and the love of my family were not the same as love for my profession. Simply put, I missed my life as a doctor and soldier.

Dr. Hall encouraged me to look beyond the loss of my career. As

I did, I found that the core of my passion for medicine was an un-quenchable desire for knowledge. It had driven me and pushed me since my childhood. So when he told me in the first few minutes of our therapy session that we needed to explore my vocational options, it didn't totally surprise me, although I didn't completely understand the gist of his conversation. I thought he had opened a channel for exploring a reentry into medicine, but I knew that topic had been closed for some time.

"I can't practice medicine," I reminded him. "I can't retrain in another specialty. I still have gait and balance issues. I still can't think worth crap. I don't think I have any vocational options."

"If you did, what would you like to do?" he asked.

"I don't know. Learn to read more books, maybe."

"Have you ever thought about writing? It has the potential of becoming a natural outgrowth of your reading. The MFA program here is interested in helping veterans."

I was thinking in a vacuum when he said that. Writing had given me fits. Did he think I could learn to write?

"I can't write and I can't go back to school. I can barely read at the sixth-grade level. I think you have to read and write in an MFA program."

"Dr. Kerstetter, our progress has not stalled out. You have the intellect and the motivation to learn more. What if we tried it for a semester?" He was serious about it. And he was talking in the fast-paced voice that he used when he was excited.

"I don't think it works that way," I said. "I can't just sign up for classes."

"Wait a minute," he said. "Don't jump to conclusions yet. Let's think about it for a week and see how you feel about the idea."

How I felt was bewildered. I couldn't imagine myself in grad school again.

"I just don't think it would work," I concluded.

I did think about my future in the days that followed. I saw it as foggy. I could no longer work as a physician. There were absolutely no prospects of returning to anything related to the field of medical

science, and writing seemed far-fetched. I could imagine myself as
a burger flipper, a library assistant, or an artist, but not as a writer.
Writing never held any vocational interest for me. I had taken a poetry class once at the Iowa Summer Writing Festival, but that was a
one-week fling with words that didn't even add up to fully formed
sentences. Dr. Hall and Heather were both inclined toward writing
as therapy, and I had done some therapeutic journaling, but doing so
as an author strained the limits of therapeutic feasibility. At the very
least, it demanded sustained attention that I did not possess.

Yet there it was, the idea that I could learn to write. Dr. Hall had
spoken the words, released the idea like a falconer releasing a bird.
He let the idea take flight, and my mind followed. Could I accomplish
such a complex task? What would writing mean to me? To others?
What if I could not learn fast enough? What if I could? The possible
answers frightened me. I conjured up excuses why I should not go
to graduate school. Age: at fifty-nine years old, I felt a bit out of my
prime for going back to school. Reading ability: grade level 5.3 worked
for reading young adult novels. It would not suffice for graduate-level
reading. Rehab: I was still in rehab. Would I put my therapy on hold?
What would happen to my brain if I did? Speed: I wasn't very fast
at anything: reading, thinking, walking, planning. Graduate school
required speed. I would have to keep up a fast pace with a slow brain.

The whole idea seemed to me nothing more than delusional happy
talk and therapeutic silliness, an exercise in positive mental attitudes
encountering impenetrable negative forces. But Dr. Hall thought I
could do more. I *wanted* to do more. Therapy had paid off. I was actually making significant cognitive gains. I surpassed a clinical plateau about every six months. When I passed one plateau, we defined a
new limit, and then another, and then one more. With each crossing,
we wondered if that might become the final boundary, my true limit
of recovery. It made me question the legitimacy of clinical plateaus.
What was the limit of stroke recovery? Were limits real or therapeutic
constructs? If they were real, how would I know when I arrived at a
point beyond which no further gains were possible or practical? There
was no answer.

My entire life had been about redefining limits and pushing against boundaries. In two years of cognitive therapy, I had learned to read and think well beyond my abilities in the immediate aftermath of my stroke. Dr. Hall tested my gains, showed me the results, and said I could learn more. And just as air bubbles had floated into my brain and changed my life two years earlier, an idea surfaced that carried the same potential for change: I could learn to write. It was a nutty idea, intangible, unrealistic—a dream. It was undeniably beyond reach, but it was there. So I grabbed hold of every damn crazy notion and cognitive nuance of what writing could mean and what it promised. With every firing neuron in my brain, I calculated how and why and if I could learn to write, and then I decided to cross that line separating all things possible from all things unknown.

As a way of validating my decision, I reread some of the stories in my short story anthology and restarted the *Hunger Games* book. One thing grabbed me immediately; good literature pulled me into the fabric of the story. It made me relate to myself on a deeper level, made me think about thinking and about divergent perspectives. It left me wanting more, just as it had when I was in high school reading J. D. Salinger and in college studying Shakespeare. If I could learn to write, that would be the metacognitive coup of a lifetime—not a vocational milestone, but a therapeutic crossing that would challenge the presumptive limitations of clinical plateaus. Writing at a graduate level would mean going well beyond the limits of therapeutic writing and cognitive brain exercises.

When I met with Dr. Hall again, I told him I might like going back to school but was unsure how it would work. I was less bewildered than when he first mentioned the idea, but it still seemed so outrageous. He had already consulted with the vocational rehabilitation counselors, who said that their department would pay for my training and, if necessary, provide tutoring if I were accepted into a writing program. It didn't have to be an MFA program, but it did have to meet their educational requirements of college or trade school education. Initially, I was excited about the idea, but I still wondered if I could perform at a graduate level of education. I had my level: 5.3. I felt it dictated my ability for reading and, by extension, learning. Dr. Hall suggested an informal interview with the staff of the MFA program at Iowa as a way forward. I agreed. Within two weeks I had three informal meetings with the director and two professors in the program. I met with several faculty in casual meetings. They told me about the demands of the program and asked if I had done any writing.

"I've been writing about my stroke a bit," I said.

They all asked about my publications.

"I have three academic papers in medical journals," I replied. When asked about my stroke writing, I told them the nutshell version.

In the end, the faculty were gracious but blunt. They didn't think I would be able to sustain the workload of reading and writing to successfully complete the program, even if I were to gain admission. That level of graduate education was highly competitive and academically rigorous. They were right. I did not have the attention and focus to sit in a classroom and listen to lectures or read numerous hours a day.

When Dr. Hall and I discussed the meetings afterward, we were both disappointed, but he said there were alternative, distance education programs. I concluded he meant correspondence courses like the ones offered when I was in college. He told me that distance education had changed and that numerous schools offered their MFA programs entirely through distance education and short residencies.

In June, I dedicated myself to contacting MFA programs with low-residency distance education curricula. Most told me to send in writing samples, fill in the application, and wait for an answer. But Ashland University in Ashland, Ohio, was different. Theirs was a relatively new program, and the director, Stephen Haven, and the program administrator, Sarah Wells, both talked to me on the phone and encouraged me to apply. They both promised that I would receive any individual attention required. I was a little suspicious, so I asked for an in-person interview. At their request, I sent them my required writing sample. I hadn't written anything except therapeutic journal entries since my stroke, so I sent them a short critical essay I had written before I went to Iraq.

During my campus visit, Sarah, who in person was even more excited than on the phone, talked with a wide smile and expressive hand gestures as she gave me a tour and answered all my technical questions relating to an Ashland MFA. She had graduated from Ashland in their undergraduate writing program and had also written poetry. Her knowledge about MFA programs and the needs of graduate students I thought remarkable. When I asked her if my stroke might create issues, she reassured me that the school could make any adjustments necessary to help me.

Professor Stephen Haven was a soft-spoken mid-career academic with numerous publications and experience teaching in China. He had published several volumes of poetry and a memoir about his boyhood among the Mohawk in New York. That caught my attention; the Mohawks and Oneidas were both part of the Iroquois Nation. I had lunch with him and we talked about my goals and cognitive deficits. He had a welcoming and collegial personality, and his refined manner and casual speech gave him the aura of a professor who was completely in touch and relevant to students. He reminded me of Dr. Hall. When Professor Haven asked about my situation and why I wanted to write, I told him about my career as a military doctor and my stroke rehab. I thought he would be put off, but he wasn't. Instead, he asked me to tell him a short vignette about being a doctor in Iraq. I told him about my medevac flight home and he listened intently. He said if I could learn to write with the same passion and intensity, I could make an impact with my writing. I had never heard that idea before, that *my* writing could possibly make an impact. I understood that was the purpose of literature, but not specifically of literature *I* might create. He sounded serious. I believed him. That was enough.

Before I left campus that afternoon, Sarah gave me a letter of acceptance into their creative writing MFA program. I would start in late July with the first of three annual two-week residencies. Excited, I called Collin at home. "I'm in! I'm in! They actually accepted me into the program." We both laughed and cheered on the phone. On the drive home I wondered what I had done.

— — —

IN THE FIRST week of my summer residency, I felt sure that I had suffered a cognitive relapse. If it were possible to beam me to a Colorado ski slope, I would have been the old man tangled in the rope tow or sliding down the hill on his ass. My fellow students were scary-smart. They seemed to know everything and possessed skills in literature and writing that made mine look paltry at best, critically anemic at worst. I sat next to two English majors who taught English in high school. I didn't dare ask them questions for fear of revealing my stupidity. Could I ask where commas were supposed to go in a sentence? What did the lecturer mean by narrative arc? What was the precise difference between an essay and a memoir? I made a quick ally of Dave MacWilliams, a college professor with a PhD in English who specialized in grammar. Grammar! I could hardly tell the difference between a comma and a colon, except that one could get cancer the other could not. There was a contingent of poets in the class who dissected words as if they were literary surgeons. They even found meaning in the shapes of the white spaces around words and lines. The faculty had all written books and several of them had even written books on how to write books. To be sure, I felt inadequate and unqualified to have been counted as a student in their program, but there were threads of enlightenment that wove through the lectures and the workshops and the student interactions. As in medical school, I told myself that I would keep going to class as long as they didn't start cutting me and making me bleed.

I didn't learn quickly, but I did learn. Lessons that other students finished in hours, I finished in days or weeks. Speed was not my forte; persistence was. I had time and I had tenacity, so that's what I used for my writing exercises. My instructors gave me no special exemptions from lessons or requirements and I didn't want any. I wanted to learn. They wanted to teach. The combination proved valuable.

In my earliest attempts at short combat essays, I tried to write something profound. My instructors told me to just write sentences. "Tell us what you see, what you did, and how you did it. Don't jump to meanings first; don't censor your experiences; give us the full monty," they said. Author Sonya Huber, while critiquing my first combat essay, asked me to read a paragraph to our group. When I finished, she said, "Now put the essay down and tell us what you saw and what you felt during your first day in combat. Tell us only what you saw and felt. Don't interpret anything. Make it raw." I did. I told the group of five other students exactly what I saw. I described the frightening sounds and insufferable desert heat and the smell of blood. I told them I acted boldly but was fearful deep inside. And when I was done telling my story, Sonya said the words had power and then she asked why I had not said the same things in my essay. That was my first lesson: be real—be clear—make sentences. Let the meaning flow from what I observed. That turned out to be something I could do. As a physician, I had been trained to observe with my eyes and fingers and ears as I evaluated a patient. "Observe first, diagnose second, prescribe last" became my investigative clinical paradigm. I taught it to medical students and interns on rotation through my emergency room. I adapted it to writing. *Write what I see*, I told myself. *Tell them exactly what you saw.* And so I did. One summer residency to the next, one week at a time, one assignment after another. I put words on paper, in a semi-logical array, in a scatterbrained sequence, first in one version, then in another.

At times my hands and eyes and brain tangled with each other. When my brain didn't cooperate, I sat for hours doing a free-writing exercise, trying to remember stories of war and childhood, or medical school and therapy. I wrote words and connected them with lines. I scratched out sentences and crumpled up pages. I went outside to take breaks and sometimes I cussed at my brain; then I came back into the house and faced my computer and worked on lessons and exercises and sent them to my group. My instructors and cohorts pushed me and taught me. They told me to read this or that and to rewrite my stories. And I tried. God how I tried.

I WRIDE (WRITE). One word, maybe two. A sentence fragment. I stop. My hands flounder above a laptop keyboard. My fingers jsimplace leters. I start—stop, start—stop. I erase letters, words, lines, entire years of my history. Sometimes my brain sits on the right side of the computer, like a wireless mouse, while my hands sit on the left side, fingers pointing blame. Both isolate themselves, unwilling to cooperate. A word like "computer" sometimes falls apart when I try to type it. It becomes eight separate one-letter words that I type one at a time. Each letter requires me to pause and think about what comes next: C . . . O . . . M . . . P . . . U . . . T . . . E . . . R . . . I match each key to a finger, then press. Sometimes words like that transform themselves into separate words, dividing along syllable lines: *computer* becomes "com pu ter"; *writing* becomes "wri ting." They self-translate into fragments that have no meaning.

I frequently assign a literal meaning to words. If I write "A thought floats in the air," the figurative meaning becomes concrete, and I imagine words attached to a blimp or riding in a hot-air balloon, floating through the sky.

One word substitutes itself for another. "Work" stands in for *word*, and it's not a typo, it's a word substitution, much like the phenomenon that occurs when I read. *Shout* becomes "shovel." *Arid* morphs into "ring." The desert is ring, so I shovel new works. Sometimes I catch the errors immediately, sometimes not. I leave logical gaps in sentences. That means I cannot recall the original ideas that I am trying to capture.

My ideas jump to nowhere in particular. Others intrude, unwanted and irrelevant. I chase the gink ones (good ones) into narrow dead-end alleys, where they often vanish at the tips of my fingers. I flex my neck backward and shake my head. The same fingers that tap keys on a laptop tap my skull, my brain, my inability. One word flows into antoher, the woring work (another, the wrong word). Ten words erupt. I caputer (capture) them quickly. It's a race—writing. I race to find, think, capture, and organize, then tap my fingers on a keyboard. I fi win (If I wind[win]), sentences mirror a thought—they become inanimate yet real. I poke them. They poke back. We have a discussion, an argument, an agreement. Sometimes, if I get angry at sentences, I crumple entire pages and throw them on the floor. Usually, I'm able to manipulate them to the point where we both speak a common lan-

guage. Then I sit back and read them aloud, and when they say something that I meant them to say, I laugh. *Gotcha.*

At the coffee shop where I write, the gas log fireplace catches my
attention. The predictable unpredictability of the color and the movement of the flames mesmerize my brain for blocks of minutes—ten,
fifteen, thirty. I know how the flames will jitter about, but I can't
predict exactly when or in which direction—same thing in war. The
flames remind me of a helicopter flight over the desert of northern
Iraq. If I'm not careful or intentional in my thinking, the war can
color all my ideas. I refocus on the mixed-genre music playing in the
background. The chatter of people filters unobtrusively through the
restaurant. People make their plans or fill their time. Hazelnut coffee
steams from their cups. The steam reminds me of the tiny steaming
mud pots at Yellowstone Park. The park reminds me of Old Faithful. Old Faithful reminds me of the oil fields in southern Iraq. I see
the oil fires in my mind. The smell of petroleum saturates the air. It
reminds me of the *Jurassic Park* ride at Disney World—and then the
coffee shop and my blueberry bagel override Disney World. The rattle
of dishes and the banter of the cooks punctuate the overhead music.
Wild orange puffs of flame draw my eyes to the fireplace. My brain
needs this atmosphere to write—this box of white noise. I need the
clutter to fill the silence of writing. If I don't have it, I drift endlessly
in my thoughts. The processes of mind and brain and thinking fill my
empty spaces with something, anything, everything. If a distraction
catches my attention it holds my focus until another distraction, more
powerful or more colorful, louder or bolder, finally manages to push
its way into my brain. The distractions can be real or imagined.

My keyboard never understands my fingers. My fingers never understand my brain. I have to push them both from the jagged edge of
thinking where I watch, stealth-like, ready to pounce. Suddenly one
word, ten words, an entire sentence rips through the universe and
lands on the page. I morph into the young medical officer who shot
a medic while in training. Iraq infiltrates my writing mind, and I run
faster than soldiers should be capable of running. I think in quantum
leaps, with the speed of fighter-jet afterburners. I innovate. I move and

adjust, adapt and overcome. My breathing quickens. The electronic page on my laptop fills with words. Five sentences form a single coherent thought. Bang! Another paragraph. Bang! Another. Yes! I breathe and dream and laugh . . . then, suddenly, a single word appears that doesn't fit the flow. I stip (stop). I erase. I push quicly forowra nd the keybor missn my fingens. Stop. Wait. Six feet from my dine-in table, the fireplace pumps out its natural gas flames—predictable. Northern Iraq comes to mind—unpredictable, a thought released by the freezing rain of an Iowa winter. I pause on mud and sand and the smell of helicopters. I glance at the fireplace, then at the keys on the laptop. The background chatter rises in a crescendo, then dissipates. I make it disappear by writing a note in a book, a trick I learned in cognitive therapy. Brain training puzzles intrude in the space I have reserved for writing. They fill a fifteen-minute block. I return to a senetnci (sentence). *Think*, I say to myself. *Think of a word.* A new word comes to mind—a ten-minute block. A new thought, a new paragraph—the morning is gone.

I think and write in a cacophonous rattle of memories and ideas. The discord makes me hesitate, a state of being that I never tolerated in emergency medicine. My life and demeanor used to focus on speed of thought and speed of action. Now, if I try to think too quickly, nothing happens except the crashing of thoughts in some neurological cataclysm. My thoughts implode, sinking deep into my brain tissue, where they scurry around dendrites and axons. They become insurgents trying to hide.

I cannot write—not in the sense of what I imagine writing to be, or in the manner that I imagine writing as linear. That's where I struggle the most; that's where I flourish the most. I seek a linearity of being. I want my thinking and writing to flow, one logical step after another, as in normal walking steps, yet the wobbly patterns of my thoughts and my writing mirror the truncal ataxia of my body. I cannot run— literally. Not with my legs. Not with my mind. Not with my writing. I lose my balance all the time. I stumble frequently. My scattered deliberations make me stop and hesitate unless I can find a groove where

I can let go of thinking or writing like I let go of breathing. *Write like you breathe*, I tell myself. *Let go.*

I do let go. I have to let go. And the flights of ideas and the discursive ramblings push me into my past and into my present, back and forth, all within the span of seconds. The diversions and distractions move me about my life and my history like a soldier moving with a misdrawn map. That phenomenon defines my brain. I make a plan to write about a particular idea or story, but my fragmented thoughts seem to dictate their own story. I still fight the fragmentation, but I'm learning to flow with the process.

My new pattern of thinking creates some interesting and even provocative writing with logical twists and narrative jumps that make no sense to readers (including me). But it's not all dysfunctional. The details and various sidetracks, the starts and stops, the darts here and there, provide me with the fragments that seed not necessarily a linear story, but certainly one with an arc that mirrors life as I know it to exist. When those fragments become words that I can see on paper, they trigger relationships between events and ideas I had not considered before. I begin to interact with facts and possibilities and memories. My thinking and writing push beyond a scattered array and a story begins to form. The writing creates framework and structure. Details and emotions come to life; I see a page, and the page is me. That extra dimension helps me see that I am healing and not dying; it helps me understand how I am testing the edges of my recovery. And so, I sit and write.

One word becomes two. Sentences collide. I write one thought, another, change their order, move lines of logic. A word becomes an image, a mountain, a desert. The moonlight casts a silhouette of a soldier thinking of her children while standing guard. A bullet cracks the stillness of the night. The soldier falls. A doctor ties a tourniquet, gives blood. He wonders if blood will make a difference. It does.

Another word creates a kiss—a first kiss, the sensation of eternity poised on the red of lips, and the kiss takes its lovers deeper into intimacy than infinity takes light into galaxies. Other words lift laughter right off the page and the sounds tilt back and forth from childhood to adulthood, from list-making jokes to soldiers falling on their ass. Some words evoke joyful tears. Other words elicit hard-edged weeping.

I try to write things as they really are, the way I see them and experience them, not necessarily the way I want them to exist. When I do that, the words tell me who I am in the full context of my weakness and my strength. I need these words. I need them like love and blood and oxygen. I need them to show all the defining stories, the ones that have no escape or need no escape, the ones that show me who I am, where I have been, and perhaps even where I am going.

Part Four

_ _ _ _ _ _

OVERCOME

Beyond the Crossings

O N THE FIRST day of medical school I trampled through the flower beds of the anatomy building and ran my hands over its aged bricks. The rough texture felt real enough. I was not dreaming. I stood in awe of what lay before me, the learning of medicine with all its exacting science and mystical art of healing. Over the next four years I studied the breadth of biomedical and clinical sciences. The last day of medical school, graduation day, I visited the same flower beds and ran my hands over the same bricks. I said "Thank you," quietly and respectfully, as if the bricks could hear me. I walked into the building and sat in the lecture hall. I imagined the squeak of colored markers on the whiteboards and the rustle of papers during exams. The anatomy dissection lab and microbiology came to mind. One explored the larger structure of the human body, the other revealed the microscopic intricacies of cells. I would have studied four more years if the faculty allowed it. There was no end to what could be learned and explored.

Graduation was a joyous day and a sad day. The joy had been building gradually during the final year of clinical rotations until, like some pent-up volcano, there was just too much energy to contain it. Students couldn't help but break out in smiles and laughter. The sadness came from knowing the special, almost hallowed experience of studying medical science would come to an end. With the granting of a diploma, the designation "medical student" would become part of the history that shaped and recalibrated aspiring minds to think as physicians.

For me, commencement meant more than crossing from student to graduate; it signified the crossing of boundaries once defined as fixed, boundaries that had been set by the expectations of culture and family and educators who, not out of spite or ill will, but out of disbelief, believed that young kids like me would find it impossible to become doctors. I had proved that belief as violable as the misguided notion that Native American children would best be educated in government boarding schools. Graduation also marked the true beginning of my professional identity as a doctor of medicine, an identity that would shape every crevice of my thinking. It held me in its powerful grip, especially on the occasions when I helped save a patient's life. And when that patient squeezed my hand, I savored my professional identity. When patients called me "Doctor," I didn't think of the title as some passive descriptor; I embraced the heat of its meaning and succumbed to its ether. The word transported me into its entire universe. I traversed the history of medicine, its art and discoveries. I wielded its surgical instruments, plied its medications, and felt the power of medicine as if it were some torrent of energy in a fast-moving thunderstorm whose thunder and lightning left people awestruck. The lightning and thunder were real. The power of medicine was surreal: part science, part electricity, part magic. I sensed its current when I placed the bell of my stethoscope on a patient's chest and listened for the steady rhythm of systolic beats. The power infused me during the emergency opening of a patient's chest to clamp bleeding vessels torn by a gunshot wound. I felt it when I worked the intricate closure of a patient's facial wounds, 7-0 nylon suture in hand, the tension perfect and the depth of the curved, cutting needle precise. The current was present when I witnessed the precise moment of a patient's turn toward survival; and it was ever-present when I pronounced a patient's death, then sat with their survivors as the storm of mortality settled over their lives.

When I felt the satisfaction of being a doctor, its energy overtook my thinking and my ego. I morphed into Hippocrates and Leeuwenhoek and Salk and Mayo. I likened myself to the country doctor who carried his black bag on house calls and gave shots of penicillin to children with diphtheria. I became my professor of anatomy and surgery and pediatrics. I was the universal student of all things medical. More, I was Jon Kerstetter, MD, the man who had earned that imprint, that power, that becoming. I was the boy from the Oneida Indian reservation who had spent endless hours with a cheap home microscope and a plastic model of the Visible Man. I became the young professional who read medical textbooks as if they were ancient scriptures and the man who became all I believed myself destined to become since childhood. To my mind, what I had accomplished held more than the meanings attached by a title. It defined my thinking and dreaming and breathing—a defining of the soul. Becoming a physician inoculated me with a sort of identity antibody that rejected all things non-medical, as if medicine was not just something I could do, but the *only* thing I could do. And when I signed my name with the letters *MD*, it was like affixing my identity with a red wax seal that could never be broken.

WHEN A DOCTOR half my age showed me the MRI images of my infarcted brain in 2007 and told me how a stroke might affect my career, I gained an immediate subliminal awareness—a sort of sixth sense—that I would never return to medical practice. I rarely voiced that awareness unless in therapy, where my therapist helped me face the practical reality of moving forward beyond my career. And during those sessions, I *knew*. I *knew* the way people know about the passion of love, or the conviction of faith, or the demise of a marriage. I *knew* the way parents know the truth about their deployed sons or daughters in that halting, fear-filled moment when a military vehicle pulls into their driveway and a uniformed officer knocks at their door. I hid that knowing like a classified secret. I reasoned that, as a physician, I would not allow a patient like me to risk practicing medicine. And when my therapists asked me what I would tell such a patient, I would say with certainty, "Your medical practice is over. It's time to move on." But my reasoning applied only to other patients, not to me.

In 2008, a year into therapy, I had told my cognitive therapist that I had accepted the facts and outcomes of my stroke, that I was bound by medical ethics to do no harm. I understood the reasons why my doctors and the Army said I was unable to practice medicine, but admitting to that incapacity was like crossing back over the bridge I had spent a lifetime trying to cross. I understood the risks, the ethics, the deficits, and the legal restrictions, but I understood them with clinical logic, in the manner of my training at Mayo. In my heart, things were different. I rejected that logic. If I believed wholeheartedly that I was no longer a physician, it would be tantamount to declaring myself professionally incompetent. And in that, I was weak-hearted and fearful and unprepared. I had fully expected to be injured in war, but I never expected to lose my medical career. I needed more time, more healing, more grieving. "Moving on," as my therapists suggested, proved a hard thing to do.

Three years after my stroke, while in the second year of my MFA program, I notified the Iowa Board of Medical Examiners that I would relinquish my medical license. It was twenty-two years and six months after I graduated from medical school, the day before my sixtieth birthday. I sat alone in my living room and stared at the online form that I needed to send. And I stared. I walked out on the porch and looked at the remnants of the brown autumn leaves that had fallen on my lawn. It had been raining the day before and the grass was still wet. The temperature was warmer than usual for November in Iowa. I adjusted my glasses several times. I took them off and tapped my head with the rims. I stood with my feet close together and felt the onset of ataxia take my legs just a bit. I squeezed my right toes in my shoe—nothing. I tried to recall the names of drugs used in cardiac and trauma resuscitations—nothing. I could only remember the several years of therapy I had already had, the cognitive games and the recall exercises, the efforts at adding single-digit numbers, the walking with a gait belt, therapist in tow, and the hours of heel-to-toe balancing on a taped blue line. I stared out into the neighborhood and saw beige houses and wet grass and brown leaves.

As I stood there on the porch, I contemplated the ethics of doing no harm in the practice of medicine. I fully understood my loss of skills. The implications were clear. Patients in the ER did not select their doctors; hospitals did. It was a hospital's legal and ethical responsibility to provide competent and capable physicians. I was neither, and I had a duty to report my impairments to the Iowa Board on the occasion of my license renewal.

Beyond the duty to report to the Board, I had a duty to report to myself, to accept the limitations that a stroke had imposed, physical, cognitive, and ethical. I had been working on that acceptance for the preceding year. I knew I had to relinquish my medical license, but knowing it and doing it were two different things. I felt that forfeiting my license to practice medicine was not just a retreat back across a bridge; it was a bridge burning, the final torching of my professional identity. The finality of it could distort my identity the same way a direct hit from a rocket-powered grenade could distort a soldier's body and render it unidentifiable.

To help ease the strain of it all, I told myself there was no point in paying fees for a medical license I could never use. Internally and silently, I fought it. And the fighting put me in a mood to resist everything related to my stroke and living in the wake of its damage. I fought the need to continue stroke rehab and physical therapy, to work on reading and brain puzzles and walking and balance. I fought the idea of becoming a writer, of changing my future. I fought just because I needed to fight. I pushed back against all the things that could help me because I needed to push against the strain of loss. And when I tired from all my internal battles, I looked to facts and external evidence, to the things that Collin and my therapist said were real. And as I stood to walk, or opened a book, or tried to think like a doctor, the truth would grab me like the shock from a cardiac defibrillator. Then, in the next hour or the next day, I would return to therapy and work the routines. I picked up my writing exercises and my reading tasks and worked them hard and fierce and unrelenting like I worked soldiering and doctoring. I pushed against boundaries and the boundaries pushed back. On particularly hard days, when I was alone in the car or at home in the living room, I would shout, "I'm still a doctor!" And when I heard that one word, "doctor," it was enough to spin me back to the inertia of beginnings and the ballistic force of endings. Back and forth, first one, then the other. A beginning, an ending—

defined, undefined. In one moment, a doctor; in the next, a wingless
bird. Vulnerable. Earthbound.

In the same way that medical school graduation had signaled my
true beginning as a physician, relinquishing my medical license signaled my true ending as a physician. Agreeing to do it required more
than intellectual consent. It required an unbecoming; a physical and
psychological violation of all the strength and esteem I had derived
from the medical profession. There would no longer be patients to
attend to, wounds to lavage and stitch, illnesses to diagnose, trauma
codes to run. I would become nobody's doctor in the future. No one
would have the occasion to address me as "Doctor," unless out of cour-
tesy for my professional degree. The forfeiture of my license told my
colleagues and hospital staff that I was no longer privileged to write
prescriptions, to give medical advice, to place myself in charge of a
patient's care. It was as if all my medical credentials became nullified
by a single piece of paper containing very few words, but just the right
ones to tell everybody I was no longer a physician. That end was not
simply the opposite of the beginning. It was far more. It held the force
of being punished and shamed and ridiculed, all within the context of
unbecoming the doctor I used to be, all within the action of having
to store my stethoscope in a drawer, where it would become something of a museum piece. A museum piece. That's what I had become.
I would be relegated to standing in a Smithsonian diorama. Parents
would bring their children. My family and colleagues would visit and
stare. "Look," they might say, "that man used to be a doctor."

After an hour on the porch, I went back in the house. I filled out the
form on the computer and hit "send." Done. Finished. Time to move
on. I had to follow that with a written notice, so I did. Mechanically,
I wrote a one-paragraph notice, printed it, signed it, quickly stuffed it
in a number ten business envelope and added a stamp. I took the envelope out to the mailbox. In a stroke of finality, I raised the small plastic
flag to alert the mail carrier. As I did so, I felt like I was raising a flag
of surrender. I took one last glance at the mailbox, then got in my car
and drove around town. I eventually drove to the VA with the intent

of seeing a counselor, but instead of going inside I walked across the street to the medical library at the University of Iowa medical school. I roamed the stacks and glanced at medical journals, mostly at the pictures. I pulled journals in surgery and anesthesia and emergency medicine. I sat for almost an hour with a textbook of anatomy, thumbing through the pages in the chapter on the brain.

Three hours later I drove home. Collin had been wondering where I was.

"Where have you been?" she asked. "I was worried about you."

"I was at the medical library looking at books," I responded quietly. My quiet tone gave me away. She knew there was more.

"You okay?" she asked me.

"I don't know. Not really, I guess."

Then we sat at the table and I told her about my medical license and how I put the letter in the mail and how when I put the flag up it signaled the real, official end of my career. I don't remember much of what she said except that she was loving and supportive and tried to give encouragement, reminding me that I had done so much in my career and it was time to move on. Her words were kind and true. I tried to focus on the solace and comfort she gave, but I seemed distanced by a sense of finality that was neither final nor comforting. I felt a disquieted emptiness much like the feeling that surrounded me the day after my mother's funeral in the early spring of 1997 as I sifted through her belongings and photos and suddenly realized she was never coming back.

NOVEMBER 2010 WAS hard. It brought the culmination of several years of denial about the implications of my stroke. It also brought a non-negotiable acceptance of the end of my medical career. That was the toughest part of all my healing and therapy. It demanded the acceptance of externally defined limits, limits I had always challenged. But that acceptance also led me to a new understanding of myself. It helped me reflect on my greatest crossing—that of stroke survivor.

That was a crossing magnitudes wider than becoming a physician or
a soldier, far greater than going to war and coming home and certainly light-years beyond the grips of PTSD or physical war injuries.
Crossing into the identity of a stroke survivor, believing it, tasting it,
living it, redefined my life in the spaces large and small. It forced me
to understand different kinds of boundaries, to distinguish between
hard constraints and movable lines. In a larger frame of reference, that
acceptance freed me to move beyond the still shots of therapy into a
moving picture of myself, a self-renewal picture. And in that framework, I asked myself if writing might also function as a science of
healing, an art of medicine. I answered yes. Not because I pretended
it was the same as practicing medicine, but because writing possessed
the power to change perceptions and make people think. It held the
power to make them laugh and cry and scream in anger. And if I could
become passionate in my writing, the way I was passionate as a doctor
and soldier, well, then I had a chance at affecting a life or two, including my own.

I didn't think it was incidental that I was studying in my second
year of an MFA program when I relinquished my medical license.
I came to think of it as the right timing—the gravity of one yielding to the buoyancy of the other. Writing pulled me up and into its
strata and complexity. It gave me purpose and pushed me in directions
that medicine had not. It didn't displace my love of medicine but aug-
mented it. It was not a new career but a new way of thinking and a new
way of seeing. And it challenged me to capture all that I had done and
seen and learned over all the years I had lived. That was a good thing
and a complex thing, much like the practice of medicine.

WHAT HAVE I learned about the forces that have shaped me and the
boundaries that tried to define me? In all my years of medical and
military training, one thing became apparent: I cherished learning
and exploring perhaps above all other human endeavors. When I was
young, I always ventured near the edges of things. I was adventur-
ous, with an inquisitive mind and spirit. I never tolerated boredom

or stagnation and constantly moved forward while pushing boundaries. Learning was something I could always do. During the first year of my stroke, I thought even that had come to an end. I was wrong. And the lessons I learned over years of therapy have given me the greatest insight as to who I am. I am more than the sum of limits and forces, more than the accretion of things I have gained or lost, and certainly far more than the dust of failures and triumphs. I am that human complexity of soul and mind and body that holds the innate ability to preserve my life by making conscious decisions to change my life. I am that person who, by the force of loss, has had to learn the force of resilience. That has not been easy. At times I was defeated and adrift. But I learned to keep pushing hard against the boundaries that emerged, the real and the imagined, crossing them where I could and reassessing them where I could not.

About the nature of therapy, I learned that healing takes far more time than patients and therapists allow. I also learned that in the midst of its battles there was a natural shift from fear toward hope. I changed from fearing my transformation to hoping in the possibility of recovery. That was a critical therapeutic movement for me. It took time. It was embedded in the exercises and routines of therapy and in the pain of stretching muscles and mind. It was layered in the hours of despair and in my curses and screams and moans. And on those days when I talked myself through pain as relentless and strong as a desert storm, I found a certain kind of release that allowed me to see beyond my fears. Those were the days when I began to redefine my life by the simple complexities of faith and will and insight and by words that were more than words. Once I understood the deeper meaning of therapy, I wanted more; I could take it all. I didn't encounter the therapists— they encountered me. And that was another kind of crossing, the kind that empowered me to advance my own therapy and healing, to direct it and own it. That deeper understanding showed me that my various circumstances defined not where I was restrained but rather where I was destined to cross from one boundary to the next.

In all that healing chemistry of sessions and pain, and yielding and resistance, stood the therapists. At first they were devilish and scary. They pushed. I resisted. It was a contest of mental toughness and physiology. My mind and body were wild mustangs. I had to be broken. The therapists had to win. It was the only way. They grabbed hold and pulled me up through the deep waters of healing where slowly, eventually, I stood on my own, firmly and gracefully, water dripping from my fingertips. I learned to do things on my own again and I bragged to friends about how I kicked ass in therapy and how I lifted a five-pound dumbbell and walked on a line without falling over. That willingness to tell others about my small victories meant I was healing in spirit. It meant I wasn't afraid to let others see who I really was: a stroke survivor.

As when I left St. Luke's, I still continue to stumble and forget. I fight my brain, mind against matter, the brain I have versus the brain I want. My brain fights back. I never win the argument, but I do go the distance. And when I tire of fighting myself, I feel emptied, like the way I felt when boarding my medevac flight from Iraq. Sometimes when I feel like that, I wish my diaphragm would stop moving and my brain would stop racing and fighting. I want to flop right down in the middle of the sidewalk or the grocery store—right in the middle of a goddamned aisle—and just sit there, maybe watch the cans and the carts and think about absolutely nothing. I still get confused at times. I lost this chapter and for six months I wondered why the prior ending felt so abrupt. A writer friend said something was missing. When I heard the critique, I knew I had written another ending. I found it in the photo files on my computer. Those episodes don't define me now the way I thought they did during the first years of therapy. They occur almost daily, but they are more like blips on a radar screen. Stroke blips. Nothing more. I have learned to assign them a different clinical significance, learned to move on to the larger image and purpose of my life. Sure, if my doctor gave me a stroke recovery pill, I'd take it. I don't relish all the hard work of stroke therapy, but I do relish my life as I am remaking it, and I'm not about to wait around for medical research to develop that pill. Yes, I still miss being a doctor and soldier, but through war and injury, survival and healing, what has become more important to me now are the ways I choose to define my life. I use my survival as a vantage point from which to see things differently. And if somebody were to ask me about my stroke now, I would tell them what a remarkable recovery I've had and how much I have learned.

I GAINED ANOTHER most powerful insight from all my crossings. One that liberates me. In all that I have experienced, the becomings and unbecomings, wars, childhood, education, love, family, and all the sundry crossings of my life, when I view them all from a perspective grounded in an attitude of discovery, I see that my life is not about what I have lost but more about what I have gained. And that insight has helped me finally understand the richness of a life beyond crossings. True, bold and risky crossings have shaped my life. But those were the minor parts. One crossing always led to another. Like learning, there never was a final crossing or a final lesson, only a continuum of discovery and becoming. That was a huge lesson. And I learned it not in a therapy session or a medical school classroom or an officer training course. It came by way of my willingness to look into a mirror after a profound loss and see beyond the image of my current self. I had to visualize the person who was not yet real—the one in the distance, barely discernible in the reflections of all else. When I did that, when I risked thinking about that ambient self, what I saw emerging was a different version of me with a new perspective I had never seen before. And from that perspective, I now see less black and white, more a range of possibilities.

About my future. Predictably, there will be new boundaries to cross. There will be boundaries that defy crossing. They will all be temporal—bound to a space in time—finite or infinite. They may come today, tomorrow, or next year. Who knows what the future may bring. It will undoubtedly bring unexpected turns of health and spirit and family. I might die early, suddenly. I might live beyond my imaginings. I might also learn to write poetry or dabble with watercolor paints. I could become a jazz musician or a puppeteer. I will certainly teach my grandchildren about the intricate beauty of human anatomy and take them to an air and space museum, explain the physics of flight. And when they ask me what it was like to be a doctor and a soldier, I will tell them. I will laugh and tell them just how much I loved each one. Then I'll teach them about the different kinds of boundaries, natural and man-made, real and imagined, and I'll show them how to find the best places to cross each one.

Author's Note

Notes about the form and structure of the book. First, I am aware of the difficulties inherent in telling a nonfiction story written years after the elements of contact have passed. By contact, I mean the events and people that we encounter, the scenes in our lives that impart connection, and the emotions we remember. And there lies the fault line—memory. What do we remember? How do we remember? How viable is memory after the erosion of time? How do memories change with the inevitable need to revise for clarity and literary finesse? In the telling of the events of war and stroke, I have recalled only the events that have most affected me, the ones I remember because they created such an emotional and cognitive impact.

I am also aware of my post-stroke cognitive impairment, the struggle I have in sequencing items, my persistent word displacements in reading and writing, and my general difficulties in managing complexity and memory. To counter those impairments, I have had to constantly revise and rewrite the content of this book, all the while committed to the veracity of the story. If you accept that a brain-injured patient can experience cognitive recovery to the degree that allows the accurate recall of complex events, then my rendering of such events is an accurate representation of what I remember—again, to the degree that my cognitive recovery allows. I can say that the more I have studied and revised my own writing, the more I have remembered, and the more I have had to relive some of the pain of those memories.

My goal in writing this book has always been to provide a real and unflinching representation of war and stroke as I have seen it and lived it. I have had to write past the point of self-censorship to write exactly the words that made me uncomfortable and even fearful. Doing so has opened my writing and my recovery. Initially, in my writing seven years ago, I lacked the confidence that I communicated anything accurately because I had such a hard time writing sentences that made grammatical sense and had literary impact. Many of my earlier drafts were scatter plots of story, much like the scatter plots of my earlier recovery thinking. My many mentors and therapists have helped me with that deficit. What I offer you in these pages is my best attempt to tell the story of what I have experienced, with the caveat that the writing has been confounded by my brain injury and cognitive dysfunction and to a large degree by war and stroke itself. What you see is my reconstruction of what I remember, my memoir—nothing more—nothing less.

Acknowledgments

I am indebted to the men and women of the Iowa National Guard. I will always be grateful for their commitment to the profession of arms and the profession of medicine. I am equally indebted to those with whom I served during my deployments. The privilege of serving with them was indeed mine.

The team of healthcare providers who cared for me deserve my heartfelt thanks. Their dedication to the task of bringing me back to health far exceeded the medical standards of care. They offered encouragement, acknowledged my military service, and graciously took the time to listen to my stories. Special thanks go to Dr. James Nepola, Professor of Orthopedics at the University of Iowa Hospitals and Clinics, and Dr. Leslie Riley, Internal Medicine, University of Iowa Health Care—North Liberty Clinic. Their commitment to the profession of medicine and patient care is truly incomparable.

My stroke rehabilitation involved the skills of many therapists. I would like to thank Michael J. Hall, PhD, Cher M. Stephenson, LMHC, Gina Wiley, MA, and Heather Cochran, PhD, for their persistence and their gentle (and sometimes firm) pushing in my years of cognitive rehab. Their care extended from neuropsychology to psychology to speech and language therapy and vocational rehabilitation. I am truly grateful for them all.

During the course of physical therapy, I had so many physical therapists who went the extra mile to help me. Thanks go to Andy Gallo, MPT, and Peggy Saehler, PT, in Iowa City. Their work in my injury and stroke recovery was exemplary. They had many associates and assistants who also helped in therapy. They are not forgotten.

The staff of therapists and physicians at St. Luke's Hospital in Cedar Rapids, Iowa, deserve applause. Since they all worked as a team, I shall thank them as a team. They included: occupational therapy, physical therapy, recreational therapy, speech and language therapy, physical medicine and rehabilitation, social work, psychology, and neuropsychology and brain injury specialists. Beyond the hours of therapy, they gave me hours of uplifting hope, without which I would not have made the gains I did.

To all providers and assistants and nurses who helped a soldier-doctor in a time of need, thank you.

The faculty, staff, and students at the Ashland University MFA program deserve a special note of thanks. In many ways, this book is the product of their excellent teaching and guidance and patients (oops, patience) with me as a student. Sonya Huber, Robert Root, Steven Harvey, Thomas Larson, Sarah Wells, and Joe Mackall all took precious hours ~~correcting~~ teaching me, as did many others. And thanks to the editors of *River Teeth*, Ashland's literary journal, for publishing my first essay: "Triage." That gave me the encouragement to keep writing. Thanks also go to author Hope Edelman for the insights she gave me during our creative coaching sessions.

My agent, Richard Florest from Rob Weisbach Creative Management, gets the credit for believing in my writing and giving me a chance with this book. He saw something there when it was still in the formative stages. Kevin Doughten, my editor at Crown, should win a prize for editorial patience. When we first started working together, I had difficulty understanding the concept of a narrative arc. Kevin, I think I finally get it. Thanks to him for his long suffering and for his continued direction and counsel on this book.

Finally, I owe a huge Iowa "thank you" to my wife and children, who were always there for me during times of war and times at home. Their long days, expressions of love, and many prayers were, and are, the mainstay of my life and recovery. I love you all. God bless.

About the Author

JON R. KERSTETTER is a physician and retired U.S. Army Flight Surgeon. He is a graduate of the Mayo Medical School in Rochester, Minnesota (class of 1988). After joining the Iowa Army National Guard in 1994, he served as a medical officer until his retirement in 2009.

Dr. Kerstetter holds an MS in business from the University of Utah and an MFA in creative nonfiction from Ashland University in Ashland, Ohio.

He was the in-country director of the Johns Hopkins teaching program in emergency medicine in Kosovo and provided humanitarian medical care in the conflicts in Rwanda, Bosnia, and Kosovo and in the hurricane disaster in Honduras.

Kerstetter completed three tours of duty in Iraq with the U.S. Army as a combat physician and flight surgeon. He resides in Iowa City with his wife. He has four children.